Maya after War

Conflict, Power, and Politics in Guatemala

BY JENNIFER L. BURRELL

University of Texas Press ⬥ *Austin*

Requests for permission to reproduce material from this work should be sent to:
　　Permissions
　　University of Texas Press
　　P.O. Box 7819
　　Austin, TX 78713-7819
　　utpress.utexas.edu/index.php/rp-form

♾ The paper used in this book meets the minimum requirements of ANSI/NISO
Z39.48-1992 (R1997) (Permanence of Paper).

Library of Congress Cataloging-in-Publication Data
Burrell, Jennifer L.
　　Maya after war : conflict, power, and politics in Guatemala /
by Jennifer L. Burrell. — 1st ed.
　　　　p.　　cm.
　　Includes bibliographical references and index.
　　ISBN 978-0-292-76201-5
　　　1. Mayas—Crimes against—Guatemala.　2. Mayas—Violence against—
Guatemala.　3. Social conflict—Guatemala.　4. Ethnic conflict—Guatemala.
5. Guatemala—Politics and government.　6. Guatemala—Race relations.
7. Guatemala—Ethnic relations.　I. Title.
　　F1435.3.C75B87　2013
　　305.80097281—dc23　　　　　　　　　　　　　　　　2012035821

doi:10.7560/745674

　　First paperback edition, 2014

In memory of Ernest Dupuy

Contents

Acknowledgments

In the Mam language of Todos Santos, *be'*, the path, is a central metaphor for movement through the joys, obstacles, hardships, and digressions of life. *Tuj be' te 'uj*, the path of this book, has been a long and circuitous one, and I have traveled it only by accruing far more debts than I can acknowledge here. *Ch'jonta tey tuj tnom.*

Todosanteros shared their lives, stories, histories, and experiences with me, and I can never adequately thank them for this. I deeply admire their struggles for identity and community, and their insistence on the centrality of these things. In lieu of thanking individuals, I thank the many people who are friends, family, colleagues, teachers, students, and advocates who have shared lives, dreams, visions, and much else with me. It is an honor to have developed such deeply rooted relationships with you and to now share these across generations. Thanks and gratitude to the participants of the mapmaking workshop (and to their parents for facilitating after-school participation); to the translation team and to those who attended the history workshops. And thanks to all the people I knew as children in Todos Santos, who are now graduating from high schools and universities in Guatemala and the United States, setting off on your own life adventures. It's most delightful to be connected to you!

Resident *turistas* and *antropólogos* of various generations shared local news, history, experiences, and *chisme* from various perspectives. Thanks to Laurel Bossen, Cory Lockhart (and Shannon, Bob, and Dottie), David Salomon, Stacia Shiffler, Summer Sands, Jim 'el ti'j' Robinson, Carolina Gallant, Jacqui Clark, Katinka Hoeg, Adriana Dingman, Emma Reuter, Peter Chase, Olivia Carrescia, Deborah Clearman, Becca Young, Annemieke Kroone, Gavin Weston, and Ellen Sharp. Frank Taylor's friendship and generosity in sharing a vast wealth of knowledge based on long-standing ties to Todos Santos in particular and Guatemala in general offered distinctive historical perspectives. Visiting friends Rob Marlowe, Elyse Weiner, and Betsy Brody provided new perspectives, reading material, and pretzels. Special thanks to Rob for reading and editing Chapter 1.

Among the many colleagues I crossed paths with in Guatemala, or around issues Guatemalan, I especially want to thank Carol Hendrickson and Gail Ament—then and now, you are inspiring! Thanks also to Abigail Adams, Diane Nelson, Liza Grandia, Linda Green, Tim Smith, Ted Fischer, Victoria Sanford, Gabriela Torres, Kay Warren, Richard Wilson, Deborah Levenson, Deborah Rodman, Patricia Foxen, and David Stoll.

At the germination stage, I was inspired and challenged at The New School in New York by professors and fellow travelers. I especially thank Lindsay DuBois, Kim Clark, Liz Fitting, Chandana Mathur, Saloni Mathur, Laura Roush, and Steve Striffler for friendship and ideas. Kamari Clarke and Mihri Inal Cakir have been intellectual interlocutors and friends since this project was incipient. Deborah Poole, Rayna Rapp, and Linda Green, my steadfast committee members in times of departmental chaos, were instrumental in helping shape the dissertation that engaged my first years of fieldwork in Todos Santos. I owe a special debt, the magnitude of which only becomes clearer with time, to the late Bill Roseberry. I hope that his insistence on the blend of careful ethnography and rigorous theoretical political-economic analysis is reflected in this book. More recently, I thank Susana Narotzky for taking the time to think through some of Bill's later work with me, and for extremely thoughtful advice on bridging theoretical and methodological divides.

In and around Albany, Alethia Jones, Rachel Harris, Barbara Sutton, Elise Andaya, Jim Collins, Bob Jarvenpa, Walt Little, Bob Carmack, and Kendra Smith-Howard provided engaged commentary on earlier versions of a variety of chapters. My thanks to Louise Burkhart for close reading of the entire manuscript, and for especially illuminating comments on Chapter 3. The Department of Anthropology has provided much logistical and administrative support in the production of this book. A special thanks to Linda Goodwin for coordinating the various pieces involved in its production.

I thank the many people who have invited me to participate in stimulating gatherings over the years. I especially want to thank the organizers and participants of the Harvest of Violence workshop at Duke in 2004, the Global Vigilantes workshop in Brighton in 2005, and the participants of After the Handshakes, held at UAlbany in 2008, particularly Ellen Moodie, Jennifer Bickham Mendez, Florence Babb, and Marc Anderson. Thanks to Wenner Gren for funding such generative events. Ted Fischer and Tom Offit provided thoughtful commentary on the manuscript that made this a much better book. My sincere thanks to Theresa May for championing this project and seeing it through to publication.

It was a stroke of luck to write this book and raise children along with fellow Folsom Library lockdown *compañeras* Katya Haskins and Abby Kinchy, as well as Eliza Kent (and Mari Shopsis and Dereck Haskins). It is a rare gift to have friends who understand when the rigors of academia mean stepping out of regularly scheduled life for a while, and who stand by to celebrate upon reemergence!

My research in Todos Santos has received crucial financial support from Fulbright, the Janey Program in Latin American Studies at the New School, and faculty research awards from UAlbany. An earlier version of Chapter 6 was published in *Mayas in Postwar Guatemala: Harvest of Violence Revisited* (2009), edited by Walter E. Little and Timothy J. Smith, University of Alabama Press, and parts of Alfonso's story were published in "In and Out of Rights," in *The Journal of Latin American and Caribbean Anthropology*, Vol. 15, No. 1 and *"Ephemeral Rights" in Central America in the New Millennium* (2013), a volume I coedited with Ellen Moodie published by Berghahn. Material from Chapter 4 appears in "Migration and the Transnationalization of Fiesta Customs in Todos Santos Cuchumatán," in *Latin American Perspectives*, Vol. 32, No. 5. Thank you to the editors for kind permission to reprint.

My parents, Dennis and Jeannette Burrell, my aunt Carol Janis, and my brother Jeff Burrell all visited Todos Santos while I lived there, and have supported the writing of this book in sometimes extraordinary ways. Thanks especially to my parents for embracing grandparenthood with such great gusto all the time, and especially while I was writing. Ernest and Blaise Dupuy, Anne Hopkins, and Gerald Weales likewise ventured to the Cuchumatanes and shared life with me there. In particular, Ernest Dupuy provided home and hearth, making it possible to move between New York and Todos Santos for many years. A cartographer extraordinaire, he also inspired the mapmaking workshop discussed in Chapter 2.

Alex Dupuy has been by my side on this decades-long journey, sharing the highs and lows of fieldwork, language learning, *and* writing. *Ch'jonta tey, tat*. More recently, Lila accompanies us on our path through life, and has grown with this book, from her first voyage to Todos Santos at five months old to her more recent wish to have me read passages from the manuscript. Bean, you can read these words on your own now! This book is finished. I love you. Let's go have an adventure!

Maya after War

Introduction

On December 29, 1996, I spent much of the morning in the central park in Todos Santos, a Mam Mayan town tucked into the Cuchumatanes mountain range in northwestern Guatemala. I was chatting with a group of young community leaders who were responsible for decorating the plaza in front of the church for the local celebration of the end of the country's thirty-six-year civil war. As they walked by with banners, paper decorations, pine needles, and other materials that would be used to adorn the area, I joined them to help with the preparations. They were looking forward to the dance that would be held that evening with a live musical group from a nearby town. The group hadn't been advertised sufficiently, so they insisted that I remind whomever I saw during the day to attend. "What about *la paz*?" I asked them, referring to "the peace," as the postwar period was called. "Aren't you excited about it?" "Who knows what will happen?" one answered. "It depends," said another. A third shrugged, reminding me: "Don't forget to tell people about the dance, and see you there."

Later that afternoon, the local ceremony to celebrate the signing of a set of peace accords by the government, the high command of the Guatemalan military, and the Guatemalan National Revolutionary Unity (a coalition of four socialist insurgent groups) began at the same time as the larger ceremony being held in the capital. I watched as the mayor and local leaders sat at a long table on the steps of the church and gave speeches in which they emphasized their role as *trabajadores* (workers), invited community members to sign a local peace document with their names or fingerprints, and, finally, released a number of doves and set off firecrackers and bombas (bags of gunpowder released from metal can-

Central Todos Santos from above, 2006 (J. Burrell)

isters), an essential finale to any celebration in the town. The event was rather solemn, especially by local standards. As acquaintances and friends returned from signing the document, I congratulated them on the end of the long war and on their participation in the local event. "I'm quite doubtful," one friend said to me. Another commented: "As long as we're still poor, peace hasn't arrived for us." A third observed: "Signing this document doesn't erase the past."

This commemoration and the reactions it evoked were a far cry from the jubilation in the capital, where members of the military, government officials, guerillas, and thousands of ordinary citizens celebrated war's end. Nor did they reflect the reportedly raucous spirit of fanfare in the guerilla camps. Throughout Guatemala, people marked this occasion in different ways, dividing along axes of urban and rural, ladino and indigenous, between genocide survivors and those who had been engaged in armed conflict, and between poor, largely agricultural Maya and those involved in the Pan-Mayanist Movement. These distinctions, which only begin to hint at the complexity of Guatemalans' engagement in and experience of war and its aftermath, spoke to how what came to be glossed as "the peace process" permeated unevenly in various national and local spaces. *La paz*, as Todosanteros made clear, resonated individually and was experienced in myriad ways.

In articulating their doubts, commenting on the impossible task of surmounting the past, and linking these sentiments to the current grim economic situation, which showed no immediate promise of improvement, Todosanteros highlighted central conundrums for post-war Guatemala, and for all states in transition. How should the complicated and widening space between what Scheper-Hughes and Bourgois (2004:27) categorize as the goals of justice and reconciliation, and redistributive justice—objectives that would ideally be considered complementary—be negotiated? Authentic democratization requires a radical redistribution of wealth and power, but the Guatemalan Peace Accords reaffirmed the economic status quo (Robinson 2003). What are we to make of the arbitrariness of separating war and peace, of imagining something called "post-conflict," as if there was an interregnum between the one ending and the other beginning? Finally, how do we maintain the hope of war's end and transitions—hope for inclusion, security, something better—in the face of the violence, crime, and impunity that came to redefine Guatemalan lives, livelihoods, and possibilities for the future during these periods? As Ellen Moodie (2010) movingly writes about El Salvador, a heady mix of expectation, nostalgia, and desire brews in periods after conflict; when this effervescent hope is thwarted by unprecedented murder rates, feminicide, narcotrafficking, and poverty, post-war periods come to be seen as "worse than the war." Questions and doubts about *la paz* rose to the surface in Todos Santos on the late December afternoon when those of us who had gathered watched the doves of peace soar into the cerulean sky toward Mexico.

We stand on the cusp of a number of ostensible transitions from war to peace and from unchecked power to representative governance. The countries of Central America are often invoked as an example of successful regional transition from war to democracy, but in the wake of the initial fanfare and handshaking, the region was left wracked by economic upheaval, violence, and insecurity (Burrell and Moodie 2013).[1] Guatemala's experiences of the tensions and ambivalence that characterize the "post-conflict" period are the latest manifestations in the region. Well into the second post-war decade, attempts were being made to understand and quantify the achievements and failures of the past years. These attempts at auditing and measuring, by their nature, often exclude the everyday experiences and struggles of the vast majority of Guatemalans—the cultural practices and lived realities that render the aftermath of war and genocide knowable (Hinton and O'Neill 2009, Nelson 2009, Sanford 2004, Lubke-mann 2007, Theidon 1012). To understand what the transition from war to post-war has meant, and how it has been experienced in Guatemala, I refocus our gaze toward communities and the individuals who comprise them, to the spaces where fear and grief intermingle very specifically with power and state control. How life is lived and how suffering is experienced in everyday ways, and what people struggle over historically and into the present, emerge as crucial factors in defining possibilities for the present and the future.

There is substantial debate about how to conceptualize, analyze, and investigate periods after war. Should we call these epochs "post-conflict," "post-war," "transition," or something else? What is the "data" of these periods, and how do we work with it to express the stories of so many disparate experiences? What comes next? These questions raise important points. Political process is only one of many aspects of these eras, and yet the vocabulary and the idioms of after war emerge from and are defined by it. The concepts and terms that we have for referring to a constellation of desirable outcomes that ideally lead to "democracy" imply the existence of some sort of transitional interval between two clearly bounded orders. This space is "an exceptional moment wherein the political body leaves behind the violence and arbitrariness of the past and enters into a newly inaugurated present" (Rojas-Perez 2008:254).

Lived realities and social suffering point to something considerably more complex. The space of transition, where the fragility of power and the possibility of alternatives are negotiated in everyday life, is the subject of this book, which explores the years leading up to and following the end of armed conflict (from 1994 to the present), and explains how this period was experienced in Todos Santos Cuchumatán, a Mam Mayan village in the northwestern highlands.

Todos Santos is well known for its picturesque setting and the hand-woven clothing worn by women and men, and is a destination for tourists who want to travel off the beaten track. It is known to generations of students and travelers through the prize-winning ethnographic films directed by Olivia Carrescia (1978, 1989, and 2011); a classic ethnography, *The Two Crosses of Todos Santos* (1951), written by Maud Oakes; and the photographs taken by Hans Namuth in 1947 and from 1978 to 1987, compiled in the book *Los Todos Santeros* (1989). Todos Santos is, in short, an iconic Mayan village. It is a particularly good place for exploring the effects of the transition from war to after war, as many of the conflicts and forms of violence that characterize contemporary Guatemala (and other places in the region) have occurred here: lynching, the rise of gangs, re-paramilitarization in the form of security committees, massive wage-labor migration to the United States, and conflicts about which historical narratives will come to represent community members' vastly disparate experiences of war. The vicissitudes of transition, after war and after genocide, resonate very particularly among the Maya, for whom the state techniques of governance may combine in uneasy tension with community-level structures of power and hierarchies of authority to reshape local conceptions of belonging, kinship, gender, and generation.

As recent history makes clear, political transitions are often marked by consequences that are surprising, unsettling, and even profoundly disappointing. In Guatemala, these include the emergence of new forms of violence, the distortion or malfunction of democratic processes, and massive wage-labor exodus and other kinds of population movements. Ongoing impunity has contributed to one of the highest crime rates in the Western Hemisphere, while only two percent of all crimes make it to court (Grupo de Apoyo Mutuo 2009).

The imperatives and mandates of establishing "democracy" and "keeping the peace" during these periods frequently clash with the actual struggles of everyday life. The welter of expectations and anxieties produced at transitional moments is typically understood as part of a series of failures and shortfalls due to the ongoing cessation of normality—the state of emergency and exception (Benjamin 1940, Taussig 1992)—in the face of violence. As many of these situations worsen rather than resolve, a different assessment of violence is called for, one that privileges the temporal and spatial dimensions and dynamics of power and politics.

Conflict and Power

Conflicts are central to social life. They are how we know history. Through them, we see the resonances of history, and we come to understand their importance in enabling us to comprehend the present and imagine the future. The details of conflicts are what the archives are full of and are what people tell us about when they narrate their lives. Conflicts—with controlling parents or out-of-control children, with the dominant or absent state, with the uncaring or overly strict legal system, with exploitative bosses—are what consume people in quotidian ways.[2] These grievances are fundamental and universal, although their details are particular. Most importantly, they show how power and violence operate through time and in particular places. They comprise the local motives that inform politics, lending violence an intimate character (Roseberry 2004:134).

Todosanteros Edna and Estéban[3] share a history of conflict that is a good example. They quarreled over land in the 1960s, during the retrenchment of agrarian reforms initiated in 1950s Guatemala. Their dispute arose from long-standing antagonisms that began with their grandparents, if not earlier. After Estéban lost this battle with Edna and she obtained legal title to the disputed plot, he migrated to the Ixcán, a fertile valley to the north of Todos Santos where many people settled beginning in the 1960s. There, he lived with other Todosanteros who did not have adequate subsistence plots (*milpa*) within the municipality. The fertile lands of the Ixcán attracted settlers from throughout the country, who used cooperative methods to forge lives for themselves. As a result, the Ixcán was thought to be a hotbed of revolutionary fervor and was targeted by the Guatemalan army in the 1970s and 1980s. Many settlers were either killed, lived in communities of populations in resistance (CPRs), or were forced into exile in Mexico. Todosanteros, including two of Estéban's three children and his wife, were among the victims of the genocidal massacres carried out in this region. In Estéban's mind, his misfortunes were the result of his quarrel with Edna, so he waited for an opportunity to even the score. Several decades later, he was living again in the municipality, and when a relative of Edna's began to hang out with the so-called *mareros*, or gang members, in Todos Santos, Estéban saw his chance and publically blamed the young man for a variety of crimes. The man was jailed, and subsequently, in a separate incident, he was killed by the national civil police.

There is nothing particularly extraordinary about conflict, especially conflicts over land and other resources. Their everyday, mundane nature is precisely the point. They are woven into the social fabric and are profoundly *normal*. Indeed, as Gluckman (1955) notes, a certain degree of conflict is necessary for society to function. Historically and into the present, as part of a community or as families and individuals, everyone engages in disputes. These would hardly bear mention or notice except that during the lifetimes of Edna and Estéban, and of many other contemporary Guatemalans, conflicts occurred in the contexts of a long-running civil war, changing forms of state and local authority, and the unprecedented levels of crime and violence that occurred after the war. Disputes that had been ongoing for generations seethed in different registers and became newly consequential. The forms and significances they took gave violence its shape during the war and into the present. These disputes emerged from and were formed by mechanisms of power. They contributed to and created the local fractures that produced internal difference and ever-deepening struggles, re-forming families, communities, and the domain of the local. Conflicts shaped war and its aftermath, and they continue to shape millennial politics and possibilities in Guatemala.

Conflicts reveal the dynamic nature of communities, which is often hidden by appeals to collectivity. When people argue over water rights with their family members, neighbors, and the municipality, appealing to the past and revealing future imaginaries, they expose fields of "dense, overlapping relationships" (Creed 2004) and a "stew of overlapping and competing rights" (Roseberry 2004). William Roseberry advocated for the construction of typologies of contentious issues for investigating the concerns that infuse conflicts. Consideration of a range of disputes, he suggested, was critical to understanding local agency and significant lines of tension as well as sources of concern and activism. Revealing complexities inherent in the production of conflict would give weight to local experience. Rather than focusing on a strict typology of conflicts, which would be another form of enumerating the aftermath of war (Nelson 2009), I refocus the lens of conflict itself, with its tremendous agentive capacity, on relationships and their embeddedness within particular fields of power and force. While typologies generally engage abstraction for the sake of comparison, I emphasize the idea of range coupled with the specificity of ethnographic data. Through this shift in definition and mechanics, I draw on the productive tension between the generality of classifying types and the actual embeddedness of real, specific cases of conflict and violence that allow us to see how categories are made and remade, taken up and challenged.[4] Ethnography, then, functions as a mode of inquiry *and* as a form of political engagement; it requires a fine-tuned attention to people's lives and the currents of power to which they respond.[5]

Maya After War examines different kinds of conflicts that occur between members of a community and between community and state. Taken together, these conflicts demonstrate the forms of power and politics that are not revealed in the official documentation and accounting of war. Perhaps most importantly, they animate what matters to Todosanteros in their everyday lives, and how Todosanteros negotiate power in the spaces they inhabit. For analysts of post-war and transitional periods, with our own investments and hopes for aftermaths, this methodology provides one way of seeing the people we work with as "the authors of their *own* dramas, not necessarily the dramas we are most interested in" (Roseberry 2004:14).

Studying places like Todos Santos allows us to relate these everyday, community based conflicts, in their specificity and diversity, to national post-war contexts in Guatemala and beyond. The municipality was neither exceedingly revolutionary (although, at first, Todosanteros widely supported the guerillas and some joined their ranks) nor particularly pro-military (although paramilitary civil patrols, or PACs, functioned there until they were disbanded in 1996). There were no organized groups of nationally based Pan-Mayanists, collectives of widows, or exhumations of clandestine graves. Nonetheless, Todos Santos does have cultural activists, widows, a large percentage of households run by women, and a high rate of migration. There also have been various local attempts to deal with the past, live peacefully in the present, and forge a collective future. Todos Santos is neither obscure nor so well known that it thrives from tourism. Though it has experienced vast waves of migration, it has not become a ghost town. It witnessed the fierce schisms and expulsions that routinely occur in marginal communities, as well as sincere attempts by its citizens to craft collective strategies. In short, Todos Santos is like many places in the world where coping with transitions and aftermaths has become a way of life. But it is also particular in the terrain and contour of its experience.

The contemporary confluences that Todosanteros struggle with—identity, history, and community—are the very things that social scientists, development specialists, and government representatives have employed for understanding the Maya, marking how these categories are the results of dynamic processes and political decisions. The strategies embraced by Todosanteros for creating lives, livelihoods, and a community for themselves arise from their everyday choices and actions and occur within contexts of extreme structural inequality and violence. Understanding Mayan experiences of war and after war requires recognizing the inspirations and goals of their struggles.

Community, Conflict, and the State

Community and conflict among the Maya are often thought of as antithetical (Grandin 2000:217). However, even the most cursory of surveys of ethnographic and historical Mayan literature demonstrates that both have continuously been at the center of Mayan life.[6] Within and outside of communities, sources of conflict in Guatemala range from power, age, land, ethnicity, religion, gender, and agrarian issues to disputes citizens engage in with the state, municipal governments, and regional and international institutions. Shared conflicts, including conflicts with one an-

The main street and central park, 2006 (J. Burrell)

other, bind individuals to their communities as much as shared culture and mutual survival.

Communities are produced and defined relative to the state. In particular, several concepts of the state are useful for thinking about how power is newly configured after war. The everyday state (Joseph and Nugent 1994), with its outposts and techniques of governance, provides the most consistent face of national power for Todosanteros. In post offices, health clinics, bilingual education classes, and even in banks, Mayan citizens gain fluency in waiting for visits and services and adjusting expectations—powerful practical tools of the state (Auyero 2011).[7] In these sites, they are taught what it means to be indigenous relative to the definitions of the state. In response, they develop forms of agency and power that allow informed local action to be taken on the ground (Postero 2006, Fischer 2007, Colloredo-Mansfeld 2007, Gustafson 2009, García 2005).

The state is also a process (Trouillot 2003), a producer of effects direct and indirect (Scott 1998), and at the margins of the state's influence and regulatory mechanisms, its uneven nature is experienced as intermittently powerful (Das and Poole 2004). Thus, the state is recognized to be organized differently depending on the subjectivity of its citizens at a given time—whether they assume the role of citizens of the newly democratic Guatemalan nation, indigenous subjects (Mamdani 1997), or actors in multicultural projects (Van Cott 2000, Yashar 2005, Hale 2006). Citizens/subjects may alternately be empowered, without rights, waiting, and/or subordinated, depending on what projects and tropes of power are being invoked by the state. They may be granted certain rights in an attempt to silence portions of larger political agendas, or they may be upheld as arbiters of national inclusiveness and successful incorporation. These possibilities set the stage and provide the tools for the development of local political practice and the array of options available to communities in the aftermath of war.

This transition period after war is characterized by ambiguity and uncertainty and is further complicated by geographical and infrastructural considerations and the construction of difference and interstitiality, which are conceptualized as "margins" (Das and Poole 2004) and "frontiers" (Abrams 1988, Camus 2012, Cole and Wolf 1974, Ong 1999, Scott 1998). Having a paved road or one that is dirt, traveling eight hours to the national capital or two to the regional capital: these factors contribute to how difference is experienced and lived, and to how it plays out in terms of power and politics. These frontiers, margins, and interstices are cultural, economic, and physical. In their spaces, the rights and responsibilities of citizenship are negotiated. The state takes on more or less definition, and self-governance may flourish. State effects—how the state is made real and felt in everyday life—contribute to fundamental reorderings of personhood and sociality that normalize and legitimize political rule (Nugent 2010, Stoler 2002, Trouillot 2003). These effects, together with a range of state actions and citizen relationships with the state, may be experienced as fleeting, inconsistent, or vague.

When state power was available to them, Todosanteros engaged it in the service of their conflicts with one another. In the aftermath of the mob lynching of a Japanese tourist and his Guatemalan guide in 2000, community members eagerly took part in the investigation, turning one another in to state investigators. This directly contradicted the usual, accepted anonymity of mob crimes; yet, for Todosanteros, the intermittent presence of the state was a powerful incentive in the pursuit of long-term disputes with one another, particularly when it was unclear whether or not individuals had participated in the lynchings.

Mayan communities throughout the highlands eagerly welcomed the national civil police appointed in the first years after the war. However, many of the police lacked authority or were poorly suited for their assignments (they didn't have the local knowledge and language skills that would have made them effective), resulting in their eventual widespread rejection and, often, expulsion from the communities. In the wake of their removal from many places by the mid-2000s, citizens were encouraged to actively participate in their own governance. Although police returned to Todos Santos intermittently, community members took self-governing to heart. When reprimanded for human rights violations early in the 2000s, in relation to the development of security committees and their clandestine imprisonment of captives, Todosanteros responded that the state had not assisted with citizen safety or the security needed to combat gangs (*Prensa Libre*, February 22, 2003), and as a result, the community had been forced to assume additional responsibilities, which they were unwilling to negotiate. In this case, the state ceded the realm of citizen safety to Todosanteros and a new subjectivity relative to the state developed. Once the line between state governing and self-governing became less clear, criminality bled into the state, contributing to corruption, confusion, and a sense that state power was mercurial and inconsistent.

The concept of community and its elasticity or solidity with regard to state power is critical to Mayan identity—to how Maya understand themselves in the world and to the development of Mayan political, economic, and cultural subjectivities. Communities and their conflicts, with one another and with the state, demonstrate how struggle contributes to the creation of social meaning by aiding the formation of new alliances and new possibilities for political action. These are processes that, when traced, expose how classifications and ways of categorizing are shattered and subsequently replaced with understandings that reflect local realities.

The community is also at the heart of the investigation into the particularities of various processes that are described as neoliberal. In Veltmeyer's (2001:40) view, a community constitutes a unit to serve as "the basis of efforts by governments, NGOs, and outside agencies" seeking to promote economic development. This form of development extends to monitoring human rights, implementing best practices in governance, and a host of additional efforts, and "the community" comes to resonate in newly important ways—as a resource and a site for understanding traditional and emerging forms of local politics and struggle.

Contexts and Keywords After War: Neoliberalism, Democratic Governance, and Violence

Guatemala's after-war period has been indelibly shaped by neoliberalism. Indeed, many otherwise disarticulated factors can be linked under its umbrella, providing new depth and complexity for the working of power. The difficulty with this is in identifying and analyzing the myriad ways in which things might be linked, what *differences* neoliberalism produces, and, in particular, how it has given new resonance to extant conflicts. A genealogy of neoliberalism in the Western Hemisphere begins with the theories of economist Milton Friedman, who, together with a cohort of University of Chicago colleagues, worked on a challenge to Keynesian interventionist policies in the late 1940s, one that would develop the democratic possibilities of the free market (Friedman 1962). The ideas they generated swiftly made their way "toward the heart of government" (Gledhill 2004), through foundations and think tanks in the United States and Europe, gaining practical form in Latin America, especially through the International Monetary Fund (IMF) and the World Bank. By the 1980s, neoliberalism was associated with structural adjustment policies that focused on privatizing publically owned entities, courting foreign investment, and opening markets, with the goal of promoting fiscal balance for repaying loans. This early form of neoliberalism and the increasing immiseration that resulted from structural adjustment did not plague Guatemala as it did many other countries, in part because Guatemala did not receive loans. However, as structural adjustment policies were being imposed in neighboring countries, genocide against the Maya was taking place in Guatemala, carried out by the army in a systematic counterinsurgency campaign that peaked in 1982–1983. Beginning in the late 1980s, military-backed dictators began to implement new economic initiatives, like maquiladora assembly plants and export agriculture, and a small group of entrepreneurs started to emerge (Offit and Cook 2010:46).[8] By 1996, when the war officially ended, Guatemala's "transnational elite" (Robinson 2003) had gained control and implemented neoliberal economic policies that culminated in the signing of CAFTA-DR (the Dominican Republic-Central America Free Trade Agreement) in 2005.

The end of the war corresponded with a shift in neoliberalism, with the movement from open-market economic policies to a substitution of the market for the state and society—from neoliberalism to neoliberalization, as Gledhill (2004:340) puts it. The repercussions for post-war society in Guatemala were profound. Democracy "as ideology, as experience, as expectation, as policy" met with the market to coproduce "free-market democracies" (Paley 2001:13). With this linkage, governance became "a nonpolitical problem in need of technical solution" (Moodie 2010:43). Guatemalans were already uncertain about the role of the state after war, and democracy was upheld and supported by the legions of on-the-ground international peace workers who offered workshops, training, and pamphlets on what to expect (or not expect) from democratic governance. The workshops, at least as they were experienced by some Todosanteros, functioned to set limits on citizenship and the idea of state largesse. They were not nearly as popular as the meetings held by aid and development organizations, where concrete assistance and training were offered.

Another emphasis of neoliberalism that trickled into the post-war era was on maximizing outcomes and achieving efficiency rather than promoting democratic participation or expanding citizen rights. This move cast citizens, many encountering "democracy" for the first time, as individuals with a moral duty to adapt to the market. It defined "rationality" in market terms, as the willingness to take risks, to self-discipline, and to self-police. Thus, new, self-auditing subjectivities were created. The very poor, who often lived in rural locations like the hamlets of Todos Santos, were, in this rubric, required to take responsibility for their poverty. Among the first to engage in the post-war migration exodus were residents of these locations. Long before migration was visible in the center, its intensification was notable in rural places.

Nikolas Rose (1999:10) shows how citizens of the liberal democracies of the European post-war period regulated themselves to become "active participants in the process rather than objects of domination." Within this framework of self-auditing, personal objectives and institutional goals intermingle until it is no longer clear where boundaries and functions of power are located. This book is a testament to how this aspect of personhood and subject making as it is expressed through community have functioned for Todosanteros, with the twist that transnational capitalism and the imposition of security regimes in the United States—where the state regulates migrants—and in Todos Santos—where community members regulate one another—have shaped a very different contemporary vision.

The rationale of self-regulation posits "failure" as the fault of the individual; the market will raise all boats. This is the concept of "neoliberal" governance now prevalent in most of the world. Pierre Bourdieu has described it as driven by the "structural violence of unemployment, of insecure employment, and of the fear provoked by the threat of losing employment" (1998:98). For many Todosanteros, this resulted in massive wage-labor migration, an important vector after war. Elsewhere in Guatemala, where rates of migration were not as high—for example, among the Momostecos described by Offit and Cook—neoliberal governance provoked such a climate of economic insecurity and anxiety that individuals retreated into a personal, private struggle for survival, which contributed to the methodical destruction of the collectives that sustained them (2010:43). This signals the manner in which neoliberalism also promotes new relationships among people, often erasing traditional or historical ties and alliances in favor of others that may be based, for example, on the (legitimate) desire to consume. Neoliberalism, says Gledhill, "is the ideology of the period in which capitalism deepened to embrace the production of social life itself, seeking to commoditize the most intimate of human relations and the production of identity and personhood" (2004:340).

By now, the concept of neoliberalism has become almost meaningless without ethnographic particularities. Ong's (1999) emphasis on cultural specificity, Gledhill's (2004) and Harvey's (2005) theoretical interventions, and a host of pointed critiques, such as Hale's neoliberal multiculturalism (2006), Postero's post-multiculturalism (2006), and Kipnis's discussion of audit cultures (2008), have indubitably changed the way we think about political-economic interconnections. Market forces have now become the forces of the transnational state (Robinson 2003), of governance, and of everyday life. In recent decades, scholars have convincingly demonstrated how neoliberal regimes create new forms of citizens and citizenship (Seider 2005, Yashar 2005, Ong 1999 and 2006, Fischer 2007). A rich body of ethnographic literature illustrates the effects this has engendered among indigenous people throughout the Americas, showing a range of power and agency. Neoliberal multiculturalism has been broadly embraced to pinpoint the state-sponsored incorporation of historically marginalized populations. Inclusion occurs on a limited basis; certain identities are permitted, while others are not (Hale 2005). Following Hale's analysis, this technique for upholding racial hierarchies in Guatemala (while appearing to promote widespread incorporation) has produced a series of interventions and relationships that have governance and management applications and control the modes and mechanisms of indigenous inclusion.

Permitido (permitted) or not, however, indigenous actors engage in everyday hegemonic battles that establish and shift balances of power and politics, taking informed action on the ground and exercising agency and power. Indigenous Bolivian peasants have used neoliberal political reforms to recast the racist exclusions of the past. Through the language of citizenship and their expectation of rights, they have demanded radical changes to the structural inequalities that have shaped their society historically and into the present (Postero 2006, Gustafson 2009). Likewise, indigenous Ecuadorians operating within civil society have utilized "vernacular statecraft" to challenge the formation of coherent national projects (Colloredo-Mansfeld 2007).

Within the constraints of neoliberalism, people create their own lives. Revitalization and recuperation of culture and the cultural, like fiestas and traditional dances, are particularly acute after war. A key state project is to establish which practices will represent the nation and how they will be incorporated. Migrants in Guatemala have taken up culture, understood as a commodity within this framework, as a way of securing membership in communities, in the process fulfilling goals that the state has outsourced (Burrell 2005).

Several decades into its role as an overarching doctrine for our times, neoliberalism has become an indispensable political-economic backdrop. Much is attributed to the cluster of techniques, practices, and effects that I have discussed in terms of their resonance for Todosanteros. By now, many analyses ascribe almost any constellation of political-economic relationships to the long arm of neoliberalism. It has become difficult, if not impossible, to discern its limits (Kingfisher and Maskovsky 2008). Perhaps this is because, as a philosophy and practice, it is extraordinarily able to infiltrate public and private spheres; and, as recent data from the United States and many other places in the world indicate, as an "ideological project" (Gledhill 2004, Harvey 2005) that fosters greater inequality by establishing the conditions of capitalism under which elites amass more wealth, it has been wildly successful. That Guatemala has one of the highest rates of inequality in the world is in large part a specific function of this epoch and a national economic history that has aided such projects. Additionally, neoliberalism functions as a popular discourse as well as an academic one—embraced by activists, popular movements, and people in struggle throughout the world, it is at the center of how many people understand their own forms of marginalization and oppression relative to transnational forces.

In its catchall capacity as a backdrop to almost anything, "neoliberal" has become an adjective, the assumption being that it means the same thing to all of us and refers to similar sets of histories that document its role in various places. After all, who can resist David Harvey's key analytical moment in *A Brief History of Neoliberalism* (2005), when the bankruptcy of New York City, Madonna, and artist Jean-Michel Basquiat all figure in making sense of the structural adjustment underway in most of the global south? This is *Process*![9] The point is that neoliberalism and the state of being neoliberal (or being a neoliberal state, to stretch my point a tiny bit more) means *something*. Whatever analytical specificity is or is not found in this meaning, it encourages the simultaneous consideration of the social, the political, and the economic.

More than thirty years into neoliberalism's ascendancy, some suggest that it is now on the wane. There are a number of contenders for the next all-encompassing theory. Of them, and in terms of the experiences of Todosanteros after war and into the new millennium, Daniel Goldstein's argument that "security" is the next orienting paradigm is particularly provocative. Security, he contends, calls on the power of fear to fill the ruptures produced by neoliberalism (and neoliberalization) (2010:487). In this sense, security is part and parcel of neoliberalism, and Goldstein substantiates his claim by tracking different kinds of violence. Security, including the reemergence in Todos Santos of patrols called "*seguridad*," is the topic of Chapter 6, but different kinds of anxieties about security and insecurity are expressed throughout this book. O'Neill, Thomas, and Offit observe that the delegation of law enforcement to communities and private enterprises has led to the development of a shared common sense that involves blaming gangs for an atmosphere of danger and chronic insecurity, and the embedding of idioms of morality and self-discipline within the problem of violence (2011:2). The recent historical processes that I trace in Todos Santos provide an unusually clear example of how these have occurred in one place, demonstrating the formation of a local "securityscape"[10] of global circulation, national patterns, the past and the present, militarism and its everyday effects, and community moral imperatives that arise from histories of ongoing conflict.

Security and insecurity naturally intertwine with the preoccupations with violence and crime rampant in Guatemala. Every day, Guatemalans are reminded that no one is safe. As a UN official recently commented: "Guatemala is a good place to commit murder because you will almost certainly get away with it" (Alston 2007).[11] As murder rates escalate, it is rare for suspected perpetrators to be investigated, let alone brought to trial.[12] For many Guatemalans, it is more likely now that they will be killed than it was during the war.

The various kinds of violence in Guatemala, their periodicity, and their local contexts make investigating this topic difficult. There is the violence of war, post-war violence, violence related to crime and to transnational entities like gangs and narco-traffickers, collective violence, intimate gender violence, and intergenerational violence. The state also perpetrates violence directly, through ongoing impunity or in other, more subversive ways. For the purpose of capturing some of the complexity of this arena and promoting linkages, violence is often categorized and classified in such a way as to make sense of its multiple forms. Violence has been "neoliberalized" outside of state actors (Benson et al. 2008) and produced by the scarcities and deficiencies of the privatizing state, mixed with the logic of transnational capitalism (Goldstein 2005). In the hands of security forces, gangs, and mobs, it has been "democratized" (Snodgrass Godoy 2002). "Structural violence," which refers to a form of violence where political, social, and/or economic structures keep people from meeting their basic needs, harming them in the process, has been ongoing since the arrival of the Spanish; half of the Guatemalan population still lives in extreme poverty, the vast majority being rural Maya. Structural violence takes form systemically and often indirectly, and is experienced "by everyone who belongs to a certain social order" (Farmer 2003:307). It is referred to as structural, writes Torres-Rivas, "because it is reproduced in the context of the market, in exploitative labor relations, when income is precarious and it is concealed as underemployment, or is the result of educational segmentation and of multiple inequalities that block access to success" (1998:49).

In their foundational contribution to the study of violence, Nancy Scheper-Hughes and Phillippe Bourgois write: "Violence is a slippery concept—nonlinear, productive, destructive, and re-productive" (2004:2). But perhaps it need not be so slippery. Indeed, rooting violence firmly within processes of power and politics renders it less elusive and slick and connects it to normal, unrecognized, everyday forms of suffering. Cecilia Menjívar, writing of ladina women's lives in eastern Guatemala, shows the violence embedded in institutions and everyday life—the corrosive onslaught of overwork, verbal insults, humiliations, denigrations, and women's lack of self-esteem, and suggests that these may be more enduring and traumatic than injuries caused by direct physical violence (2011:9). This kind of radical rehistorization allows us to see incidents of violence as the outcome of particular cultural, political, and economic struggles (Donham 2006:18–19). It presents a challenge to the idea that violence is exceptional, or, as Scheper-Hughes and Bourgois suggest, that what goes around comes around (2004:3). Getting a firm grasp on violence—on what it produces and how it works—means "staring at suffering," as Donham (2006) writes, and acknowledging that it is part of a whole fabric—one that is produced by processes that are deeply historical.

Violence constituted in this way attends to the historicity of conflicts, their resolutions (or not), and their periodic resurgences. This approach to the details and processes that compose and create violence resolves some of the issues around the "data" of this topic, which is produced, as many have noted, in ways that are different from the protocols of other modes of social scientific inquiry.[13] Often, people are silent about their histories and experiences, or, for one or another reason, cannot tell their stories. At other times, contradictory resources or competing narratives result in a history of violence that is not necessarily the one that people would tell about themselves. These understandings of violence raise ethical as well as methodological dilemmas that require sensitivity to suffering and trauma, as well as analytical rigor. They call for ethnographic investigation that establishes respect, contributes to restoring dignity, and refocuses our gaze on the everyday aspects of life (and death) while locating conflict and struggle within larger contexts.

Conflict After War in Todos Santos

Maya After War is organized around a range of conflicts experienced in Todos Santos, many of which reflect local, national, and regional preoccupations. Focusing on these conflicts accomplishes two goals: First, it reveals forms of power and politics that shape how the post-war period was experienced in a particular community. These forms remain hidden in official narratives and accounts. Second, considering a range of conflicts exposes how they are linked to one another, or are convergent and overlapping processes. When examined together, they provide a broader and more complex view of the after-war decades and emphasize the commonplace. To paraphrase Carolyn Nordstrom (1997), this is a different kind of after-war story.

The first section of this book introduces Todos Santos in two specific contexts: as a place where violence was experienced and counterinsurgency was lived, and as a specifically Mayan place. The first chapter provides a narrative of *"la violencia,"* the word that is commonly used in Guatemala to refer to the counterinsurgency campaign that began in the early 1980s. (There is also a parallel word, *"el ochenta,"* [the eighties] that Todosanteros are more apt to use.)[14] In detailing local experiences, I emphasize how living under the army's counterinsurgency campaign sparked crucial redefinitions in social and political life.

In Chapter 2, I trace the construction of locality and the mapping of space figuratively and literally. I contextualize spatial understandings and their role in the war-to-post-war years in relation to the mapmaking workshop I conducted with primary and middle school students in July and August 1994, prior to the end of the war. At the time, spatial control and state artifacts (maps) were politically constituted in drastically different ways. The politics of mapmaking were complex in Todos Santos and in the capital, and showed a level of wartime state control that was, by then, on the wane. This chapter is an important marker in charting the rapidity and density of change in Todosanteros' experiences with the state in relation to everyday considerations and conflicts.

Understanding the specific experiences of war, violence, and everyday life in the context of the wartime state provides a foundation for understanding the conflicts that followed. Chapters 3 and 4 chart two issues that dominated the national terrain of Guatemala following war: the establishment of official historical narratives of the country's civil war, and the issue of massive wage-labor migration and some of its effects on communities. These two chapters are organized around a cluster of issues addressing cultural revitalization and recuperation in relation to the larger contexts in which local processes occurred.

Chapter 3 takes up the issue of contested histories about *costumbre* (Mayan religious/spiritual practices and beliefs) and the silences that developed in relation to an informal translation of Maud Oakes's ethnography *The Two Crosses of Todos Santos* (1951), an iconic account of Mayan spiritual practices in the 1940s that subsequently faded from public life. In the history workshops that followed the book's translation into Spanish and distribution throughout Todos Santos (cassette tapes in Spanish and Mam were provided for those who didn't read), Todosanteros analyzed the wellspring of discord that erupted around the book, as well as the suppression of public expressions of culture that were once such an integral part of community life—a phenomena the book helped to bring into public discourse. Foregrounding the special role of history in processes of transition, I explore Todosanteros' view of historical knowledge as a resource to be deployed for a collective future. As versions of history are debated and conflicts emerge over which will be favored, people search for a way to articulate a mutual, conflict-laden past silenced through wartime experiences of domination.

At the center of Chapter 4 is the renowned Todos Santos fiesta, where migrants' roles in perpetuating particular parts of it are analyzed relative to state projects of neoliberal multiculturalism. Transnationalism is radically reshaping contemporary notions of community, but some migrants are invested in orthodox forms of celebration that bring them legitimacy and authenticity. This relationship with tradition is in direct contrast to the challenges Todosanteros face in reconciling history with the present in other domains, such as the realm of historical forms of power, the ability to speak silenced histories, and the reconfiguration of transnational families, as discussed throughout the chapters.

The final chapters take up the most controversial "conflicts": lynching, the issue of gangs, and what I call re-paramilitarization, the establishment of security committees in which adult men are required to serve. Exploring these causes of regional anxiety ethnographically shows the deep-seated currents of community power and politics and the long-term histories of conflict that come into play through these processes.

Lynching has come to dominate the landscape of after-war Guatemala. In 2000, a particularly infamous incident left a Japanese tourist and his Guatemalan bus driver dead at the hands of a violent mob in Todos Santos. Although perpetrators of lynching often enjoy the anonymity of the mob, in this case, Todosanteros turned fellow citizens in during the investigation, taking advantage of the intermittent presence and power of the state to address age-old conflicts with one another. Villagers spoke of the climate of terror that they likened to *el ochenta* in reference to its ambiguity—at any moment, one could be accused of participating in or of having witnessed the actual lynching despite having been nowhere near the crime or the mob. Seeking to understand why some people cooperated against others, Todosanteros turned to their community's history of conflict to account for actions in the present.

In Chapter 5, "After Lynching," I consider rumors, panic, poverty, and encounters with the legal system as domains of analysis for understanding the aftermath of the lynchings, and I look at how Todosanteros accounted for the murders that occurred in their village. After living in Todos Santos for more than thirty months, I left just three weeks before the lynchings. I initially read about the incident in the *New York Times* and followed it in various dailies in Guatemala which culminated in a return trip months later. In Chapter 5, I scrutinize published accounts of the lynchings as a stark moment during which the fault lines of the multiculturalist project were revealed in startling ways.

Intergenerational conflict and the repressive tactics used to staunch its newest forms in Todos Santos are the topics of Chapter 6. Labeling rebellious youth and returned migrants as *mareros* (gang members) enabled community members to tap into regional and national anxieties about crime, security, and the "youth problem," and to justify using increasingly harsh tactics against youth, including establishing security committees to carry out illegal acts, like clandestine imprisonment. Ultimately, ongoing antigang measures led to the re-paramilitarization of Todos Santos, in forms very much like those imposed during war. Methods for "gang control" implemented during this period were ultimately considered so successful that they have been incorporated nationally. In this chapter, the story of Alfonso shows how this long-term community process is, in its current iteration, also about conflict between generations. Wage-labor migration, post-war transition, and transnational lives mix together to unsettle historical forms of authority and hierarchies of power.

These conflicts have been organized as individual chapters, but their relatedness quickly becomes clear and demonstrates the flows of power that continue to animate the after-war period in many rural places throughout Guatemala.

Notes on Method

Between 1993 and 2007, I spent thirty-eight months in Todos Santos, in periods ranging from a few weeks to more than a year. Most of this was from May 1996 to April 2000, the critical period leading up to the signing of the final Accords, the dismantling of the civil patrol, and other local promotions of transition to democracy. I also visited places in the United States where Todosanteros lived, like San Francisco and Oakland, California, and Grand Rapids, Michigan. During this period, I confronted a number of methodological complexities that are commonplace for anthropologists conducting community-based studies, but were especially so during this epoch—difficulties including establishing the trust of Todosanteros, attempting to locate and then avoid axes of local conflict, and, eventually, noting what was left unsaid as much as what was said. By 1999, I was able to converse in Mam,[15] exchange pleasantries, and tell jokes. (Until this time, I had communicated in Spanish, using the occasional Mam word and phrase.) So many people had played a part in my learning the language that there was much collective pride in this achievement. The benefits of knowing Mam were many, including deeper relationships with locals, especially with older Todosanteros.

With a mapmaking project conducted in 1994 and discussed at length in Chapter 2, I began an approach dedicated to long-term fieldwork: I listened to Todosanteros as they suggested how my anthropological training might be useful to them. As a result, my ethnographic practice and methodology became unusually inclusive, a conscious strategy, on my part, about how I would do the fieldwork.[16] In July and August 1994, at the behest of a friend who later became my *compadre* (fictive kin), I taught the mapmaking workshop to primary and middle school students. The workshop illuminated a local spatial topography and the kinds of concerns and historical experiences that had shaped it. In 1999, I worked with a group of young Todosanteros to informally translate *The Two Crosses of Todos Santos* (1951) from English to Spanish. Following the distribution of the book and recordings of it in Spanish and Mam, I convened and facilitated a series of history workshops from November 1999 to March 2000, the topic of Chapter 3.

I also engaged in the more traditional cultural-anthropological methods of participant observation and interviewing. In 1994, I conducted interviews and asked to record them. I was almost always refused permission and the formality of these encounters produced stilted and unnatural conversations. A much more effective and open-ended interview style gradually evolved. In addition to these interviews, over the years, I bartered translation, editing, and graphic design work for free Mam lessons; taught an occasional English class in the middle school; participated in a number of language exchanges; attended meetings of local women's groups; and baked cookies in borrowed ovens and cooked food (that was never salty or sweet enough) in my pressure cooker for friends. I also attended a *cursillo*, a two-week series of nightly lectures (all in Mam) that served as preparation for godparents and others participating in sacraments in the Catholic church, *tuj be' tey dios* (on the path of God). This was an intensive initiation into an important vector of power and politics.

Given the contemporary movement of villagers, especially between Guatemala and the United States, my association with Todos Santos and Todosanteros hardly ended when I returned to New York after conducting fieldwork. In fact, in the United States, through my research in Guatemala, I met people I hadn't previously known, maintained contact with friends who moved *elna* (the Mam word for West, used to refer to the United States), and deepened and broadened my knowledge of migration and the material and political conditions that shaped choices made by migrants. More recently, I am reencountering, through social media like Facebook, people I knew as children, and instant messaging with friends who are still living in Todos Santos, something that was unimaginable just over a decade ago. This is a clear indicator of the difference that transnationalism and "free-market democracy" makes.

CHAPTER 1

War and *La Violencia* in Todos Santos: Accounting for the Past

I went to Todos Santos for the first time with two vivid images in my mind that defined the town for me as a particular place on the map and as a place with a wartime history. Both of the images were from Olivia Carrescia's 1989 film, *Todos Santos: The Survivors*. The first was a pile of stones in the street, meant to block army vehicles from reaching the town center in 1982. The second was the burned-out hull of a school bus, its jagged edges like a scar on the village landscape. The roadblock was long gone by the time I arrived in 1993, but the bus was parked in front of the cemetery — a silent, ever-present reminder of the war.

My own understanding of *la violencia* in Todos Santos developed in many ways, over an extended period. I didn't hear many testimonies, explicit civil war stories, or accounts of genocidal violence. For many years, I knew only the very basic histories of some key events. The army locked men in the church. Stones spelling "Todos Santos" were placed into the mountainside so the town could be quickly identified in the army's Cuchumatanes flyovers. Todosanteros lived in exile in Guatemala and Mexico. I gradually came to realize that I had been hearing about *la violencia* consistently, since my first summer of fieldwork in 1994. I was told the subtle details that evoked the variety of feelings, shifts in daily life, and ruptures in relationships that had occurred. These weren't testimonies. Instead, they conjured a sense of lived and shared experience in the present that was indelibly shaped by the past. It took me some time to realize that these were war stories.

In 1999, the much-anticipated *Memoria del Silencio*, the exhaustively researched ten-volume report prepared by the UN-sponsored Committee for Historical Clarification (CEH), was released. From 1981 to 1983, the committee determined, genocide was carried out against the Maya, leaving approximately two hundred thousand dead in the wake of 626 army-perpetrated massacres (CEH 1999).[1] One million of Guatemala's 7.5 million people, mostly in the western highlands, were at least temporarily displaced. Importantly, Guatemala's long history of severe social inequality was officially acknowledged in the report as being among the causes of the war. With this, the CEH became the first commission of inquiry to make explicit the connections among structural violence and war and its aftermath. The committee demonstrated these connections by showing how the escalating civil war was linked to local conflicts and their fault lines: grievances among families, villagers, and communities (Grandin 2010).

The "scorched earth" campaign that came to define the brutality of the war was a systematic attempt to break down community structures and thereby destroy any possibility of nurturing insurgency (Schirmer 1998). The military killed through acts so heinous they are difficult to recount. They destroyed sacred sites, ceremonial spaces, and cultural artifacts. Indigenous language and dress were repressed. Bases of traditional authority were undermined and communal forms of power were shattered (Grandin 2010). Much of this destruction was performed in an ongoing spectacle of terror, one that was particularly successful because the military assiduously cultivated parties already engaged in local conflicts, and forcibly inducted indigenous men and boys into military service, harvesting their insider knowledge while producing some of the fiercest killers in all of Latin America.

The National Picture: Prelude to Genocide

In 1954, following a decade of social and political progress, land redistribution throughout the Guatemalan countryside, unionization, and representative democracy, reformist president Jacobo Árbenz Guzmán was overthrown in a U.S.-backed "anticommunist" coup. It was designed to protect the interests of U.S. investors in the country, particularly the United Fruit Company and their Guatemalan supporters (Schlesinger and Kinzer 1982, Smith and Adams 2011). Colonel Carlos Castillo Armas was initially placed in power, following an "invasion" from Honduras and the implementation of an experimental strategy involving diplomatic, economic, and propagandized campaigns that utilized radio broadcasting and pamphleteering. After Castillo's assassination in 1957, and an irregular election, General José Miguel Ramón Ydígoras Fuentes was placed in power. He would be widely considered a puppet president who supported U.S. business interests (Schlesinger and Kinzer 1982). An unsuccessful coup d'etat against Fuentes on November 13, 1960, by disaffected army officers, many of them trained in the United States, spurred the creation of the counterinsurgency Guatemalan state, thereby initiating the armed conflict that was to last for the next thirty-six years. Popular resistance and the government's repression of organized gatherings escalated after this point (Handy 1994, Grandin 2000, Smith 2011).

The war shifted in character and intensity over the almost four decades of its duration. It is often characterized as arising from a popular response to a conservative, U.S.-centric government that was almost entirely taken over by the military. However, Ball, Kobrak, and Spirer suggest that, at first, the conflict was "a 'Gentleman's War,' limited in scope and fought largely between members of the urban middle classes" (1999:16). A key moment was the replacement of the police by the military (Smith and Adams 2011). Eventually, the insurgents, particularly the Guerrilla Army of the Poor (EGP) and the Organization of the People in Arms (ORPA),[2] expanded into the countryside. This development coincided with the growth of local liberation movements, particularly liberation theology and Catholic Action, organized groups of lay Catholics who attempted to bring a Christian influence to their environment.

The 1970s were marked by mounting repression at the national level, beginning with the declaration of a state of siege and the suspension of constitutional rights under then-president Arana Osorio (Levenson-Estrada 1994). In February 1976, a massive earthquake devastated the central highlands. Relief efforts transformed social alliances, bringing student volunteers and union members into closer contact with peasant villagers, who were the population most affected by the destruction (Ball et al. 1999). Although Todos Santos was not near the epicenter, aftershocks were felt in the Cuchumatanes range and the earthquake remains an important historical marker there as in the rest of the country. The quake catalyzed community-based development and organizing, strengthening an already growing cooperative movement.

As the Guatemalan economy began to expand in the mid-1970s, a time of overall growth in Central America, more workers became involved in organized labor actions, and some seventy thousand went on strike in 1977, more than ever before in Guatemala's history (Levenson-Estrada 1994, Ball et al. 1999:20). At the end of that year, a labor protest march originating with miners from Ixtahuacán, a Mam-speaking municipality in Huehuetenango, attracted thousands of participants en route to Guatemala City, demonstrating the burgeoning potential of a united front that combined participation from the city and the countryside. Within months, three student labor organizers from Huehuetenango who had worked with the strikers were killed (Levenson-Estrada 1994:127–129, Konefal 2010). In 1978, the multiethnic, popular Committee for Peasant Unity (CUC) emerged in the western highlands, propounding a nationally based struggle and uniting poor ladinos, coastal plantation workers, and others who were mobilizing around a vision of social and economic change. The CUC quickly grew in membership, advancing the slogan "a clear head, a heart of solidarity, and a clenched fist" (Ball et al. 1999). Indigenous activism, however, was met with swift retribution when 140 Q'eqchi' peasants were massacred in Panzós, Alta Verapaz, in the department of El Quiché, in May 1978, signaling how the state would respond to opposition under General Fernando Romeo Lucas García (Grandin 2004, Sanford 2010). In January 1980, CUC activists and university students occupied the Spanish embassy to call attention to the violence in El Quiché, and thirty-seven people were burned to death when state security forces stormed the building.[3]

Following the 1979 Sandinista victory in Nicaragua, and guerilla offensives in neighboring El Salvador, the Guatemalan guerillas, especially the EGP, underwent a massive expansion. Within several years, the EGP claimed to have six operating guerilla fronts (Figueroa and Martí 2007:46). By October 1981, General Fernando Romeo Lucas García had initiated a counterinsurgency campaign in Guatemala that was continued by his successors Generals José Efraín Ríos Montt (March 1982–1983) and Óscar Humberto Mejía Victores (1983–1986). While the war in Guatemala lasted almost four decades, it was the early to mid-1980s that definitively changed the scope and terms of the conflict. A new concept of "internal enemy" was defined, one that explicitly included the Maya as an ethnic group that the army intended to destroy in whole or in part (Schirmer 1998). Mayan communities were identified by color according to their suspected guerilla presence, ranging from "white," indicating villages thought to have no rebel influence, and that therefore would be spared, to "red," indicating villages with extensive rebel influence, which were designated for destruction, with the execution of all residents (Carmack 1988, Schirmer 1998). Huehuetenango, where Todos Santos is located, was targeted by the army as a problem zone and was therefore subjected to campaigns of massacre and "scorched earth," which reached their zenith during this period.

El Ochenta and Beyond in Todos Santos

"In Todos Santos (the town), sixty to eighty people were killed in 1981–1982. The army also burned an estimated 150 or more houses. Many of these houses remained destroyed and abandoned. We were told that the land of people who were killed is generally being used by relatives and not outsiders. Land does not appear to be available to buy, and this shortage may make it difficult for anyone returning from Mexico to obtain land."
MANZ, 1988

"In Todos Santos the shells of destroyed houses have remained in the town center for almost four years. No one either has been allowed or is willing to re-inhabit these sites."
MANZ, 1988

In Todos Santos in the 1970s, there was no national police or military presence, and young men were not drafted or forcibly conscripted into the military, despite this being the practice in many other parts of the country (Bossen 1984:101). In search of arable land, many Todosanteros—according to the parish priest at the time, up to one-third of Todos Santos's total population of about twenty thousand—migrated to the Ixcán, which was a two-day walk from Todos Santos (Perera 1993:145). Located in the northeastern foothills of the Cuchumatanes range, in El Quiché, the Ixcán attracted Guatemalans from various parts of the country who were lured by the fertile agricultural land that the Guatemalan government offered for free to those willing to clear and settle it. By the mid-1970s, however, following a steep rise in the price of oil, the army, with the support of the Guatemalan oligarchy, instigated a campaign to retake the land for drilling, dispossessing the settlers (Falla 1994). Some of the earliest migrants to the area eventually became members of Communities of Populations in Resistance, mobile communities that formed to flee the "scorched earth" policies implemented by the army in this area.[4] In Todos Santos, new, local forms of organizing, such as cooperatives, arose. However, the most successful local organization, a weaving cooperative, Estrella de Occidente, was mired in conflict over leadership. Tensions existed between those who sold weavings locally and those who sold in regional market centers.[5] Concurrent to these developments was the spread of evangelical churches, although this occurred more rapidly at the end of the decade and into the 1980s.[6]

The EGP became publicly active in Todos Santos in the early 1980s.[7] Initially, they drew sympathy and support from the more educated, especially the teachers, and from agriculturalists who were swayed by their ideology of land redistribution and economic and social justice. The first group of guerillas, which included both men and women, appeared during the Saturday market in early 1981. Community-based contacts mobilized large crowds who came to the central park to listen to their message. The rousing speech made that morning ended with a warmly received call to "release the land to the people" (Ikeda 1999:8).

During these first months, clandestine military training was conducted for boys and young men, and by mid-year, the guerillas had placed their own Justice of the Peace in the town hall. At this point, some claimed that the group's philosophy, particularly regarding arbitration of local land disputes, had changed. Businesspeople and landowners were increasingly targeted, and some were eventually killed, among them one of the few prominent indigenous shopkeepers and *cantina* (bar) owners and a couple whose son was serving in the army. The corpses of victims were left in the town square, sometimes hanging.

On March 16, 1982, after community members and the guerillas put boulders in the road in an attempt to block army vehicles from entering the town, six men were captured and held in the church by the army. The following day, they were moved to Santa Isabel, an *aldea* of San Juan Ixcoy, a neighboring township, where they were executed. Their bodies showed signs of torture (CEH case #5031). Father James Flaherty, a Catholic priest who resided in Todos Santos at the time, recounted: "In the spring of 1982, the army barricaded the road and no one could get in or out. I remember seeing EGP supporters scattering large rocks and boulders in the church courtyard, so the army helicopters could not land there. But of course, they landed anyway" (Perera 1993:145). The army also placed white-painted stones spelling "Todos Santos" on the mountain above the center of town in order to more easily find the community while patrolling by helicopter.[8]

In early 1982, two to three hundred elite army operatives, called *Kaibiles* (the Q'eqchi' term for warrior) and identifiable by their red berets, moved in and conducted a swift and devastating campaign in which 150 houses were burned, the vast majority of them in the hamlet of El Rancho. The guerillas had been active in this *aldea*, the most heavily populated in Todos Santos. On the way from El Rancho to the town center, the soldiers raped and otherwise attacked women, some of whom later died of their injuries (Ikeda 1999). Residents were called to a meeting in the Catholic church in the center of Todos Santos, at which they were told that the army had come in retaliation for executions perpetrated by the guerillas that January and February. The captain of the *Kaibil* unit claimed that the army knew who the guerillas and their sympathizers were, and called out more than two hundred names of "subversives" that had been collected by local informers. He then ordered guerilla leaders to identify themselves, threatening to strafe the town from helicopters if they did not. Several men stepped forward. The *Kaibiles* systematically began to torture them in the middle of the meeting, and a number of the men were killed.[9] That night, the bodies of the victims were carried to the cemetery and buried by other Todosanteros.

After this visit by the army, many people disappeared and others were abducted and murdered. Still others left to join the EGP. No one knew for sure who was responsible for the abductions and killings during these months. Some suspected army supporters; others thought the guerillas were seeking retribution for the devastation wrought by the army. On April 5, 1982, on the road from San Lucas, Ixcán, to Todos Santos, guerillas stopped the truck that shopkeeper Hilario Pérez Pablo was driving and beat him to death, burning the truck before leaving the scene (CEH case #11128). Shortly thereafter, two more men, Augustín Mendoza and Pedro Mendoza, were executed by the military (CEH case #15239).

Many other Todosanteros were massacred in the Ixcán. Father Flaherty claimed that of the thousands of Todosanteros living in that region, the army killed at least two hundred during the late 1970s and early 1980s in campaigns to deny the guerillas a popular base of support (Perera 1993:146). Following those massacres, many of the Todosanteros who had migrated to the Ixcán left to live in refugee camps, especially in Campeche, Mexico.[10] Others returned to Todos Santos.[11]

In Todos Santos, on March 23, 1982, the army gathered villagers in front of the church to announce that all of the town would be burned. Adult males were locked inside the church and told that they would not live to see the next day. Threatened with immediate death if they tried to exit the building, the men waited out the long night, and when the first rays of morning light filtered through the stained glass windows, they noted the silence and slowly opened the doors. The army was gone and the town was intact. Turning on the radio, they discovered that General Efraín Ríos Montt had toppled General Romeo Lucas García in a coup the previous day, and all army units had been called back to their bases.

By July 1982, Ríos Montt had appointed rural mayors, often by force, who were to be integral to implementing permanent counterinsurgency

Church, 2006 (J. Burrell)

measures locally. In conformance with *Appendix H: Standing Orders for the Development of Anti-Subversive Operations of the National Plan of Security and Development*, a long-term, elaborate, counterinsurgency campaign, these appointees were central to the philosophy of fighting the war on all fronts: "military, political but above all socio-economic. The minds of the population are our main target . . ." (Schirmer 1998:24). Abuses continued. In November 1982, in the *caserío* of Txanxmil, a hamlet of San Martín, Todos Santos, the army captured a man and brought him to the office of the military command, where he was beaten and deprived of food and water for three days, after which he was released. The victim was detained because the soldiers couldn't find his grandson, who was working on a farm in Mexico (CEH case #5408).

People most often talk about this period in relation to the nuances and suffering of day-to-day life. While *la violencia* is always a crucial marker in life histories and personal narratives, a typical detail slipped in might reference the way that Don Idelfonso went to his *milpa* every day. Even during *el ochenta*, after his family left for Huehuetenango, he continued to work his land. Such an act was dangerous; another man, while working in his *milpa*, missed the six p.m. curfew imposed by the army and was executed.

His *milpa* was far from the town center and he had encountered an obstacle on the path home. Another anecdote might be how Don Javier, the carpenter, could not make coffins quickly enough, so sometimes multiple bodies were buried in a single coffin, or individuals were buried without one. This situation was so unimaginable that it had to be hidden from the elders. Other details: the market continued to operate, but most women were afraid to attend it alone, and there was little to buy; since some teachers had been ladinos from Chiantla and Huehuetenango who left Todos Santos at the height of the counterinsurgency campaign, children did not attend school for long stretches of time and instead would do housework and agricultural work and accompany their mothers on errands; because it was difficult to purchase thread, many women stopped weaving during *el ochenta* and no one had new clothing. There was nothing extra to sell through the weaving cooperative, which, because cooperatives were targeted by the military, shuttered its windows and remained closed for much of the period along with the buildings and businesses that had been owned by the ladinos who fled during the military incursion.

I found these details particularly important and poignant because they spoke to the ways in which everyday life for Todosanteros was affected during genocidal wartime conditions: men continued to work in the *milpa*, but adapted to curfews; women continued to patronize the market (not the shuttered stores), but were always accompanied; Todosanteros continued to bury their dead, but corpses often shared or went without coffins; and women living in Todos Santos stopped weaving. People suffered unspeakable horrors, yet they continued to strategize daily lives for themselves, while fear, as Green (1999) has described, became a way of life. One older woman summarized the situation in the late 1980s: "Here, it used to be good. People worked very hard and the land gave us our necessities. But now we are distracted. Our children and grandchildren have left for their safety or to look for better living conditions elsewhere. And we who remain are still frightened" (Perera 1993:147).

Many physical reminders of *la violencia* dotted the everyday landscape of village life: burned houses, scorched fields, rusting hulks of the aforementioned bus and other abandoned vehicles. To these, Todosanteros added another. To accompany the two crosses in front of the church that Oakes immortalized in her ethnography, a third cross was erected among the unexcavated mounds—the center of the *twi' witz* (sacred ground), where communication with ancestors most commonly took place—to commemorate the victims of *la violencia*.

Politicization of Local Conflicts

In 1988, *Harvest of Violence: The Mayan Indians and the Guatemalan Crisis*, a collection edited by Robert Carmack, was published. The volume, written by U.S. anthropologists who had extensive pre-war fieldwork experience, comprised ten before-and-after accounts of the effects of violence in particular indigenous communities. One emphasis of the contributors was to distinguish how they, as anthropologists, had obtained the information on which they based their case studies—through listening to the Indians—from how the U.S. government had acquired its data supporting the war—often through newspapers or helicopter trips with the Guatemalan military. Even news from the guerillas, they pointed out, "took precedence over the Indians as sources of information" (1988:xiii). This pioneering insight for wartime anthropology was incorporated into the methodology of anthropologists who worked among the Maya beginning in the 1990s, and yielded the crucial observation that what people did not say was often as important as the stories they *could* tell (Carlsen 1997, Green 1999, Sanford 2009, Warren 1993, Zur 1998). In constructing this account, I have been sensitive to both of these ethically informed methodological approaches.

Anthropologists who "listened to the Indians" during the war revealed how personal and community-based conflicts were politicized by both the Maya Indians and the military to fuel the intensification of warfare during the early 1980s. People almost always knew who was behind a denunciation that led to the death of a loved one and often could identify the conflict that likely precipitated the accusation. Conflicts commonly occurred over land disputes, water rights, unpaid debts, and internal tensions produced by class differences. Some people felt guilt over the consequences of their actions, while others brazenly confronted survivors. One woman recounted to me what occurred following her parents' murder by the army. She and her brother had remained hidden, watching the event. The following day, she went to the store to purchase candles to mark her parents' deaths. She encountered neighbors with whom her family had recently engaged in a serious conflict, who inquired into her parents' whereabouts. Eleven years old, scared, and unsure of what to say, she told the neighbors that her parents were at home. The neighbors began to laugh. "These were very solemn days," the woman recounted. "People didn't just laugh like that."

As survival of the brutal counterinsurgency began to seem possible by the late 1980s, the character of people's conflicts and the ways in which they were related were notably more vehement. Discussing the struggle between evangelicals and Catholics, an evangelical man referred to Catholics as "devils with wings" (Carrescia 1989). For many evangelicals, Catholic Action and liberation theology, with their underlying ideology of social justice, were seen as having directed the wrath of God and the generals onto the Maya. Scorn for the Todosanteros who went to the Ixcán to eke out livelihoods for themselves and their families was close to the surface; by accepting land in a place that became a base of support for the guerillas, these villagers had provoked the vengeance of the army.

In their tellings, many Todosanteros professed to care less about whether military forces or guerillas killed their family members than about the neighbor or community member who might have been responsible. These latter accounts usually remained unspoken, emerging only at extraordinary times, as in the aftermath of the lynchings discussed in Chapter 5. Emphasizing the ways in which these conflicts remained central even while they were repressed reminds us that the histories people try to make for themselves as communities, as neighbors, and as households are not necessarily the histories they have experienced. Instead, daily life occurs in concordance with the tension of shared values and culture and the unspoken and unspeakable past. Understanding the parameters, axes, and historicity of these conflicts among fellow villagers and with the state shapes the resources that are available for political action, agency, and struggle in the present. Ultimately, what the Indians have to say may not always be what they want to say, or what those of us who listen expect to hear, a point discussed in greater depth in Chapter 3.

Civil Patrols and the Breakdown of Justice

"Our strategic goal has been to reverse Clausewitz's philosophy of war to state that in Guatemala, politics must be the continuation of war."
GENERAL HÉCTOR GRAMAJO, MINISTER OF DEFENSE, IN *THE GUATEMALAN MILITARY PROJECT: A VIOLENCE CALLED DEMOCRACY* (SCHIRMER 1998)

In the 1982 *Thesis of National Stability*, a document marking a strategic shift in philosophy, the Guatemalan army acknowledged "the poverty and discrimination at the roots of the insurgency" and vowed to "address these by way of eliminating further threats to national security" (Schirmer 1998:238). Central to this project was the implementation of government on the village level.

By the end of 1982, under army direction, all able-bodied men between eighteen and sixty years of age were organized into civil patrols (PACs) that were expected to spend "one day every 8–15 days protecting roads and inhabitants in their villages from guerilla intrusions" (Carmack 1988). This was a labor obligation of approximately forty-five to fifty days per year, representing a labor tax equivalent to anywhere from one-fifth to one-half of a family's monetary income at that time, a devastating state of affairs for most peasants as well as a crushing blow to the rural peasant economy (Davis 1988:29).[12] As a result, mandatory participation in the civil patrols was not only a way of suppressing the guerilla movement, but a method of controlling rural indigenous populations (Ibid.). In addition to patrolling in *pelotónes* (platoons) in twenty-four-hour rounds, males were also required to build roads and carry out other community-based rural development projects for the army's counterinsurgency program, or to work for the local military commanders in nearby garrisons. These obligatory "search operations" forced men to be prepared to serve the army at any moment without knowing precisely when they would be needed or for how long (Schirmer 1998:32). While a "Food for Work" (FFW) program, *Fusiles y Frijoles* (Bullets and Beans), paid for the men's labor with food (and other items, such as metal sheeting for roofs) between 1982 and 1985, after 1986, when the patrols officially became "voluntary committees," the work went unpaid and men provided their own food and sometimes their own guns (Schirmer 1998). In the early years of their formation, the patrols were presented as a sure way of divorcing communities from any association with the guerillas in the eyes of the army. Eventually, however, these organizations often came to be sources of abuse of power and authority, used to settle interpersonal or interfamilial rivalries. Davis points out how the civil patrol system "replaced the national judicial system as an institution for resolving local conflicts and disputes" (1988:29). The national judicial system was always a last resort because of widespread discrimination and corruption, but at least theoretically, it provided a nonviolent, codified alternative for dispute resolution. By 1985, Davis reports, disputes were settled "through arbitrary acts of violence by local civil patrol commanders, members of civil patrol units, or, in the final instance, local or regional army commanders" (Ibid.). Rural villagers thus became completely cut off from legal processes: they were effectively removed from democratic practice and, as a military officer explained, subjected to the imposition of "the discipline of the army on the pueblo [town]" (Schirmer 1998:255).

The army had planned for civil patrol leaders to assume civilian leadership positions as soon as they became available. Patrol leaders, however, refused to step down from their paramilitary leadership positions as long as the war was ongoing. This led to the growth of a strong sense of local- ized sovereignty within communities, precisely what the army wanted to achieve as part of a project of localized statism: from Bullets and Beans to the construction of a pan-highlands network of *centrally controlled but seemingly localized security*, this situation was "development within a con- text of rational and effective security" (Schirmer 1998:225, Remijnse 2002, Kobrak 1997).

In Todos Santos, Don Gaspar,[13] the head of the civil patrol during its first decade, had come to the attention of commanders at the local military base in Chiantla, at the foot of the Cuchumatanes range, after soldiers seized his car in 1982. Making visit after visit to the base in an effort to reclaim the car, he was eventually told that it had been "blown up after serving in undercover operations by G-2 [secret service] agents" (Perera 1993:152). As Perera points out, while Gaspar lost his car, his visits to the base had taught him how to "curry favor" with the commanders (1993:153). As a result, after he and his nephew Benito Ramírez went to the base to heroically offer themselves up in exchange for the two hun- dred people on the "subversives" list, Gaspar was invited to lead the new civil patrol (Perera 1993:153). As he tells it, he saw this as another oppor- tunity to protect his community. While he became very adept at "singing the army's praises and denouncing the guerillas" to his bosses (the army commanders), behind their backs, Perera reports, he advised his patrollers to "look the other way if they encountered *non-belligerent* (my emphasis) guerillas on their patrols" (1993:152).

Both Perera (1993) and Carrescia (1989) mention that the civil patrol in Todos Santos did not engage in armed combat once during its first seven years of existence, which is consistent with reports that Todosanteros served in the PACs without protest or rebellion but, unlike patrols else- where in the country, were nonaggressive. In 1995, asked when the patrols had last spotted subversive activity in the municipality, a twenty-year-old patroller in the *altiplano* (high altitude) hamlet of La Ventosa answered: "*Mil novecientos ochenta y dos* [1982]." Whether or not the patrols found or killed guerillas in the mountains, their leadership wielded substantial power in the village, and, as paramilitarized entities, the patrols contrib- uted to undermining any remaining sense of community trust.[14] Addi- tionally, corruption was often rampant among the PAC leadership. Al- though the kinds of blatant get-rich-quick extortionist schemes described elsewhere in the country weren't reported in Todos Santos, Gaspar was exceptionally well-off and remained so throughout his leadership (Perera 1993). His status as a former *caporal* (agent for the coastal plantations) who owned a car in 1982 indicates that he was substantially better-off than the vast majority of townspeople, even before *la violencia*.

Intracommunal and even intrafamilial distrust, the omnipresent threat of denunciation by parties to a conflict, financial pressures, lack of democratic alternatives, continuing impunity, rumors of *orejas* (literally "ears," but used colloquially to refer to spies), and the accompanying economic crisis all contributed to the earliest wave of men migrating to the United States from Todos Santos. As people returned from the refugee camps in Mexico and from the Ixcán, new pressures emerged on already stressed land and resources. A long period of economic decline further exacerbated local tensions. Early wage-labor migrants to the United States almost always identified the ongoing war and uneasy political situation as a major contributing factor to why they left. And yet, migration to the United States at that time was looked upon with criticism: responsible citizens and workers were expected to farm their *milpa* plots and serve in the civil patrol.

Despite the wishes of Don Gaspar and his patrollers to view and present themselves as neutral protectors of the community, in 1993, they were challenged by the appearance of a Todosantero who had allegedly served as an EGP commander in the early 1980s.[15] Now a representative of the Guatemalan refugee community in Mexico, and a member of the land committee of the UN Commission on Refugee Status, Joaquín Jiménez came back to the town while in the area surveying land available for returning refugees.[16] He was nearly lynched by an angry mob, then taken into custody, tortured, and later released by civil patrollers who alleged that they had saved him from certain death at the hands of the crowd. The civil patrollers also alleged that Jiménez was responsible for the murder of eighty-three residents of Todos Santos in 1982 (CERIGUA 1993). The PAC later turned Jiménez over to the local military base, where he was briefly detained and then released by order of the Minister of Government. He returned to Mexico at the end of August. The Huehuetenango attorney general filed charges against the civil patrol over this incident. Coming to the defense of the PAC, Defense Minister Enríquez claimed that "guerilla or ex-guerilla," Jiménez was "rescued" by civil patrollers from enraged villagers who "remembered the terror he sowed" in the early 1980s (Ibid.). At the time, refugee leaders argued that the defense minister's charges aimed to discredit them.

Jiménez continued to polarize community members in a way that neither the PACs nor their current incarnation, the Comites de Seguridad, do. The fault lines of historical conflict run deep. While these latter entities have engendered substantial ambiguity, both during wartime and after, part of their continuing power in places like Todos Santos—indeed, throughout the country, as *seguridad* is now being implemented nationwide—lies in the spaces they provide for the negotiation of power. During the war, patrol leaders refused to put down their arms and assume leadership positions until the war was over. Although the PACs were officially demobilized in 1995, and they returned their weapons to the army, the social capital and political power that the patrol members had accrued over the years was, quite naturally, difficult to surrender. It is no accident, nor is it surprising, that a resurgence of the PACs emerged after only a few years, albeit with quite a different resonance in the post-Accords world of neoliberal democracy. From their experience participating in and engaging with the patrols, Todosanteros had adopted a particular form of political subjectivity, one that was hypermasculine and adaptable across a range of anxieties, worries, and contexts. In the post-9/11 world, as it turns out, concerns with security and the state's failure to provide it rendered this in-place and available set of alliances and networks extraordinarily useful, and they were quickly implemented: in a particularly neoliberal turn, pre-existing resources and knowledge could be engaged in the project of outsourcing security to communities. The civil patrol set a precedent for the kinds of repertoires that could be considered acceptable for dealing with conflict in the post-Accords era. The reactions to the alleged ex-guerilla provided the impetus to engage in the spectacle of control and reaffirmed the patrol's place and importance in local hierarchies of power.

CHAPTER 2

Localities in Conflict: Spaces and the Politics of Mapmaking

Localities are always political and struggled over. This is especially true among the rural Maya, where specific conceptions and local knowledge of space are central to the construction of identity and subjectivity. An individual is Mayan in part due to her relationship to a particular place, constructed from the memories and experiences that connect people through shared knowledge: the family *milpa*, the secret hiding places of childhood, the out-of-the-way courting grounds of teenagers, and the sacred peaks and valleys. Each plays a part in what it means to be a Todosantero. Because locality is shaped so precisely and in relation to myriad understandings about space, place, and politics, it is also a locus of inevitable conflict among community members and between neighboring villages and citizens and the state, in part over what Harvey categorizes as "the proper sense of space that should be used to regulate social life and give meaning to concepts such as territorial rights" (1989:203).

Culture and power have particular forms of spatialization that are best understood by examining the changing meanings that space has for people over time. As Gastón Gordillo has demonstrated in his work on the Tobá and Guaraní of the Argentinean Chaco, the sedimentation of historical processes of confrontation are lodged in the physical textures of landscapes (2004). This is particularly meaningful among the rural Maya in the post-war period, since sacred signifiers, associations, and histories have been so severely disrupted and even manipulated through long-term experiences of military occupation. Relationships to the land have been in flux over the course of the last century, especially with the increasing privatization of commons and the brief nationalization of agricultural land in the 1950s. The Catholic Church sought to eradicate signs of intimate connection with ancestors and spirits located in the sacred places of Todos Santos by often brutally destroying the symbols and offerings people placed there. During *la violencia*, the space of Todos Santos was invested with memories of violence and the land was saturated with blood. As a result, histories of recent struggle and conflict can be read through space and the multifaceted meanings it holds for Todosanteros.

As I have shown in the previous chapter, the Guatemalan army carried out a project that systematically "destroyed, reconstructed and penetrated the geographic and cultural fabric of villages" (Schirmer 1998:95). To accomplish their agenda required fundamentally altering local spatial understandings and patterns of use. While space, place, and the imagination of locality are dynamic and constantly shifting processes, *la violencia* represented a deep-seated break with many historical connections. Since then, the tensions of the post-war period, such as migration and the rise of gangs, have been built upon the changes introduced by *la violencia*, incorporating spatial relations and patterns of use and control that have been developing since the early 1980s.

Understandings, uses, and representations of space, as Wood (2003) has shown in the case of post-war El Salvador, are personal, often varying among individuals and groups who share similar experiences. Histories of communities, families, and other overlapping groups, such as agriculturalists or religious practitioners, are clearly reflected in space, in relation to local practices, cosmology, and agrarian patterns. This local knowledge contributes to the significance of space in the construction of Mayan subjectivities (Watanabe 1992, Warren 1978, Little 2004).

Stemming in large part from Foucault's study of the emergence of the modern prison (1979), recent scholarship has highlighted the use of control through the management of space (Merry 2001, Gupta and Ferguson 1997, Smart 2001, Low 2001). For Foucault, space functioned as a container of power: within it, subjects were incarcerated, disciplined, or otherwise socially controlled (Foucault 1986, cf. Watts 1992, Harvey 1989:211). By considering space in such a way, Foucault made the organic connection between spatial concepts and the microphysics of power— that is, the relationship between the map and surveillance, with all territorial concepts implying the exercise of power (Foucault 1986, cf. Sack 1986 in Watts 1992). While spatial governmentality is often viewed as an urban phenomenon (Merry 2001, Low 1999, Caldeira 1999, O'Neill and Thomas 2011, Perry 2000, Perry and Sanchez 1998), conflict in rural community life also develops around space, with tensions along lines of class, ethnicity, gender, and age, among others.

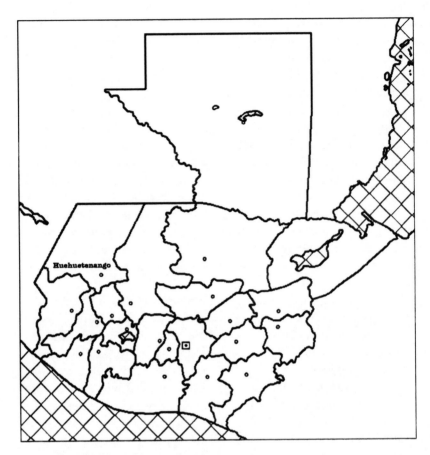

Map of Guatemala and Huehuetenango

Todos Santos as a Place on the Map

Todos Santos cleaves to the mountainside in a dramatic valley of the Cuchumatanes, the highest nonvolcanic range in Central America, located in the department of Huehuetenango in northwestern Guatemala. The highest nonvolcanic peak between Guatemala and the Andes is within municipal boundaries. The town center is located at close to three thousand meters (8,500 feet) and surrounded by four-thousand-meter (twelve thousand feet) peaks.

The municipal center of Todos Santos is twenty-three miles from the departmental and administrative capital of Huehuetenango, a distance now traveled on a single, paved road in approximately an hour or two.[1] The main road goes through the town center and continues on to various hamlets within the municipality.

The town's population was 33,619 people (2010 census),[2] with 2,980 of them living in the town center. Of these, about one-tenth were ladino (non-Maya), with the majority of them living in the village of San Martín. Ladinos dominated political and economic spheres in Todos Santos for most of its recent history, but in 1982, during the height of the genocidal counterinsurgency campaign, many left, not to return. Mayan Todosanteros took over their commercial establishments and business interests. The center, referred to as *tnom*, contained only about ten percent of the town's population, and one hamlet alone is home to several times more people (2002 census). The valley, *twi' witz*, is surrounded by a number of peaks central to local cosmovision.[3]

Beyond the dramatic valley setting, Todos Santos is famous for being

Map of Huehuetenango and Todos Santos

Market day, 2006 (J. Burrell)

one of the few townships in Guatemala where both men and women continue to wear *traje*, clothing that identifies its wearers as being from a particular town. *Traje* is among the reasons Todos Santos is one of the most photographed municipalities in all of Guatemala, as well as an attraction for those desiring to visit a less-developed region. While most Mayan women continue to wear *huipiles*, hand-woven and embroidered shirts, there are few other towns in Guatemala where men have likewise continued this tradition of distinctive shirts and pants that mark them as Maya.

Land, Space, and Conflict

"When eighteenth-century Indian petitioners or litigants addressed why they wanted or needed land, they did so in a very specific context, using terms borrowed from a language with which they had limited familiarity and in the manner most calculated to ingratiate themselves with their superiors. Probably, if asked in a general way, the whole question would have struck them as absurd, for the utility of land was self-evident and eternal: land meant everything."
DAVID MCCREERY, *RURAL GUATEMALA*

Land—or the shortage of it—has historically been the single greatest on-going concern in Todos Santos, as it is for many Mayan communities. While the quote above refers to the eighteenth century, it remains applicable today. Indeed, neoliberal economics has only exacerbated land shortages as regional trade agreements open the doors to corporate interests that engage in mining and industrial, agricultural, and other forms of resource extraction that displaces the Maya (Grandia 2012). The majority of migrant narratives include this situation as a concern, suggesting that chronic land scarcity remains a primary push factor for massive out-migration throughout the Guatemalan highlands. Land often remains, in one way or another, at the heart of the conflicts that animate the post-war period.

In noting land's historical centrality in local conflict, scholars of Guatemala have advanced various conceptions of how Maya understand and ascribe meaning to land, documenting historical land-use patterns, beliefs, cosmologies, and clashes. Falla notes that for community representatives who filed land claims following the liberal reforms of the 1870s and the advent of the coffee oligarchy, land was understood as a series of concentric circles (1978:280, see also McCreery 1994:237). The center of two overlapping circles represented land passed down directly to the individual through the *parcialidad*, an "ancestor estate" (Ibid.). This plot denoted the sacred relationship between the living and their forebearers. On this plot, the ancestors could be called upon to advise in a number of different capacities and to provide assistance in times of need. During her research in Chichicastenango, Bunzel noted that this type of plot "has a shrine, where offerings are made; [it is] a place where one can approach the supernaturals" (1952:17). Losing contact with this spiritually imbued parcel, and thus with the ancestors, could have disastrous consequences for the lives of individuals and families, but controlling access to it was a source of local power, usually held by the father of a group of sons. The intergenerational and sibling tensions that this created were built into Mayan social life and, Bunzel noted, were so insurmountable that they had the capacity to tear asunder the social fabric of communities.

Recognizing this tension in his model, Falla suggests that the land in the first circle was for a man who might argue with his father but still remain part of the community by using open and available fields in the village commons. The second circle represented *tierra caliente* (hot low-country land) that, while not strictly part of the community, might be used by the people from it; however, farming this land meant only indirect participation in community life (McCreery 1994:237). This conception of local land ownership and use is similar to what John Watanabe found in Santiago Chimaltenango. In the grid that he constructed for understanding space and social relations, the area of the municipality extends in concentric rings of decreasing familiarity from the village to the most distant volcanoes (1992:61–63). Four broad categories of space include the house, the town, the *milpa*, and wilds/forest area. While Chimaltecos spend most time in their houses and in the town, wilds and forest can be brought into the realm of familiarity through the work of clearing and cultivating them (1992:63). Todosanteros similarly divide the space of the *twi' witz*, often according to growing zones, and village spaces are imbued with cosmological significance.

While individuals construct their own personal spatial orientations, they do so relative to essential and historical understandings and uses of land. In this sense, the social construction of space is central to the development of community and local subjectivities on the one hand, and on the other, it ensures that conflict, especially intergenerational conflict, is guaranteed. Social geographers stress the need for mapping procedures that incorporate this complexity, suggesting that the wealth of social texture and experience find representation in space. Alan Pred and Michael Watts, for example, insightfully call for mapping procedures that incorporate multiculturalism, hybrid cultures, migrant workers, and the diaspora community (1992:12). The application of these expanded spatial understandings connects the mountain peaks and valleys of Todos Santos with regional capitals and marketplaces in Guatemala; former refugee camps in Chiapas and Campeche, Mexico; the migratory pathways through Mexico; the coast of the Mexican state Quintana Roo (the so-called Mayan Riviera), where in-transit migrants and deportees find refuge; and the vast territory *elna*, where Todosanteros settle in places like Oakland, Grand Rapids, and Boston. Such perceptions of space and place have led scholars to advocate for thinking about cultures and nations as occupying naturally discontinuous spaces (Gupta 1992). In their doing so, region emerges as the result of historically contingent processes where space is culturally (re)invented.[4] While this expanded model is useful for understanding broad political-economic changes brought about by transnational capitalism and neoliberal state practices, particularly as these play out in the post-war period in Guatemala, it is significant that the town center of Todos Santos is always located in the middle of the map. Recognizing the political, cultural, and symbolic significance of the town center, army and guerillas fiercely sought to control downtown Todos Santos. War wrought substantial reconfigurations in how the center was used, remembered, and controlled.

These included the implementation of various forms of surveillance, the patrolling of perimeters, forced citizen relocations to the town center, and the reconstitution of local power and economic life after many ladinos fled to the regional capital. In contrast to the Benthamite, and, later, Foucauldian notions of the panopticon, where the sentiment of invisible omniscience meant that observers could not always be seen, after 1983, the army was constantly present, either directly, through paramilitarization of villages, or through the presence of *orejas* (spies). Military bases were constructed all over Guatemala during the 1980s, and troops were stationed throughout cities, towns and their perimeters, and the countryside. Curfews were imposed nationwide to control movement and at strategic posts were negotiated on a case-by-case basis (Green 1999). Just outside the departmental capital, Huehuetenango, a garrison in Chiantla controlled access to the Cuchumatanes range and to Todos Santos. The places to which individuals were granted access were often dependent upon the whims of individual soldiers. Warren (1978) writes of severe restrictions imposed on the Trixanos of San Andrés, who were allowed outside of certain physical boundaries only if they convinced soldiers of their legitimate need to work, which was often accomplished by carrying machetes or tumplines (a strap used to carry heavy loads on one's back). Risking discovery outside of permissible boundaries was potentially fatal. Green (1994) describes meeting with local military personnel in order to seek permission to work with the widows of Xec'aj, only to be allowed to circulate among them under constant observation. Spatial control beyond the jurisdiction of garrisons rested with civil patrols.

State Rules and Tools

The Guatemalan state after war is powerful but poorly delimited, promoting in its citizens a sense of uncertainty about what it does or is responsible for, or what can be expected from it. This is in marked contrast to the wartime state, which sought to unambiguously control many aspects of social, political, and economic life. State power, its operations, and frequently the rules, regulations, and strategies for surviving within such a regime were clear (Schirmer 1998, Carmack 1988). The state interpolated itself into village life through everyday manifestations of state formation (Joseph and Nugent 1994), which included outposts such as schools, health clinics, and the post office, and also through its developmental agenda.

One of the ways that the state constructs itself, making itself evident, is through official documents and maps, by which it creates and recreates a vision, or visions, of its own existence. These material forms constitute "the primary paraphernalia of modern states" and are emblematic sites for statecraft (Navaro-Yashin 2012:84). The document and the map, artifacts of the state constituted by (usually) routine data compilation and interpretation, are part of the nexus of complex underlying cultural significations and classificatory practices that give life to the art of the state (Carter 1994). Maps are symbols of the state that assert unity; the map as national atlas and as symbol of nationhood was a concept that was prominently revived after World War II and the creation of new states. The map is an intellectual tool that often serves to legitimize territorial conquest, economic exploitation, and cultural imperialism, usually embodying a language of power (Harley 1988).

In both their content and their modes of representation, maps have been pervaded by ideology (Harley 1988:300). The practical actions carried out with the use of maps—warfare, boundary making, the dissemination of propaganda, or the preservation of law and order—are documented in the history of mapmaking. The abstract quality of maps often removes face-to-face contact from the exercise of power, making it easier to dehumanize the people in a landscape (Dym and Offen 2011, Harley 1988:303). Maps may "desocialize" the territory they represent, fostering a notion of space that is devoid of "real people doing real things," as Sherry Ortner put it (1989:144). The undeclared processes of domination through maps are subtle and elusive, yet powerful; therefore, when maps are used to understand subaltern experiences of domination and struggle, they represent particularly important artifacts of these experiences (Orlove 1991, Taylor and Steinberg 2011, Wood 2003).

Notably, in the post-war period, nationally produced maps took on very different characteristics, tending more toward the incorporation of cultural data that supported the multicultural riches of Guatemala. For example, language areas and indigenous "costumes" were frequently represented on maps. A central strategy in the presentation of the Guatemalan nation at war's end was what Benedict Anderson refers to as "logo-ization": how national maps are incorporated in postage stamps, banners, letterheads, airport decor, and tablecloths, and how ethnic imagery is appropriated to symbolize the newly constructed nation-state (1983:182).

Obtaining Maps in Wartime Guatemala

As I conducted preliminary fieldwork in Todos Santos in 1994, I anticipated doing a household census to collect data about gender statistics
in relation to household work. One of the ways that I considered order-
ing and arranging data was via maps. Through conversations with teachers and community leaders, this idea of organizational mapping morphed
into a plan to teach a brief mapmaking/social geography workshop to
students in the fifth and sixth grades, over the course of several weeks.[5] In
order to teach such a class, I set about searching for materials, especially
local maps to which the students could relate, in time discovering that
there were very few to be found locally. Maps, it quickly became clear,
were strictly controlled documents, and Todosanteros alternately feared
them (older people told me that the army could find people more easily
with them), passed them around clandestinely (only to people they knew
and trusted, in notebooks or while inside of their houses), or thought they
were useful for tourism and might, they told me, be available at the Spanish school or in the library.

While maps are often produced in the service of the powerful, as Elisabeth Wood (2003:46) notes, this is not always the case. In Todos Santos,
mapmaking did not exist as a cultural practice, as it does, for example,
among the Inuit of northwestern Canada and Alaska (Rundstrom 1990).
Nor, to my knowledge, had locally produced maps been used in land conflicts, as they had during a dispute over reed beds at Lake Titicaca (Orlove
1991 and 1993). Nevertheless, there was a tradition of what Orlove (1991)
refers to as "vernacular" maps, spatial explanations conveyed with hands,
drawn as *croquis*, or "sketch maps." Indeed, several people had hand-drawn
croquis and *planos* (street plans), which they were willing to lend to the
project. I hiked out to distant places to get them, or received them in en-
velopes or folders in the back rooms of local businesses.

My inquiries about available maps at the town hall yielded the information that there were none in town but I might acquire one in the capital if I were willing to journey eight hours each way and stay in the capital
overnight. I traveled to the offices of the National Institute of Statistics
(INE), where I waited in a cavernous technical workshop while the maps
were printed out one by one on a giant, hand-cranked mimeograph machine. My fellow map seekers, I discovered, were mostly women teachers.
I chatted with them as we waited. Several had been given a day off from
their teaching responsibilities so that they could travel to the capital specifically for the maps. On the whole, they planned to use their maps as

decoration for their classrooms. To most of them, maps were of extremely limited utility, but the prevailing feeling was that students should nevertheless be exposed to them.

The sale of maps covering zones of conflict (those officially defined in 1976) was technically illegal, I discovered, but it was permissible if the buyer came in person and could demonstrate appropriate need or credentials. When my turn came, I presented a letter signed by the mayor of Todos Santos requesting that a map be released to me for purposes of education and tourism. In a final flourish, the secretary had added that tourism was growing so much in the town that maps would be quite handy for such pursuits as hiking and horseback riding. The actual map that I received was drawn in March 1993, in preparation for the 1994 census. The scale was such that most freestanding buildings in the town center were shown. These maps were included with census materials to help enumerators find all of the houses in particular areas, and the enumerators were to mark any changes they found as they went about their work.[6] While in the capital, and now curious about the restrictions on map sales, I decided to see what, if anything, I could find by way of maps in the touristic environment of Antigua Guatemala, the colonial capital. In a local shop devoted to trekking and hiking, I purchased a complete set of fourth-generation photocopies of topographical maps at a price far beyond the means of most rural *campesinos*. The aerial photographs for these maps were taken in 1954 with assistance from the CIA, on the eve of the overthrow of the Árbenz government.

My map-finding mission exposed some of the more subtle ways (that I might not otherwise have noticed, as a *"turista"*) in which wartime conditions were indeed in effect. Both Green's (1999:68–70) observation about the silence and secrecy that underlie a "fragile" tranquility among Maya living in wartime fear and Stoll's (1993) reflection on what I think of as "touristic immunity" (even at the height of the war, ignorant travelers could hike through a "hot" zone unharmed) came to mind. Who had access to maps, when and where maps could be found, and how the information they contained was categorized were rigorously controlled while the war continued. As von Clausewitz reminds us, "the chief preparations for a theater of war afford, of course, great advantages, to which may be added the knowledge of the terrain and the possession of good maps" (1832) [1984].

The Politics of Mapmaking

Most frequently, maps do one of two things: they assert sovereignty or map localities (Black 1997, in Wood 2003:214). As cultural representations, their purpose and meaning differ by individual or group. Teaching about maps and carrying out an actual mapmaking workshop brought categories and assumptions about space, social relations, and political economy into focus. It illuminated social relations, conflicts, and tensions while clarifying local perceptions about the state and social change. I taught the class for several periods during the school day, while the teacher was away at a conference. The mapmaking workshop, in which we used handmade tools (protractor, strings, compass) to map the "center" of Todos Santos and understand concepts of representation and cartography, took place after school. Part of the workshop entailed collecting different kinds of information to include in the map: sacred sites, places that appear in local legends, workplaces, different kinds of churches, municipal buildings, and neighborhoods.

Naturally, arriving at the point of teaching this class was a process in and of itself. A friend initially suggested that I take on this project, and I suspect the fact that I was available and, it was presumed, could manage two classes of preteens in the absence of their teacher, was one motivating factor for asking me to do so. The subject matter for the class emerged from my questions to villagers regarding the feasibility of making a map to record household census data, and from one day of attempting to actually map this data. During that day, I encountered the civil patrol, and the head of the patrol cleared the project upon hearing that it was work for my studies at a university in New York.[7]

Notably, when I began to ask people about maps, and whether a mapmaking class and workshop would be useful, the first question that most Todosanteros asked was whether or not the mapmaking project had been cleared by the civil patrol. Their concern shows how space and the production of documentation pertaining to it (unlike other projects involving reforestation or the construction of ovens for bread making, for example, which didn't require the patrol's permission) were still very much under state control, and that maps were a mechanism associated with this control. Spatial governmentality was clearly in effect, and belied the commonly expressed idea that in Todos Santos the patrol was pro forma (Perera 1993, Carrescia 1989). Upon hearing that the project had been cleared, most people were happy to provide opinions about a variety of issues they felt were pertinent.

Intergenerational differences in response to this project were striking. Younger people and parents of students were enthusiastic, calculating that after the class was over and the project completed, the map could be housed in the library where people could freely go to see it. Others commented that having never had access to maps, other than those that hung in the municipality office and the *puesto de salud* (community health clinic), they were curious about how different kinds of information might be understood spatially. Many people involved in tourism thought that a map would be great for people who wanted to hike and ride horses in the area (of course, this project only encompassed the center) and others suggested that places important to tourism, like *comedores* (eating establishments, serving a set menu), hotels, the library, the bakery, and the Spanish school, be incorporated, thereby giving the map an immediate purpose and echoing a popular version of maps that they may have experienced traveling within Guatemala. Older Todosanteros objected to maps in general. Maps, one told me, were just a way for the army to find them more easily; they served no other purpose.

In teaching about maps, I sought to stress the great variety of information that could be contained within them. One weekend, interested in how local legends were spatialized, I asked students to ask their grandparents to tell them stories, to record these stories, and to be prepared to talk about them and the spaces where they took place. The idea was to map sacred or significant places enshrined in legends and to see where they were physically located relative to the places students found relevant to their everyday lives. Upon hearing about the assignment, ladino students seemed pleased with such homework, but many Mayan students groaned and began to drop their pencils on their desks. This, they told me, was an assignment they couldn't complete. When I asked why, one student replied that the Mayan grandparents wouldn't talk to them. I told the students they could ask parents, aunts, uncles, older brothers or sisters, whoever might tell them stories. They immediately cheered up, said they could do this, and moved on to their next class.

Curious about this response, especially because of the close relationships I had observed between children and grandparents—who often lived together in the same households or family compounds—and the pride that people take in storytelling, especially older people, who have had years to hone the skill of weaving narratives about the past, I asked students and friends to explain this seeming disjuncture across ethnic lines. Obviously, in some cases, grandparents had passed away, but in many others, this wasn't true. Privileging this local knowledge in a classroom was also extraordinary at that time—normally stories from grandparents would not constitute homework—and perhaps this threw some students off. I never received a satisfying explanation. The answer could have been simply that the Mayan elders were gathering at another location in the municipality on that particular day, but I marked the classroom incident as the kind of hallmark encounter that ethnographic fieldwork often presents: the challenge of understanding context and local history in shaping questions, and the issue of silences—what is not talked about, or perhaps not shared with strangers, in uncertain times. Part of the ethnographer's process is to make sense of circumstances based on what she knows. Because this was, for me, an early glimpse into the complexities of the local politics of space and the different kinds of polarizations it produced, I wonder how I might have rephrased the assignment. I wonder, too, if the Mayan elders' refusal to participate had to do with my still being a relative stranger to many Todosanteros at that time, before the signing of the Peace Accords shifted the kinds of relationships people had with the multitude of NGO and human rights workers, tourists, and government employees who spread into the most rural of locations.

Classroom Encounters and After-School Escapes

The mapmaking workshop served as a means for focusing my anthropological gaze on space as a vector of local conflict. In 1994, much of what comprised the "tourist center" in Todos Santos—where the hotels, *comedores*, and the library were located—was in the *txol* (neighborhood) Mendoza. After residing in this neighborhood and walking its streets and paths, I was at first surprised by classroom arguments over what constituted the center of Todos Santos, which I had assumed was obvious. For me, the church and the central park were located, if not at the exact physical center, then at least at the symbolic center of the town. Debates over what constituted the center were very much based on which *txol* students lived in and, to a certain extent, whether the students were indigenous or ladino. (Most ladinos lived in or around one neighborhood or along the main street.) Some students lived in *aldeas*, and these also tended to be loosely organized around kinship groups and were therefore connected to particular *txol* in the town center. Some students also emphasized that depending on the purpose of the map—whom it would serve or how it would be useful—the center might be represented by different places. As Black observes, "a map is designed to show certain points and relationships, and in doing so, creates space and spaces in the perception of the map-user and thus illustrates themes of power" (1997:12).

Whether students lived in the center or the hamlets was another significant axis of social differentiation. At the time of the mapmaking class, I observed a marked difference in how authority regarding space and its conception was granted according to where one lived. That is, when students debated about what constituted the center, the opinion of those who lived in some commonly agreed upon part of it counted more. Later, the center and the hamlets came to represent populations of "civilized" and "modern" rational behavior in contrast to the "out-of-control," "emotional," and "uninformed" actions of those from the *aldeas*. Seen another way, however, Todosanteros in the *aldeas* earned considerable respect for their "authenticity" and for the fact that they often spoke a form of Mam not heavily laden with Spanish words, were agriculturalists, kept spiritual connections, and, in general, reflected the prestige of the old ways and a shared past. This, however, was before the intensification of migration, which concentrated more wealth and transnational experience in rural locations, challenging some of the claims of authenticity and/or backwardness.

Other axes for spatial understanding were the places where family members worked, whether or not Todosanteros were employed outside of the home, where friends were located, where grandparents lived, and where favorite stores for purchasing snacks and sodas were located. Because of this, each student had her or his own very personal and unique map of "the center," which might also include such landmarks as the church, central park, market, municipal building, cemetery, *Calvario* (calvary, chapel representing the site of the crucifixion), and even more far-flung locations, like the *comedor* at the top of the *altiplano* halfway to Huehuetenango. We drew these maps on large pieces of paper as a class, and students called out various spaces that ought to be included in different depictions of the space of Todos Santos, explaining where they thought certain landmarks should be placed relative to others.

One exercise was to mark local workspaces: where did men and women in Todos Santos work? While there was a huge concentration of work in the municipal center, there were surprising numbers dotted throughout the *aldeas*, usually converging around schools, agriculture, and outposts of development projects and churches. Some students also incorporated seasonal work, emphasizing how the map shifted during the months of the coffee harvest or the *milpa* planting and harvesting seasons. Differences between work maps of indigenous and ladino Todosanteros were striking, although not unexpected. While indigenous Todosanteros might travel long distances to the *milpas*, almost all ladinos were concentrated in the town center or in the *aldea* of San Martín, and some even included Chiantla and Huehuetenango in their maps.

Sites marked by violence often evoke competing views of the past and markedly different spatial sensibilities (Gordillo 2004). The aforementioned mapping of sacred places and other sites was divided along lines of ethnicity, and ladino students often felt more confident in the validity of their knowledge in the classroom.[8] It took what I thought of at the time as considerable patience to uncover an alternative spiritual topography, and I later came to understand that this topography had been marked by violence in very particular ways that led to the undergrounding of its public expression. Because Mayan boys and men who had been forcibly conscripted comprised the lower ranks of the army, their knowledge was sometimes exploited in an attempt to co-opt and discredit local spiritual customs. *Chimanes* (shamans; spiritual leaders) and even *comodronas* (midwives), and the linking of spirituality to local spaces and places in public life, had become, as a result of wartime strategy and campaigns by the Catholic Church prior to the war, much less visible in Todos Santos.

In their local maps, regarding their conceptions of the sacred, ladinos tended to include the Catholic churches in town (and sometimes in San Martín), the cemetery, and *Calvario*. Indigenous students mentioned places located throughout the *twi' witz*, especially mountain peaks and bodies of water, although at the center were the buried mounds located just above town. Some debate ensued about whether the Mayan historic site of Zaculeu, outside of the departmental capital, should be included along with other unexcavated sites that few had ever visited but that cropped up in conversations consistently during my fieldwork. It's important to remember that although the Pan-Mayanist Movement was active by 1994, their agenda and post-Accords imperatives, such as revitalization, had not yet taken significant hold in distant locations like Todos Santos. In retrospect, in the context of ongoing experiences of war and spatial governmentality exercised by the military, it is notable that students mentioned any spiritual sites at all.

Once we had agreed on the location where we would work, we met two or three afternoons a week for a couple of weeks for the second component of the mapmaking project: working on using protractors and lines to map physical space. Not all the students could work on this at once so I conducted a lottery, in which I was particularly careful to include equal numbers of young women and men. To participate in the lottery, and hence, in the mapmaking component of the project, students were required to obtain the permission of their parents to meet after school for these few hours every week. Unfortunately, this eliminated some students who had long walks back to their *aldeas* after school, or who had to work in the fields or in shops owned by their parents. After I had secured a group of mapmakers, we conducted the first several sessions, making reasonable progress until the young women started to drop out one by one and eventually I was left with a group of boys. The girls told me that they had to work at home for various reasons, mostly to care for younger brothers and sisters. The few girls who might have continued were unwilling to be the only ones working with a large group of boys.

Because it took place on the street, this was the most public component of the mapmaking workshop, and I came to know many people through conducting it. Once students were visibly working and learning on the street, even the curmudgeons stopped to chat and to ask about the project. Sometimes they volunteered stories or descriptions of events from the past that were helpful for students in putting together the data they collected and expressed on maps. The large-scale map of parts of several streets downtown that emanated from the central park was eventually embellished by drawings and written text about community history and culture that reflected the students' various assignments and classroom exercises. The map was placed on a wall in the library. When it was first hung there, parents and community members gathered to view it as the students explained what it represented and how they had decided what should be included.[9] Years later, many of the young men who had participated in this project migrated from Todos Santos, but when they returned and we ran into each other on the street, they would always mention the mapmaking class and workshop.

Conflict, Space, and Ethnographic Sensibility

Locality "is a complex coproduction of indigenous categories by organic intellectuals, administrators, linguists, missionaries and ethnologists" (Appadurai 1996:182). Consequently, reinscribing locality, particularly under conditions of violence, indicates the dialectical nature of this coproduction and the relationships and histories that compose it. Influences of spatial control are difficult to see precisely because they eventually become normalized and incorporated into everyday routines. Local conflict, however, frequently provides greater insight into understanding how power and domination are experienced in the present. Maps, as strictly controlled artifacts of the wartime state, or as vernacular means of expressing relationships, shed light on how space is struggled over, regulated, and reinscribed with different kinds of meanings and possibilities for use. The workings of power and the parameters of local conflict emerge as categorically different in this chapter and in relation to the mapmaking project, compared to the fieldwork discussed in the following chapters. Power worked differently at this moment, and the local role of the state was considerably less ambiguous, as demonstrated in the ability of the municipal government and the civil patrol to regulate and control not only the perimeters of space, but also what went on inside of it and who had access to its representation.

Another motive has also influenced the presentation of these maps: to provide contours and texture for the development of a particular ethnographic sensibility and an inclusive methodological trajectory. I can't claim to have thought of the mapmaking workshop on my own. Instead, I was invited by Todosanteros to embark on a collective project that proved inestimably more enriching than anything I could have managed on my own in my first six weeks of fieldwork. This collaboration also laid the groundwork for thinking through other kinds of methodological possibilities, based on what people found important and wanted to engage in or follow through on while I was living in their village. This kind of ethnographic practice, emerging from local dialogues, is one way of negotiating some of the perils of ethnography during conflict: it allows us the means to make respectful, common cause with the vulnerable—what Paul Farmer calls a pragmatic solidarity (2003:230).

CHAPTER 3

Histories and Silences

"Guatemala suffers from a mutilated official memory . . . as if remembering is dangerous, because to remember is to relive the past like a nightmare."
EDUARDO GALEANO, GUATEMALA CITY, JULY 1996

"We can't agree on anything. I mean we all have our different versions of what happened, stuff we heard from our parents and grandparents. But it's always different. How are we supposed to know what really happened? And if we can't even agree on what happened here, in this one place, how is the whole country supposed to arrive at one [shared] history?"
FIELD NOTES, TODOS SANTOS, FEBRUARY 2000

Marx famously wrote in *The Eighteenth Brumaire of Louis Bonaparte*: "Men make their own history, but they do not make it just as they please; they do not make it under circumstances chosen by themselves, but under circumstances directly encountered, given and transmitted from the past. The tradition of all the dead generations weighs like a nightmare on the brain of the living" (1852). Perhaps at no time is this truer than after war. But certain versions of the past weigh more than others, and in the urgency to create official narratives—those that will speak to the vast and distinctive experiences of entire populations—contestation and divisiveness are very much a part of the process.

Historical narratives shape possibilities and visions for nations and communities. This makes them worth struggling over; it makes history powerful. From this perspective, processes of historical production and the contexts in which people after war recover, recount, or are silent about history are often as important as the histories that come to be told and heard. This is particularly true in periods of transition, when state projects seek to advance the consolidation of diverse cultures, practices, and narratives into a seamless, national past. Examining the processes by which some historical narratives emerge as dominant after war clarifies the often long-term power struggles that claiming history entails.

History and how to tell it was very much on the Guatemalan national agenda in the decade following the signing of the Peace Accords precisely because the official history of the recent past was established during that time. In the final negotiations to end the war, the Guatemalan army, like many other armies in Latin America and throughout the world, arranged for a series of broad amnesties, including the 1996 National Reconciliation Law, which extended coverage to the guerillas and was agreed to by Guatemalan National Revolutionary Unity (URNG) leadership. However, the so-called Oslo Accords, negotiated in 1994, had already established the role of the Commission for Historical Clarification (CEH) to illuminate human rights violations and acts of violence committed during the war.[1]

The CEH, which had a broad mandate that prohibited the naming of names or the preparation of cases for prosecution, would operate for only a short period and represent both the government and the guerillas. Some in civil society questioned its ability to produce the "official" truth.[2] As a result, the Catholic Church initiated a separate commission of inquiry, the Recovery of Historical Memory (REMHI), led by Bishop Juan Gerardi and meant to provide a reconstruction of the country's history from the perspective of its victims.[3] On April 24, 1998, Gerardi publicly presented the findings of the REMHI report *Guatemala: Nunca Más* to a large audience in Guatemala City. Statements from thousands of witnesses and victims of repression during the war blamed the government and the army for the vast majority of the human rights violations. Two days later, Gerardi was bludgeoned to death in his garage.[4]

The task of historical recovery that Gerardi and his team pursued was fundamental in the subsequent work of the CEH. The CEH registered 42,275 victims, 23,671 arbitrary executions, and 6,159 forced disappearances, and estimated a total of 200,000 deaths (CEH 2009). The investigation found the army guilty of conducting genocide against the Maya from 1981 to 1983, a crime not covered by the 1996 amnesty due to Guatemala's signatory status to the International Genocide Convention.

Classifying political violence as genocide may lead to further conflict and violence in post-war societies struggling with the aftermath of wartime atrocities, as perpetrators attempt to conceal or destroy evidence and eliminate witnesses.[5] Genocide designations set in motion a series of legal mechanisms that has the potential to overrule amnesties and due obedience laws put into place to protect perpetrators. History (and histor*ies*) become threatening. Extensive violence has been and continues to be mobilized to silence attempts to recover the past. Gerardi's murder and the recurrent death threats received by Rigoberta Menchú and by members of the Guatemalan Forensic Anthropology Foundation (FAFG), whose work contributes evidence to investigations and commissions of inquiry, are some of the most well-publicized examples of this phenomenon.

Career military officer Juan Fernando Cifuentes wrote: "There is a historic truth in Guatemala, which is a truth from the perspective of power and that is the one that we know and accept" (1998, in Manz 2004:231). Powerful challenges to this perspective emerge in the form of international human rights tribunals, such as the Guatemala Genocide Case in Spain;[6] the cases being heard in the Intra-American Court in Costa Rica; and the January 2012 demand by the attorney general of Guatemala, Claudia Paz y Paz, that former military dictator Ríos Montt stand trial for genocide and crimes against humanity.[7] The ability to wield national history and to cast it in one's favor became one of the most sought-after prizes following war.

Historical Terrains After War

The political contexts for the production of memory reveal some of the mechanisms through which history is created and framed and provide a basis for projects of social and political change. Significant attention has been devoted to how these processes work on the national level, especially in relation to truth commissions and other post-war investigative processes. Community-level conflicts over memories of war and violence, however, are often ignored or elided from these narratives. One reason is that the narrative that "counts" is the one that quantifies, or that produces the statistics that render war knowable—how many were massacred, when and where, how many displaced (Nelson 2009). Those who tell these accounts are portrayed as individual victims of human rights abuses (Oglesby 2007:79), rather than actors who have participated in the making of their own history (if not in circumstances of their own choosing). Within this context, experiences embedded in multiple socioeconomic contexts are narrowed to their singular expressions of trauma and death in order to be heard as legitimate histories.

In Todos Santos, reckoning with the past in this period has meant revisiting a number of contested and recuperated histories. They are not "histories of death" (Oglesby 2007), or portfolios or catalogues of trauma (James 2010), at least not originally. Some of these histories resurfaced in the wake of a Spanish translation of Maud Oakes's ethnography *The Two Crosses of Todos Santos: Survivals of Mayan Religious Ritual* (1951), from 1999 to 2000, within a context of a nationwide emphasis on cultural patrimony and revitalization. Following her sojourn in Todos Santos in the 1940s, Oakes wrote a detailed account of religious practices, customs, and spirituality, which resulted in an ethnography of a way of life that shortly thereafter was subject to intense pressures. Her account was situated against a backdrop of racism and economic hardship and was a well-respected addition to the documentation of Mayan communities. The book's informal translation from English to Spanish, and the history workshops I moderated, prompted a community discussion about cosmovision, *costumbre* (Mayan religious practice and customs that existed alongside Catholicism), and spiritual leaders. (I use the words *costumbre* and *chimanes* following the example of Oakes and the Todosanteros themselves.)

The undergrounding of *costumbre* was a controversial history that had shaped power and politics in ensuing decades. In the 1950s, Maryknoll Catholic priests established a beachhead in Todos Santos, where they trained young men as catechists. These men embarked on a systematic campaign to undermine the primacy of *costumbre* and the authority of *costumbristas*. During *la violencia*, *costumbre* and local spiritual knowledge was pushed underground, not to resurface until after the war, and then only in greatly reduced form. Although it had been the object of local contention for years, once it became an element of the Guatemalan army's "scorched earth" policy and counterinsurgency plans, public expertise and practice of *costumbre* effectively disappeared. It was the final death knell for the once renowned *chimanes* of Todos Santos, famous, among other things, for their ability to levitate to the sacred peaks that ring the municipality.

The narratives of history include silences that are as meaningful as what is said (Trouillot 1995). The long-term narration of Todos Santos history after war produced a definitive silence around some aspects of the topic of *costumbre*, the depth and breadth of which only became apparent during the workshops. By 2000, in the face of contentious debates about the role of Oakes's ethnography in the town, one Todosantero, a recently returned migrant, expressed the difficulty of discussing the historical centrality of *costumbre* in the community:

It's very difficult to get people to talk about these things [. . .] Many people were sought out and attacked for political reasons but also for cultural reasons. And later, after they were beaten up and all of this, they said, "No." We don't talk with anyone, not even among ourselves. Because the soldiers asked them [. . .] "Do spirits visit you? Demonstrate this now. We [. . .] want to see it." The majority said, "No. We don't have such beliefs." We don't even talk about it among ourselves. [. . .] It was this moment when people really stopped believing. People stopped talking about spirits like the ones in [Oakes's ethnography]. This is when the idea was contested [. . .] when the history of culture, of these beliefs, died. Lost their value. They told me it was when people were obliged to say [to the army] whether it was real or fantasy. They did it to protect themselves. That's why it's so difficult to talk about this. (history workshop, January 27, 2000)

To protect themselves, Todosanteros became adept at "knowing what not to know," a powerful form of social understanding (Taussig 1999). At this point, the history of *costumbre*, and of the conflicts associated with it, was rendered dangerous; underlying it were the disputes and actions of families, neighbors, and community members that became (or contributed to) acts of war during *la violencia*. Subsequently, when Todosanteros ceased their collective public practice and discussion of these customs, they also instituted the silencing of this history.

After more than thirty months of living in Todos Santos, "little did I know," to evoke Nelson's (2009) milieu of uncertainty that dominated the after-war epoch. The person who did know, and who was able to voice histories that no one else could, was a migrant. He had the perspective of distance and was invested in exploring this space. He showed up several times at the history workshop, before which I didn't know him. Migrants were key actors in the neoliberal multiculturalist project of revitalizing and upholding cultural practices, like fiestas, that were meant to unite a diverse nation. But perhaps it was their independence from local networks for economic livelihood, as well as their experience in negotiating social connections and knowledge in transnational contexts, that freed them to speak when others found it impossible. Once spoken, these histories had the power to heal, spark new divisions in different contexts, provide the footing for new alliances, or become the basis of claims that Todosanteros make to the state and/or to other institutions.

Cultural Revitalization and History

Negotiated peace brings an opening for new kinds of cultural dialogues. Issues of recuperation are almost always at the center of them. Debates about cultural revitalization in transitional periods in Guatemala (and elsewhere) have generally stressed the conciliatory aspects of these cultural returns. For example, Wilson (1995) writes that Q'eqchi'-speaking Maya of Alta Verapaz, Guatemala, responded to a profound sense of social dislocation by attempting to revive their ancestral traditions after abandoning them during the 1970s in response to increasing pressure from Catholic and Protestant evangelists. Pan-Mayanists in Guatemala have embraced revitalization as a way to unite across language, geographical, and cultural differences (Fischer and Brown 1996) and "utilize history to build a collective sense of nation" (Warren 1998:132). Charles Hale (2005) has suggested that these projects are consistent with a neoliberal multiculturalism that includes limited recognition of cultural rights and the endorsement of intercultural equality, usually without committing resources to mobilization or providing protection for the continuance of these rights. Nevertheless, they represent local efforts to make sense of the past in the present.

Cultural revitalization of ancestral practices, forgotten customs, and particular narratives of the past are not embraced without repercussions and struggles. If certain versions win out over others, if things once forgotten or pushed underground reemerge, this results from local processes in which a contest produces a victor. Local "winners" and "losers" then compete in larger arenas where new conflicts emerge.

Abigail Adams's research on the split among Q'eqchi' Mayan spiritual seekers in Alta Verapaz shows the group's rupture over divided interpretations of how spirituality should be practiced and presented publicly. All agreed that their worship contributed to the region's post-counterinsurgency healing, but their rift pitted those who advocated for universal and "rational" practices against those who wished to pursue more mystical forms of spirituality (Adams 2009:31–32). While investigating this split, Adams identified an additional complexity in the negotiation of Mayan *costumbre* in the post-war landscape. If practitioners were deemed to be "authentic" and "legitimate," they were seen as not fully modern, in which case they were judged unfit for the benefits of citizenship in the modern state. In other words, if they were successful at what they did, they were suspect.

In Joyabaj, Diane Nelson writes of how *costumbristas* are considered backward and are consequently dispossessed of their labor and the means to obtain a better life with the trappings of modernity. The people who pass this judgment are themselves often members of *grupos* Mayas, dedicated to the preservation of language and culture. In an incident in her book, while Nelson speaks with Alfonso García, a member of a group of organized Maya who meet to discuss culture and history, they see a man and his children hoeing a cornfield. García says to Nelson: "They are traditionalists and I feel really sorry for them, how hard they have to work. It hurts me to see it" (Nelson 209:175–176). For García, some culture is good, but too much authenticity and tradition is not.

The terrain of culture, recuperation, and revitalization is fraught with paradoxes, pitfalls, and myriad stakes. Understanding the specific circumstances from which they emerge necessitates returning to the local site of struggle and contention. It is within this framework that history reveals itself as a kind of resource. In viewing it as such, it draws our attention to how it is both a source of power and a fruit of power. The more visible the process of producing historical narratives, the less effective these histories are rendered in their function as unifying national tropes. More history does not necessarily equal more power, but history successfully manipulated does. This often unseen and deeply political (and material) aspect of the construction of historical narratives is crucial for understanding intersections between culture, power, and violence, where migrants articulate unspoken histories, organized Maya denounce the historical practices attached to identity, and *costumbristas* feud over how to be simultaneously modern and authentic. In Todos Santos, various versions of the past emerged after war; in the process, some that had been long submerged came to intermingle and were contested, challenged, and struggled over.

Costumbre, like many religions, has consistently been the subject of tension and ambiguity. However, the half century taken up in my analysis is one that demonstrates the long-term nature of community discord and contention and how it was ultimately shaped in explicit ways by *la violencia*. Focusing on history provides a way of looking at process by compelling one to move away from static notions of culture and society and from reading social and cultural forms as received or "natural." This attention to process, anthropologist Lindsay DuBois notes, "sets social life in motion, calling our attention to the dynamics and relations of power that constitute ever-shifting social terrains" (2004:22–23).

Community Contexts and Cosmologies

The Two Crosses of Todos Santos assumed a significance of its own in situ. Following its publication, Oakes sent copies of the book to Todos Santos, and over the years, additional copies trickled in, mostly as gifts from visiting and returning travelers. By the mid-1990s, there were a handful of Oakes's books in Todos Santos. For their owners and other Todosanteros, they had become objects of status and prestige[8] and were a source of community pride. At the same time, because the book was written in English, many people were familiar with its photographs and had a vague idea of its contents but remained unaware of the level of detail it contained. Occasionally, Todosanteros would ask tourists to translate passages for them, afterward discussing what they'd heard among themselves, agreeing or disagreeing, often commenting that this was something they'd been told by their grandparents.

A parallel historical trajectory involves the suppression of *costumbre* in the intervening years. Part of the knowledge that Oakes enshrined in her ethnography had to do with everyday practices. The cosmology that orients Todosanteros, connecting them with the peaks and valleys in which they live, is extraordinarily rich. The *twi' witz*, as the valley of Todos Santos is known in Mam, is anchored by the various peaks that surround it. These peaks are considered sacred and animate, and individuals may develop relationships with and pray to them. *Dueños* (owners), or guardian spirits, inhabit the *witz* (peaks). As Don Pascual, a well-known *chiman*, commented, "catechists and evangelicals come and go. Even shamans pass from the scene—both true and false—but the guardians of the four mountain peaks endure forever" (Perera 1989:20). This aspect of *costumbre*, the connections between the local environment and daily life, remains at the center of local knowledge. During my visit to a first grade classroom in 2009, students recounted the names and "duties" of the *witz* to me with great delight.

Individuals must accompany their prayers to the *witz* with *kotz*, gifts including candles, incense, eggs, alcohol, and turkey blood. These gifts were formerly administered to mountain spirits by very strong *chimanes*, who were known throughout Guatemala for their power and ability to communicate with the *witz*. Although the vast majority of *chimanes* were men, both Oakes (1951) and Bossen (1984) report that women *chimanes* were active during their sojourns. At the center of the *witz* is the unexcavated archaeological site above the town center, *Tuj qman txun* (at our father's

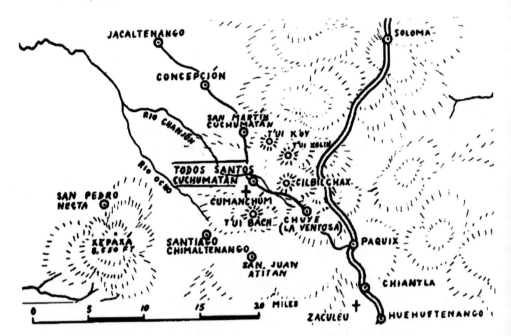

Twi' witz and sacred peaks of Todos Santos, from Oakes (1951:18a). The peaks are considered sacred and animate, are associated with resources (such as water and trees), and serve to connect the local environment with daily life.

limestone), thought to be associated with the classic Maya center of Zacu-leu, located outside the city of Huehuetenango. The mounds, proof that Maya have inhabited this valley for many centuries, are the most powerful place in the *twi' witz* at which to ask for the intercession and power of the ancestors.[9]

This cosmology and its role in local religious practices in the past and present is symbolized publicly by two crosses that stand in front of the church. These crosses are not Catholic crosses, Todosanteros explain, but Mayan crosses; on them, the intersection occurs in the middle and not slightly farther up, as in the Catholic version. In the late 1940s, dur-ing Oakes's sojourn, one cross was constructed of wood and the other of stones and whitewashed adobe, meant to symbolize the Indian and the ladino.[10] (1951:23) Two similar, smaller crosses were and continue to be located at *tuj qman txun*, and a third cross made out of wood, inscribed with the date April 15, 1982, was added by survivors in commemoration of Todosanteros killed during the violence of 1981–1982.[11] The crosses are considered sacred, and offerings are frequently made, indicated by copious wax drippings.[12] The local landscape is dotted with additional sacred sites. Todosanteros form close relationships with the environment and with nature, and individual families will often have specific places that they believe to be particularly meaningful and powerful.[13] Community identity in Todos Santos, as is true in many Mayan towns, is "imagined in relationship with the local sacred landscape" (Wilson 1995:21).

Historical Contexts

After Guatemala's independence from Spain, in 1821, the Maya continued political and social structures of authority that were implemented under Spanish colonial rule and connected to the Church and to the forced resettlement of natives. These forms were deeply attached to local tradition, and communities were organized according to systems of religious political hierarchy that were outwardly Catholic but maintained many native elements. Land was central to these forms of local power, and various kinds of ownership were recognized (McCreery 1994).

Two Crosses and a cellphone conversation, 2006 (J. Burrell)

The Liberal reforms of the 1880s brought ladinos to positions of authority in township governments in Guatemala, replacing indigenous leaders (McCreery 1994). Under the presidency of Jorge Ubico (1931–1944), *intendentes* (mayors) were appointed to oversee local administration, and although this had the effect of somewhat weakening the authority of local ladino elites, it did not return power to the traditional civil/religious hierarchies. The 1945 constitution, written and implemented under Juan José Arévalo Bermejo, Guatemala's first democratically elected president, provided for increased local autonomy and power in Guatemalan townships. During the six years of his presidency, Arévalo Bermejo carried out massive economic and social reforms, but these were only superficially felt in outlying areas (Handy 1994:4). Although they varied significantly, local power structures at the time of the revolution generally consisted of a hierarchy composed of civil and religious elements, including forms resembling the Spanish institution of *alcaldía* (a colonial form of governance), with elected village officials, including various councilors, a municipal secretary, one or two mayors, and the *cofradías*—brotherhoods organized to care for and honor various important village saints. Male community members worked their way up in the religious and civic hierarchies, and upon reaching a position of leadership of a *cofradía*, frequently joined an informal group of *principales*, or elders, who were consulted when important decisions needed to be made (McCreery 1994).

The accounts of Oakes (1951) and Raymond Stadelman (1940) indicate that by the late 1930s and early 1940s, Todos Santos, like many other townships in Guatemala, had not had an Indian mayor for decades. While *cofradías* do not seem to have been particularly powerful in these decades, the civil/traditional hierarchy was still functioning and powerful, and enjoyed substantial local support. It included the guardians of the Caja Real (the royal coffer in which the receipts for tribute payments since the seventeenth century were kept),[14] church officials, *principales*, and *chimanes*. In 1947, when Oakes collected her data, forty individuals were designated church officials.[15]

From 1951 to 1954, President Jacobo Árbenz implemented revolutionary changes in the countryside. For places like Todos Santos, this meant the gradual transfer of power from ladino to local (indigenous) power structures still closely associated with religious hierarchies, and the abolition of debt and vagrancy laws.[16] Vesting authority in these local organizations directly contradicted the reformist state agenda of incorporating

Mayas into the national government as a peasant class, but ultimately, doing so provided an on-the-ground structure of power that was immediately available (McCreery 1994).

There is generally no sense of revolutionary reform underway in the ethnographies of Guatemala during this period, and Oakes in particular highlights a system of ladino domination, rigid land control, and capitalist anguish, from which the only escape for the typical Todosantero was to work on the coastal coffee plantations for a number of months each year.[17]

Church

The hierarchy of the Catholic Church had originally encouraged the adoption of *cofradías* and the addition of local practices as a way of speeding up processes of incorporation and Hispanicization. During the late colonial period, however, the Church became increasingly alarmed by the growing divergence between native Catholicism and forms officially sanctioned by the Church (Calder 1970). Efforts to eradicate these divergent practices had been largely unsuccessful, often ending in violent confrontations. When Oakes conducted her fieldwork in Todos Santos from 1945 to 1947, although there was a Catholic church, there was no resident priest. In the past, priests from the Mercedarian order had visited Todos Santos and other townships in the department of Huehuetenango. By 1945, a Maryknoll priest was appointed to Todos Santos and was visiting a few times a year to officiate at masses and baptisms. This priest was well liked, and according to one Todosantero, the *alcalde rezador* (prayer leader), he was kind and didn't ask to be fed, as the other priests had (Oakes 1951:53). Aside from this man and the occasional clergy member passing through, Todosanteros used the church, convent, and the shrine at El Calvario to worship in their own ways; one man could chant in the Catholic fashion, according to Oakes, and this was the extent of Catholicism in the town (1951:53–54). Oakes reported that there were no Catholic altars or images of saints in the houses of Todosanteros like the ones Oliver La Farge and Douglas Byers (1931) reported seeing in nearby Jacaltenango or Santa Eulalia, and the statues in the church seemed of little importance to most Todosanteros, except for the one of "Santo Todos Santos, the patron saint of the pueblo, who has been identified with San Francisco, and perhaps also Santa Lucia and San Isidro, who are prayed to for rain" (1951:54).

Saints in the church, including Santo Todos Santos (right), 2006 (J. Burrell)

In 1957, less than a decade after Oakes departed from Todos Santos, a Maryknoll Catholic priest from the United States began to reside full-time in the village.[18] Thereafter, priests lived in Todos Santos until 1982, and have been there since 1998. Categorizing *costumbre* as "a religion of fear" and "a weird mixture of Christianity and Mayan religion," the first priest systematically initiated a crusade to eradicate its practice in Todos Santos, initially on the public level (Maryknoll Films 1960).[19] His campaign was conducted along multiple lines: desecrating and destroying sacred sites and objects, publically humiliating citizens who practiced *costumbre*, excommunicating them from the Church, and socially ostracizing them. Following the Maryknoll strategy of developing core groups to receive training in Catholic doctrine (Calder 1970:88–89), the perfidy of local catechists—who were instrumental to this project—figures prominently in Todosanteros' memories of this time. These young rebels physically ejected people from the church during mass, utilized techniques of public humiliation, and provided advice on how to most effectively destroy Todosanteros' connections with the practices and beliefs of *costumbre*. A crucial factor in the success of the priest and catechists was local conflicts between community members and members of *cofradías*. Increasing debt servitude and longer periods at coastal plantations to repay debts that had accrued for mandatory participation in fiestas, along with other expenses, meant that there was an increasing lack of faith in these institutions, and *cofradías* began to lose popular support (Behrens 2004, Warren 1989). Viewed as an alternative, with significant and important linkages to local and state power that could be beneficial to the community, Maryknoll were successful in not only converting but in quickly gaining legitimacy in communities.

Unlike the *cofradías*, who seemingly took their power for granted and exacted significant financial cooperation, catechists, especially under the Maryknolls, developed personal relationships at the household level by going to each individual home and offering to pray with families (Watanabe 1992). In this way, they succeeded in putting a local face on the imposition of Catholicism, a useful technique for implementing their agenda at the community level. Younger people found the opportunity to achieve leadership roles in community life without long apprenticeships and decades spent moving through traditional hierarchies of power and social arrangement attractive (Brintnall 1979).

Another strategy for combating *costumbre* and drawing converts away from *chimanes* was the distribution of medicine. Initially, this involved drugs for dysentery and malaria that migrant workers picked up on the coastal plantations, but eventually the Maryknolls established clinics throughout rural Huehuetenango (Calder 1970:83, Watanabe 1992:101). To further distance catechists from the *chimanes*, Maryknolls also denounced the consumption of alcohol, central to *costumbre* rituals, as immoral and wasteful. A final element of the Maryknoll program involved education. By establishing primary schools in the rural areas of Huehuetenango, and the Colegio la Salle (a secondary school) in the department capital, Maryknolls sought to overcome the linguistic and cultural barriers faced by Maya in regular public schools, hoping that education might constitute a defense for further ladino exploitation (Calder 1970:78–79, in Watanabe 1992).

Many of these strategies and programs were central to the social justice concerns espoused in liberation theology[20] and Catholic Action, which advocated for the indigenous poor and sought to raise awareness of and counteract injustice throughout Latin America, particularly in rural areas. Liberation theologists implemented their programs in communities through collective forms such as cooperatives, and these in turn were points for community organizing. Politically, many catechists were interested in transcending rather than erasing community differences, which was also true in other parts of the region.[21] From their perspective, community cohesion was based not on native traditions but on religious belief and ethnic identity and the possibilities for political organization these represented (Harvey 1998).

Producer cooperatives were also the organizational form implemented by groups of Todosantero settlers in the northern jungle areas of the Ixcán beginning in the late 1960s. Identified by the army as a source of guerilla support, cooperatives in general were targeted in an effort to wipe out this base, and "cooperative" became a dirty word synonymous with communism. Many Catholics were targeted for social justice activism and community organizing as well as for membership in cooperatives (cf. Warren 1989).

In the midst of the increasing repression of Catholics, by the 1960s, the *chimanes* of Todos Santos appealed to Oakes for advice and help in battling the onslaught against and the demise of their public roles. Oakes exhorted them to hang on, reminding them that their religion had survived for five hundred years and, based on what she had observed, would easily survive another five hundred.[22] By the 1970s, she realized her mistake, lamenting that the very fact that these proud leaders had thought to ask for the assistance of the foreign anthropologist illustrated their desperation.

Replacing Mayan religious practitioners as local power brokers with crucial access to the resources and influence of the church, the catechists quickly consolidated their power, gatekeeping not only in matters of Catholicism but also in public life. As community members, they were particularly successful in bringing the influence of the church to bear in the other community struggles and conflicts in which they participated. As community leaders, they were able to shape the contours of sectors of local development, hold high-ranking political and hierarchical roles, and produce local mayors from their ranks. To this day, they maintain authoritarian control over access to the church and to church sacraments. Any attempts to negotiate directly with the priests (who are assigned to temporary duty but are nevertheless at the top of the hierarchy during their sojourn) earn their wrath and ire.[23]

The religious landscape in Todos Santos has been significantly transformed since the days when the *costumbristas* and catechists battled over local terrain. In the 1960s and 1970s, evangelical churches began to appear in Todos Santos. As was the case throughout Guatemala, Todosanteros flocked to these churches in large numbers, especially beginning in the mid-1970s. Many sought to escape the orthodoxy of the Catholic Church; others were attracted by a different kind of work ethic and possibilities besides *cofradías* and other traditional hierarchies (Warren 1998, Annis 1988). Notably, this was the same attraction that the catechists trained by the Maryknoll had mentioned in their accounts of their conversions just two decades earlier. Still others saw it as politically expedient, noting that by the 1970s, the army was increasingly targeting Catholics (Carrescia 1989, Perera 1995). New kinds of conflicts over religion emerged and were exacerbated by the war and the experiences of *la violencia* in Todos Santos. These conflicts were particularly raw in the mid-to-late 1980s and mostly had to do with the emerging split between Catholics and evangelicals. By the early 1990s, Mormons were also present in Todos Santos and had established two churches (one in the town center and one on the main road in a municipal hamlet). They continued to send missionaries to Todos Santos until 1997, when they closed both churches due to a shortage of converts.

The undergrounding of Mayan religious practice interfered with local cosmologies and spiritual links to the environment that had long represented a living history of Todos Santos. The enormity and trauma of the destruction that was wrought during this process was captured by one Todosantero who, recounting his mother's painful experiences of public humiliation and social ostracism in the 1950s, referred to it as "*la segunda conquista de mi cultura*" (the second conquest of my culture). "This time," he told me, "it was even worse because it was her own people doing this to her." Because obliterating the oral tradition of *costumbre* was central to destroying it, the emergence of these kinds of accounts in discussion around the translation of *The Two Crosses* was notable. It also meant that Oakes's ethnography (even prior to translation) gained a new significance as the only repository for the local customs and history of religion in Todos Santos, becoming a crucial artifact in recuperation efforts. And Oakes herself became a powerful figure in local history, albeit one whose authority and legitimacy was debated and contested.

Genealogy of a Workshop

In 1999, I worked with a group of three young Todosanteros—one woman and two men—to draft an informal translation of *The Two Crosses of Todos Santos* into Spanish.[24] We did this because for many years I had been involved in discussions about how the book should be made more accessible to Todosanteros. Our work culminated in a formal presentation in the town center in November 1999, and afterward, the translation that we prepared, photocopied,[25] and bound was read and discussed by a rotating group of twenty to thirty people in conjunction with history workshops I facilitated in 1999 and 2000.[26] Parts of the translation were recorded in Spanish and Mam for those who couldn't read. Mormons, Protestants, revitalization leaders, *costumbristas*, teachers, agriculturalists, and migrants of both sexes and from different generations (most were between the ages of twenty-five and fifty) brought varying perspectives, wit, and humor to the table for two or more hours. At their request, I served as convener, moderator, and coordinator, and we met at least twice a month, usually in the library.

Initially, the workshops were divided between men and women par-

The *entrega*, the public celebration of the informal translation of Oakes's book, 1999
(J. Burrell)

Todosanteros with the Oakes translation, 2000 (J. Burrell)

ticipants, but toward the end, there were more men. In general, men and women had distinct styles of narrating history. Several women commented on how unusual it was to have the opportunity to share histories outside of their homes. They related historic periods to stories their family members told them: "It must have been at least 1938, because my grandmother had two children already." And they recounted stories in relation to how, where, and when they first heard them: "I was weaving on the patio, I remember the *huipil*, I must have been thirteen when my grandfather told me that story," or "My grandmother recounted this history while we were making tortillas, because in those days we made them everyday."

Men had a very different kind of storytelling style, often claiming that they "didn't know any history." They would immediately disprove this as they began to weave histories embroidered with levels of detail that were extraordinarily rich. It wasn't common for men to sit around the house and share histories; they were usually *en la calle* (in the street) with their sons, while women and girls pursued storytelling activities at home. Due to this different relationship to the art of storytelling and of embroidering oral histories, men were frustrated by what they saw as extraneous details in historical narrative.[27] The men's approaches were more direct; they would resort to contextual background only if they were unsure about particular details, and it was rare for a man to explain the provenance of an historical account. Men would frequently invite women to participate in elaborating on a particular community history when they knew that an individual had something to add. This was a rare act for women participants, who were more likely to narrate an entire historical episode on their own. There also were some generational differences in storytelling, perhaps related to levels of education.

Access to the information and materials contained within the *The Two Crosses*, called *el libro de los Todosanteros* by one participant,[28] provoked a number of debates, illuminating the contours of a struggle in which a dominant narrative and practice (Catholicism) had clearly taken hold while another (*costumbre*) had been erased at great social cost to many individuals. Catholics sought to replace the tradition of the ancestors, with its rich cosmology and emphasis on the value of history and social interconnectedness to one another and to the environment, with Catholic orthodoxy, in correspondence with ideas about progress, modernity, and education. In speaking about the memories of their family members during this process, Todosanteros evoked a sense of loss and violence perpetuated on one another at a transitional moment during which substantial power was at stake. Adding to this, *la violencia* had clearly suppressed both religious practice and oral tradition, creating a silence around some aspects of *costumbre* that was difficult to breach even years later.

In the new space of Mayan cultural revitalization in the post-war period, an opening was created in Todos Santos for some people to discuss, dispute, and argue over the ethnography and its subject matter. In due course, the ethnography itself became an object of conflict and contested history. Younger people as well as some teachers and community members grappling with what it meant to be Todosanteros in contemporary times embraced the ethnography as a sort of "sacred" book, a designation the translators and others argued was appropriate because the book was a history of the religion of their ancestors. It explained not only a system of beliefs, but also its practices, some of which still existed but no longer had their original meaning. Oakes's book was also sacred because it was a *written* account of a specific historical moment and set of customs and practices in their community. One participant suggested that it could potentially take on unwarranted importance because there were few such books in places like Todos Santos. Others argued that although they didn't think the ethnography should be a manual for reinvigorating a local practice of *costumbre*, it was significant as a book of stories, of information, "an inheritance for the community" (history workshop, December 18, 1999).

Having this history and data available at a key moment of national transition, when the post-war state was attempting to promote and establish a sense of a shared common past and cultural practice, was threatening for those who had participated in and benefited from local processes to push *costumbre* underground. A former catechist and political leader in Todos Santos argued that the book was history—nothing more, and nothing less. It was a story of the past that bore no relation to the present and should be read precisely as that, as what happened *antes* (before).

Excerpts: Notes on the *Taller de Historia* *Biblioteca Popular*

Todos Santos Cuchumatán
December 12, 1999

It's our first meeting and ten people attend. One elder came for the first hour or so and told us stories about "Matilde Robles" (Maud Oakes) but left a little while later. Among other things, he claims she only had one arm. He remembers this because she was the first one-armed person he saw. She held a mirror to his uncle's mouth when he fell off a horse during the *corrida*. When she saw condensation, she knew he was still alive. Matilde smoked like a Maya. She offered everyone a cigarette when she had one. (Like you, Jennifer, they tell me.) "Ladinos, they light one cigarette for themselves and don't invite anyone to join them."

We wished for more elders—we hoped to hear their stories—and we're not sure why they're not here. This becomes an agenda item—how can we persuade more elders to join us? They're the ones that we need to hear from, who lived through so much.

People realize that I am leaving Todos Santos in four months. If they want to meet to share and discuss community history, now is the time. They say that they're too busy; if I'm not around to act as coordinator, they won't meet on their own. It's not something they have ever done before. One friend tells me, "Matilde Robles would be proud of you."

At first, we talk about *The Two Crosses*. It's contentious; there are many opinions. Then, a new idea emerges: "We should try for a complete view of our pueblo now. We are on a *camino* [path] that changes us. There is so much that will be left behind. Let's figure out what is important to us as a community."

We draw up a list of themes and assign responsibility for them, but in the end, everyone tells stories. A rhythm develops. "Everyone has their own history, but there's a separate history of the pueblo that's important." We discuss *The Two Crosses* and its importance:

—"How should we think about this book? [We can] think about it as healthy spirituality so that it can be an alternative for our society or we [can] leave it [. . .] read it as things that happened, what other people said, of no value to us now. I don't know. I read this and I think, good, it really is like this."

—"There are no newspapers here. Sometimes people aren't prepared because they don't read [. . .] People are going to see [the translation] as negative and start a conflict over it and I don't know what else."

—"[It depends] on the person [. . .] For me, it's a book of histories, of information. If you're not going to use it as a guide, [thinking], "This is the right road to follow, I'm going to take this path," that's not useful. It's like the basis, a foundation, raw material, taking it as neither bad nor good, it is just material, good material in this case."

—"My point of view is that this book is not simply reading material. It's something good [. . .] If we treat it like any old book, it really won't have any value [. . .] but if we take it as something that we can build from, because it shows us something about our own society, of spirituality, it gives a sense of [. . .] how things are constructed here. On the other hand, if we're just going to leave it like any old book, well then we can't define our position in relation to it [. . .] There are the sects [evangelicals], there are the Christians, all of this, but it's not good for us to ignore our current reality."

—"[. . .] Children attend school now and they need courses that teach them history [. . .] it will serve as an important document for them to deepen their knowledge. Maybe they'll study the town, [and] then this book will be like a machete for them. I believe it will be like a machete for them. There are many people who say that this [book] isn't good, it's not useful, but things are useful. [. . .] Valuing something or giving it life, sooner or later it will be useful. Because I've realized that when we went to school, we would have to buy this book or that book and looking at [the translation], well, you realize it's worth it and finish reading. It's even better that it is part of the history of our town."

How should the knowledge within the ethnography be made more widely available? One teacher, active in Mayan religious revitalization, feels that presenting it in a *basico* (middle school) classroom is risky. In his reasoning, it should be respected, and we can't count on teenagers to show the proper deference for this knowledge. They might subject the book, its contents, and the teacher's personal efforts to teach it to ridicule. Another teacher read sections of the book discussing local cosmology and relationships to the environment to his first graders. He invited me to attend these discussions, and I was amazed at their knowledge, which showed that this history is very much alive.

Costumbristas and Conflict

As Todosanteros began to read the ethnography and meet to discuss it, a series of issues around the subject matter and its local history began to emerge. Chief among them was the role of *costumbre* in contemporary life. Younger people, whose experience of *costumbre* was limited or nonexistent, asked about its legitimacy and whether their ancestors had really believed in it at all. One man recounted that his father's visit to a *chiman* had been rife with drunkenness, debauchery, and fraud. "My father didn't have the money for this. He saved up to do this and got drunk, passed out, and fell asleep on the floor. He vowed that he would never do it again."

While the doubts expressed by younger practitioners emerged in relation to the Oakes translation, they must be understood in the context of a long period of attack directed at the *chimanes* by the Catholics, and how the *chimanes* were discredited in the process. While some continued to be respected community leaders, many more, in contemporary times, were viewed as drunkards and cheats who were incapable of discretion and gos-

Chimán performing *costumbre* in the cemetery during the fiesta, November 2, 1999 (J. Burrell)

siped about what people told them in confidence. Worse, they were also liars who charged too much money and gave little or nothing in return. The moral economy of charging for spiritual work became a topic of debate in Todos Santos, as it was in other parts of Guatemala (Little 2008). Dionisio, a participant in the workshop, said: "Many people performed ceremonies because they had a calling to help people. But now, it's for the money. Imagine it, I heard that they're charging one thousand quetzales, two thousand quetzales [$150–$300] for one visit."

Today, nostalgia is evident for a time when there was more unity and respect specifically derived from hierarchies. Although Todosanteros continue to consult with *chimanes* for some things—migration, health, agriculture, finding a spouse, intervention from ancestors—they realize that the spiritual power of this engagement is greatly diminished. *Chimanes* also serve as advisors for Todosanteros fulfilling community cargoes, such as participation in the running of the horses or dancing during the fiesta, to assist them with soliciting the powers and protection of the *twi' witz*. Because of the contested reputations of so many *chimanes* in Todos Santos, some people consult practitioners outside of the community; they desire the integrated spiritual connection, but worry about the price, the gossip, and the credibility of local options.

There were fewer disputes among workshop participants once the focus shifted to the collection of customs, practices, and stories unique to Todos Santos. Sharing these histories was ground that everyone could agree on, probably because it represented a movement away from the dangerous and silenced histories of *costumbre* and mutual betrayal, and engaged history as resource, as a means of securing a possibility for cultural recuperation and a return for future generations in the likely scenario that many of the practices that made Todos Santos unique would soon be lost. In this sense, it was a local "salvage ethnography," or a potential community survival strategy. It was, as one man put it, the creation of a new "machete" for youth, the tool that would enable the new generation to whack their way into a future in which knowledge of the past was valued and important.

Rather than rescuing a holistic culture or identity, this idea of salvage ethnography appropriated anthropology's historical liberal mission and was used to bolster an under siege ideal of collectivity that Todosanteros continued to find meaningful, underscoring how community is a shared and produced social enterprise. Conversations were organized around the annual fiesta and associated practices, inaugurations for new houses, the celebration of the first twenty days of a newborn baby's life, the *pedida* (the custom of men asking for a daughter's hand in marriage), racism, and discrimination.

In the context of these conversations, new ways of thinking about the dominance of *costumbre* by Catholicism emerged. In fact, compared to contemporary processes involving Protestant and other kinds of evangelical churches locally referred to as "*la religión*,"[29] some argued that maybe the Catholics hadn't been so bad after all, recognizing in the course of their discussion the considerable force and power that had been used by Catholics to eradicate *costumbre*. One of the participants, Eucadio, said:

> *La religión* has been expanding a lot. And these people want nothing to do with our culture. The Catholics came first and were more flexible, easier. When they realized, for example, that no one was coming to the churches, they destroyed the sacred places where our ancestors had their sacred stones [*fiadores*]. Yes, they went destroying. The Catholic religion really did do more damage, on a larger scale, I suppose. But now, with the Protestants, they really want us to change. Many of them have been marginalized, but they've marginalized themselves. Now they don't want to have anything to do with our culture. They don't want to participate. Little by little, they are contributing to the loss of our culture. (history workshop, February 27, 2000)

Costumbre is articulated here as "our culture": a culture that is shared, now under attack by those who refuse to share in or acknowledge it. Commenting on the same phenomena and adding an intergenerational twist, another young male migrant raised the issue of youthful disrespect, a threat as grave as that presented by the evangelicals. He pointed out that religious practices flourish more in the *aldeas*, among older citizens, and enjoy a greater rate of participation. There, he said, "they still appreciate culture. They still believe." Another participant remarked that in the hamlets, there are fewer options for how to spend spare time, so cultural practices and celebrations carry more weight and are more widely attended.

By the mid-to-late 1990s, in conjunction with the signing of the Peace Accords, and cultural revitalization attempts, there was an effort to recapture some of the knowledge of *costumbre* and utilize it again in public life. Even though *costumbre* in Todos Santos no longer had much of a public role in community life, people still spoke about how Todos Santos once had powerful and renowned *chimanes* who were justifiably famous for their spiritual practice and their supernatural abilities, although other places in Guatemala were now more important Mayan spiritual centers.

Some aspects of *costumbre* had been passed down and were practiced alongside Catholic or evangelical equivalents. For example, before a new house was built, candles would be lit in the four corners of the prospective house site and/or in the foundation. When I asked how he had celebrated the construction of his house, a young, recently returned migrant told me: "It was more my father who observed these things. I don't know how to do it but he knew from his grandparents because the ancestors did this thing with candles before building a new house." He went on to mention how pleased he was to practice this custom, especially after returning from the United States, saying, "I might not have done it before. Being [in the United States] gave me a new appreciation for our culture." While these kinds of observations aren't necessarily new,[30] what is notable is the frequency with which they occur among migrants and the collective power that migrants can choose to exercise in matters of local history and culture.

In workshop discussions, Todosanteros addressed the complicated ways in which the past is and is not discussed, demonstrating DuBois's observation that "historical accounts are often among the most obvious contexts in which the things people take for granted in their social worlds become domains of struggle" (2005:14). In this case, silences were negotiated, a nonthreatening narrative of history emerged, and a clear statement of cultural distinctiveness as survival strategy (the "machete" to carry into the future) was articulated.

In 1993, Victor Perera remarked that "after 1982, the cross of violence eclipsed the other two in the Todosanteros pantheon. The town's spiritual center moved from the *Caja real* in the *cofradía* and the crucified Christ in the church to the new cross standing next to the old Mayan altar [at the ruins]. Only recently have the symbols of a gentler Mayan tradition and of Christian worship begun, slowly, to reclaim their accustomed place" (1993:144). The heady mix of cultural revitalization, the rise of neoliberal ideas about culture and cultural practices, and the presence of substantial "peace dividend" funding after war meant that this project of local reclamation was sustained into the twenty-first century.

History and Transition

Exploring contested histories is particularly productive in transitional periods such as the one in post-war Guatemala. People's notions of how things were, how they become, and how they should be provide us with registers of the past, understandings of the present, and possibilities for the future (O'Brien and Roseberry 1991, Comaroff and Comaroff 1992 in DuBois 2004). Shifts from one historical period to another involve attempts to come to terms with prior history in order to move on to something new. At other times, impunity, lack of accountability, and other kinds of avoidance make this transition impossible even while questions regarding how to deal with "the past" permeate national agendas. While all national projects may seem more or less disconnected from history at various times, this is especially true in fierce post-conflict debates about peace and reconciliation versus justice. Moments of transition—with their promises of better futures in exchange for the "temporary" withdrawal of rights and services, along with other deprivations—raise memories, histories, and past violence in ways that link them to the present.

Assessing the social and cultural dynamics generated by the Peace Accords in the immediate post-war period, the Association for the Advancement of Social Sciences (AVANCSO) in Guatemala City concluded that

> The State has approached Guatemalan social diversity from an idealized point of view, unifying, forgetting—or denying—the social and economic complexity which is its distinctive feature. The attitude of the state has always placed society in comparison with an age-old way of being that as a hegemonic vision has been reproduced without interruption, and whose fundamental purpose has been the transmission of values and formative elements, standardizing citizens, making them uniform, an idealistic view of what has to be reached . . . . (1998)

Among the ironies of the process of constructing "peace culture" was that the transitional state sought "age-old ways of being" and the (re)establishment of a cultural patrimony that state violence had been responsible for silencing. "Cultures of peace" are always contrasted to "cultures of violence" (Oglesby 2006). As the narratives of Todosanteros illustrate, state violence made some histories unspeakable, and people searched for common frameworks for articulating these pasts and the experiences of domination that colored them.

Uncovering history and reclaiming the past is often thought to lead to reconciliation, but as a post-war goal, it is an ambiguous process that may often have effects that are more unsettling than cohesive. This is true not only on the national level, where history is often connected to projects of cultural revitalization, but also locally, where various versions of the past disguise the kinds of conflicts that individuals, families, and communities have with one another. Although reconciliation is a central goal of peace processes and an objective of fledgling democracies—regardless of the associated social costs—how reconciliation should be achieved is a question that polarizes after-war epochs and those who have stakes in them. At the core of this issue are competing visions of democracy: as consensus, or as debate.

Another contradiction is that while attempts are being made in Guatemala to establish new historical narratives in a "time of peace," spaces are simultaneously created for past disputes and conflicts that resurface, unsettling local relationships of power and prestige. One consequence is that history at these moments becomes threatening for earlier victors and power holders (who argue: "This is about the past and has nothing to do with the present"), and for others history becomes a powerful force or resource for addressing grievances or revalorizing marginalized perspectives. Given these different perspectives, the recuperation of historical memory and cultural revitalization is not without pitfalls, nor does it occur in isolated episodes. By characterizing historical recuperation as an *ongoing* and cumulative process—as opposed to a series of episodes provoked by politics or neoliberal multiculturalist or post-multiculturalist agendas in the post-Accords era—it is possible to understand the kinds of local conflicts and experiences of violence and domination that are unleashed through these efforts.

Todosanteros who participated in the history workshops were influenced by discussions of history and the construction of new narratives. Initially, they were concerned that cultural practices that contributed to their distinctiveness be preserved, not placed at risk like *costumbre*. Participation in the "work" of cultivating and maintaining culture was taken seriously. Membership in a cultural committee that formed in August 2000 and was charged with drafting long-range plans regarding cultural heritage and history was highly competitive. The committee's goals, some of which have been realized, included reopening a museum dedicated to the material culture of Todos Santos and continuing to gather and record history. Because of the absence of elders in the history workshops, a project to record local legends for a bilingual Mam textbook was initiated and eventually seen through to fruition.

A translator and workshop participant opened a local radio station in Todos Santos, Xolb'il Yol (Speaking for the Middle) Community Radio, which broadcast solely in Mam, with the aim of deterring "the rapid influence and hegemony of the Spanish language." Listeners enjoyed marimba music along with shows on local history, culture, health, and linguistic preservation, routinely hosted by community experts. Now, there is another station, Radio Qman Txun.

These community-level processes—local contestations of dominant narratives—challenge linear tales of the unity of the Guatemalan nation and the local community, complicating our understanding of cultural revitalization and the recuperation of history. The history of *costumbre* in Todos Santos, one contested history among many, continued to resonate in community life. In probing its contours as an axis of local conflict, we discover that there were and are alternatives to dominant narratives and hegemonic configurations of power, and that these shape subjectivities and future imaginaries.

A Future History

In 2003, Mary Jo McConahay, a journalist and longtime observer of Guatemala, characterized the battle for history as "a dramatic national struggle," writing of the radical means used to intimidate memory and competing narratives of the past. She referred to attacks on Mayan priests, who had often taken part in community reburials of victims following exhumations, and of others who challenged state forms of authority. In this case, cultural revitalization, as debates about the recuperation of history and "the past" demonstrate, is another kind of dialogue between state and local power, both of which are tied to and framed by ongoing impunity, which makes historical voices, silences, and competing versions dangerous to those who speak them.

I began this chapter with an explanation of two commissions of inquiry, one official and mandated through the Peace Accords, and the other unofficial and carried out through the auspices and networks of the Catholic Church in Guatemala. Together, these two succeeded in challenging dominant narratives put forth by the military, and created a foundation for various cases that subsequently made interventions into the ongoing impunity enjoyed by the architects of the Guatemalan genocide. However, at the time of this writing, invasive, all-encompassing impunity in everyday life rapidly closes spaces where counter-hegemonic alternatives and processes of contention flourish. In June 2012, Guatemalan government announced plans to lay off the majority of the investigative research staff of the Peace Archives, signaling their intention to close the archives. Founded in 2008 to digitize government documents related to the armed conflict, the archives have been one of the most active and important insti-tutions dedicated to creating peace, truth, and reconciliation in the wake of the Peace Accords, and provide an important source of support for human rights prosecutions in Guatemala (Doyle 2012). As Kate Doyle of the National Security Archive describes, this represents yet another move in the Guatemalan government's long-standing strategy to cede truth and reconciliation efforts to nongovernmental actors and civil society.

Histories of the war and *la violencia* that assign blame and urge for ac-countability are fragile and are subject to ongoing attempts to silence, dis-tort, and change them. While they currently function to buttress projects to end impunity and violence, and to support peace and justice in the present, perhaps their greatest power lies in the hope they provide for all Guatemalans, but especially for the youth. As Todosanteros suggested, shared histories and narratives of the past constitute an essential imple-ment and tool for the next generation. It is this generation who will sow and cultivate visions and imaginaries of the future.

CHAPTER 4

Reimagining Fiesta: Migration, Culture, and Neoliberalism

"The fiesta is something more than a date or an anniversary. It does not celebrate, but reproduces an event: it splits open normal time so that, for the space of a few short immeasurable hours, the internal present reinstates itself. The fiesta becomes creator of time. Repetition becomes conception. Time is born. The age of gold returns."
OCTAVIO PAZ, 1959, IN *CHANGING FIELDS OF ANTHROPOLOGY: FROM LOCAL TO GLOBAL* (KEARNEY 2004)

"As long as we're still poor, peace hasn't arrived for us," a Todosantero told me, when the town formally marked war's end in December 1996. This echoed the sentiment of the graffiti on the wall in downtown Huehuetenango that read: "No hay paz sin trabajo" (There's no peace without work). These words reflected the historical inequality and structural violence later identified by the Commission for Historical Clarification (CEH) as crucial to understanding the genesis and escalation of Guatemala's war. Although it stopped short of calling for reform, the peace process was meant to provide mechanisms for addressing these circumstances, as outlined in the Accord on Socioeconomic and Agrarian Issues. Officially recognizing poverty as a problem for Guatemala, this accord also indicated that the state was responsible for the economic well-being of the population. A peace process without "redistributive justice" meant that Todosanteros (and all Guatemalans) were still subject to the structural violence of poverty, a historical constant in Guatemala. The neoliberal propensity for exacerbating inequality through free-market practices intensified these conditions. In the late 1980s, military-backed dictators began to introduce a series of new economic measures, and by 1996, a Guatemalan transnational elite had assumed control of the country, pro-

Top 3 Sources	2010 Amount ($US millions)
Exports[†]	8,470
Remittances	4,130
Tourism	1,380

[†]estimated

Foreign Currency Sources in 2010
Sources: EFE *Latin American Herald Tribune*

pelling Guatemala toward a market-driven free trade agreement with the United States, which further marginalized much of its population (Robinson 2003).

Massive wage-labor migration is one of the consequences of the failure to address economic inequality and structural violence, evidenced in the severe poverty that characterizes Guatemala: more than fifty percent of the country's population is below the national poverty line and fifteen percent lives in extreme poverty. Among the Maya, these statistics are more extreme: seventy-six percent live in poverty and thirty-eight percent live in extreme poverty (UNDP 2006).[1] Guatemala also has one of the highest malnutrition rates in the world: approximately forty-three percent of children under the age of five are chronically malnourished. The country is characterized by massive inequality (it holds the second highest inequality rate in Latin America with a 0.55 Gini coefficient) and 60.6% of the income is earned by twenty percent of the population (UNDP 2008).[2]

The rich are getting richer and the poor are growing ever more miserable throughout the world. This is the result of the "success" of the neoliberal "ideological project," meant to foster greater inequality by establishing the conditions of capitalism under which elites amass more wealth (Gledhill 2004, Harvey 2005 and 2010). However, the worldwide economic crisis, the termination of "peace dividend" funds so prevalent in the immediate aftermath of the war, and the implementation of the Dominican Republic Central America Free Trade Agreement (CAFTA-DR) in July 2006 have exacerbated inequality in Guatemala. By the end of the first millennium, according to the Pew Hispanic Center in 2011, Guatemala had more citizens living in the United States than any other Central American country: as of 2009, there were 1.1 million, of a total population of 14.36 million.[3] Consequently, Guatemala receives more remittances, an

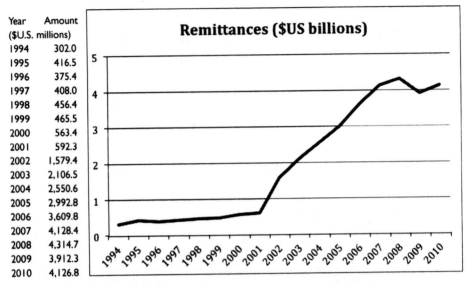

Year	Amount ($U.S. millions)
1994	302.0
1995	416.5
1996	375.4
1997	408.0
1998	456.4
1999	465.5
2000	563.4
2001	592.3
2002	1,579.4
2003	2,106.5
2004	2,550.6
2005	2,992.8
2006	3,609.8
2007	4,128.4
2008	4,314.7
2009	3,912.3
2010	4,126.8

Remittances in 1994–2010

amount nearly one-half that of exports, or one-tenth that of the national GDP. These totaled 4.13 billion U.S. dollars in 2010 (Banco de Guatemala 2011).[4]

By the mid-2000s, at least one-third of Todosanteros engaged in wage-labor migration to the United States.[5] Before changes in U.S. border and immigration policies reshaped possibilities for most migrants,[6] many individuals moved back and forth between places where they lived in the United States and in the municipality, imagining their eventual permanent return to Todos Santos. In addition to sending remittances, they also performed valuable cultural work, guaranteeing the perpetuation of certain community practices and customs. Participation in fiestas and other community events earned migrants social prestige and respect. Through this involvement and work, they ensured that they would continue to belong to their home communities, and they assumed complicated subjectivities (or politicized identities) vis-à-vis the state.

The staggering economic power of remittances to Guatemala only began to be truly harnessed for long-range national economic development and planning in the early part of the twenty-first century. Certainly there has been little centralized effort to capture the extent of community-based initiatives like the cultural work undertaken by migrants. Nevertheless, it is precisely this often unacknowledged work and sector of engagement that is critical to understanding the cultural aspects of transnational migration and the specific functions of neoliberalism, particularly its multicultural dimensions. For both migrants and the state, culture is understood as a kind of commodity per a rationale that holds culture as resource. Community functions as a particular space where culture is enacted.

The after-war Guatemalan state sought to promote particular cultural practices to represent the multicultural nation. These efforts were largely a decentralized and uncoordinated part of the agenda of shifting the regulatory functions of the state to communities. Migrants, who frequently have little other contact with the state, assumed this work in exchange for concretizing their local interests, which included identity, belonging, legitimacy, and cultural authenticity. While assuming the costs of this agenda, they became behind-the-scenes political, economic, and cultural actors and new kinds of flexible transnational citizens (Ong 1999) in promoting the transitional state's multicultural agenda. In doing so, as Karsten Paerregaard (2010) argues for Peruvian migrants to the global north, they joined the ranks of the most powerful agents for tradition and modernity.

In making this case, I turn to theories of neoliberal multiculturalism, which many scholars of Latin America argue constitute a form of governance that has the limited incorporation of indigenous populations at its core. This concept has generally been divided into two components. The first is the quintessential individualist and self-auditing subjectivity widely associated with what it means to be a neoliberal actor (Rose 2001, Gledhill 2004). The second is the acknowledgement of collective rights, granted to groups, usually as compensatory measures (Hale 2005:12). Theorists of neoliberal multiculturalism have pointed to the production of new subjectivities and of subject actors who work for the state by implementing its indigenist policies (Gustafson 2009, Postero 2006, Hale 2006). Many are not state personnel, but nevertheless engage in activities that serve the state, helping to advance an agenda that promotes cultural revitalization and recuperation while it also serves their own needs.

One theory of state-sponsored multiculturalism holds that it creates categories and spaces where indigenous actors and citizens are expected to remain. Some of these classifications include fiestas, touristic marketplaces, and national celebrations. Because they are confined by these classificatory mechanisms that establish the terms of their citizenship, citizens can be managed in ways that serve state visions of inclusivity (Postero 2006, Fischer 2008, Hale 2005).

Charles Hale (2002 and 2006) has elaborated the concept of the "authorized Indian," or the "*indio permitido*," who negotiates the spaces the state has opened to him without becoming radicalized or breaching his social boundaries. The *indio permitido* belongs in the realm of culture and labor. Participating in and sponsoring of fiestas allow migrants to be *permitido* in the eyes of the state and the community in ways that go beyond the economic influence of remittances.

Critics charge that the neoliberal multiculturalism model ignores spaces for indigenous activism and agency and instead explores the idea of indigenous civil society as a generative space for funds, national and international attention, and even indigenous citizens' own autonomy (Fischer 2008). Indigenous migrants fall between the spaces of action and activism and must navigate multisited, transnational spaces of culture and citizenship. Because they are in transition and are sometimes able to depart after fiestas, their activities in these spheres represent performances of citizenship and belonging and consitute what Renato Rosaldo, Lynn Stephen, and others have called "cultural citizenship" (Stephen 2007:238–241).

Fiestas are arguably one of the most public pieces of the neoliberal multicultural/post-multicultural agenda as it is articulated in communities. As the most visible point of migrant engagement with this schema, the festive terrain is one where migrants and the state have the common agenda of supporting authenticity in relation to cultural customs. Formerly, these celebrations of cultural affiliation, important markers of local identity, were left to communities. Although communities still carry the financial responsibility, fiestas are increasingly noted as being in the jurisdiction of the national cultural patrimony. The role of migrants in perpetuating them is located at the intersection where government gestures toward indigenous culture and post-war inclusivity run up against the devastation wrought by the same government's economic policies.

While migrant interventions may inadvertently contribute to transitional state goals, the terrain of the fiesta is at the same time an arena of local struggle and conflict. Individuals may use the fiesta setting to settle or to engage in disputes that they have with one another as well as with outsiders.[7] For example, public fights and brawls are legion, with those involved often meeting on the same ground for the first time in years. Murders have occurred. Sometimes, disagreements about modes of participation circulate as drunken gossip; for example, the appropriateness of a woman's participation in the *baile* (dance) is questioned because she is a teacher. This aspect of the fiesta situates community not only at the crossroads of shared interests and identity but also in terms of local, national, and transnational discord.

Transnationalism and Community

Migration has had enormous transformative effects throughout Mexico and Central America.[8] Many places have become veritable ghost towns, while others are mainly populated by women, children, and the elderly, who live in a landscape dotted with the new, vacant houses built by migrants who hope to return one day. Other places that have experienced massive wage-labor migration are engulfed in debt (D. Rus and J. Rus 2008, Rus 2010, Stoll 2010). Todos Santos, in comparison, is vibrant and dynamic while still experiencing many of these issues. Still other towns are marking the prodigal return of migrants who have suffered the U.S. economic crisis or who have been deported (Boehm 2011).

Recent studies have taken care to distinguish between the terms "transnational" and "global." In particular, Glick Schiller's work on transnationalism emphasizes "the ongoing interconnection or flow of people, ideas, objects, and capital across the borders of nation-states, in contexts in which the state shapes but does not contain such linkages or movements" (2004:449). Transnationalism, then, brings into play the exercise of political power by governments, specific forms of governance and subject making, and everyday instances of state formation. In addition to this crucial aspect of power, transnationalism also creates social fields that cross national boundaries (Basch et al. 1994:27) through the use of cell phones, e-mail, Facebook and other social media, traffickers of people and goods, and international wire transfers. As a result of rapid innovations in technology, new social fields and sites are constantly emerging.

As the period of migration enters its third decade in Todos Santos, the annual celebration of All Saints' Day, or the Day of the Dead, has become a firmly entrenched transnational social field shaped as a result of a continually shifting interplay of political, economic, and historical forces. Although the character and intensity of migrant participation may change relative to larger contexts, like the imposition of an ever-deepening security regime in the United States that prohibits back-and-forth passage, or economic crisis, the fiesta is consistently notable as a site for observing how community is imagined (Guss 2000:2) and how the perception of it is continually in flux (Bakhtin 1984:211).

What we see in these celebrations that otherwise remain hidden are the multistranded, changing relations that link together societies of origin and settlement, crossing the borders of nations, states, socioeconomic classes, and generations (Stephen 2007). Since the fiesta is the only ground that regularly unites Todosanteros from various locations, it is also the

A cell tower facilitating transnational communication, 2006 (J. Burrell)

site where concepts of community, family, and gender are negotiated and enacted and where terms of belonging are established. Beyond these performances, there are additional stakes that shed light on the kinds of historical and political processes that have legitimated and sustained social and economic inequality. Migrant network ties essential to establishing new lives in receiving communities are made, and individuals demonstrate their positions within these networks (Paerregaard 2010:54). In these processes, through a web of expenditures, participation, and network-building, fiestas at once unify communities and create new lines of division between those who migrate and those who do not.

After war, and under neoliberalism in Guatemala, communities have been expected to take on the role of promoting local cultural agendas that resonate with national cultural goals. Migrants have come to assume much of this work, financially and through their transnational organizational efforts. Since the role of "the community" in the multicultural nation-building project is one where national visions are enacted, mostly with local resources, this is crucial for negotiating spaces of personal belonging for individual migrants and for aspects of relationships with the state. Through its migrants, Todos Santos contributes to the state's multicultural agenda while maintaining its own cultural distinctiveness.

Although wage-labor immigrants are often vulnerable and liminal in their positions in the United States, their relative economic strength and buying power at home frees them and their families from local labor relations. Seeking to concretize their status within their home community, migrants insist on perpetuating the traditions that comprise their understanding of the "authentic," common past, in the process maintaining relationships that no longer reflect contemporary politics and structures of power. In doing so, they may uphold and/or subvert hierarchies of race, ethnicity, and local authority.

Transnational migratory imaginations tend to reinforce local-global oppositions, where the local is original, centered, authentic, and "natural," and the global is new, modern, and inauthentic (Gupta and Ferguson 1997:7). As Massey points out, these are also gendered: the local is associated with women and with a "feminized, private, domestic and natural space" (1994). The global, in contrast, is a "masculinized" intrusion. The after-war project of building multicultural national culture through community-based work has unsettled some of these notions; in the new terrain, both migrants *and the state* reify the local, so that idealized sets of relationships—from those of the domestic realm to those of the more public act of fiesta organization and participation—are now the required, or at the very least desired, qualities for successful citizenship in state-sponsored multiculturalism. Through their contribution to these requirements, migrants concretize local social spaces for themselves and national spaces for Todos Santos.

Fiesta Celebration and Labor Histories

The *corrida de caballos*, a running of the horses that takes place annually on November 1, is one of the highlights of All Saints' Day in Todos Santos. Multiple teams of ten to twenty men (*xq'atx qoya* [riders]), who have been dancing to *marimba* and drinking through the night at the home of the team captain, ride back and forth along a quarter-mile stretch on rented horses for most of the day, colored streamers and feathers flying from their hats, sheathed machetes fastened to their belts, their new clothing often spattered from the rain-muddied paths of the town and the course on which they are riding. One of their principal goals is to stay on their horse and finish the event. Large crowds gather to watch these men ride, closely observing who is participating and how the men are dressed. In the late 1940s, Maud Oakes commented that it was ". . . the hope that many riders will fall from their horses and add to the excitement of the fiesta. The riders are all so drunk that they can hardly keep their seats, and the hopes of the crowd are invariably gratified" (1951:210). That is still true.

On November 2, the fiesta moves to the cemetery, where the dead are honored with *marimbas*, *bombas*, and various other offerings, such as tortillas, sections of oranges, *cuxa* (a local alcoholic beverage), *Quetzalteca* (a popular, commercially produced, sugar-based alcohol), flowers, candles, and beer.

The fiesta is the time for Todosanteros to show off new clothing, handwoven by the women, as a testimony to prosperity and innovation. While the teams of *xq'atx qoya* still frequently wear the hats bedecked with ribbons and streamers, men and women now judge one another's clothing based on innovative weaving techniques, imaginative additions, and unique color combinations and interpretations of older styles (Hendrickson 1995). The men who participate in the running of the horses often add a personal touch to their ensemble for luck and/or to differentiate themselves: a favorite leather jacket, cowboy boots, or a Stetson-style hat.

In 1999, a young Todosantero rode back and forth on his horse attired in a denim jacket emblazoned with a large, raised, U.S. flag; a stars and stripes bandana around his head; and a full-sized U.S. flag flung across his shoulders like a cape. In choosing to wear this ensemble, he distinguished himself, followed a popular fashion trend in the United States that year involving the American flag, and made a statement about the terms of his participation in this event. Local commentary on his outfit was playful and respectful, acknowledging it as unique. "He worked hard," one woman told me, summing up the prevailing public sentiment, "and I'm

Corrida de los Caballos, November 2008 (Jean Yves Picq)

Men in the cemetery during the fiesta, November 2003 (J. Burrell)

glad that he came back to participate [in the corrida]. No one else wants to do it anymore." A local pundit remarked: "Here, he couldn't make enough money to buy a Guatemalan flag to wrap around himself."

His display captures one strategy for blending the new experiences of migration with the desire to concretize transnational community membership. While cell phones with inexpensive long distance service and data connections have now widened the range of possibilities for active participation in community life, previously, belonging was most publicly expressed through the fiesta. Its incorporation of new socioeconomic and political dynamics changed the character and meaning of social, historic, and traditional relationships and the subversions inherent in them. The traditions and practices associated with the fiesta are central to processes of culture, identity, and community, and they tie people in complex ways to a significant past. Shifting modes of participation as well as political and economic marginalization index migrants' embeddedness in changing capitalist relations, war, and after war, both as Maya in Guatemala and as (often unauthorized) Hispanics in the United States.

The fiesta provides an annual opportunity to examine how the re-visioning and the confirmation of community occur from a variety of locations that extend beyond Guatemala's borders. As such, notions of inclusion and exclusion are contested and refigured in Todos Santos and among groups of Todosanteros in places like Grand Rapids, Michigan, and Oakland, California. A particular quality composed of social experiences and relationships (Williams 1977) underlies a common past as well as an increasingly differentiated present, emphasizing the "transbordered" aspects of lives that cross ethnic, class, cultural, colonial, and state borders (Stephen 2007).

Choices made by migrants regarding fiesta participation make clear the importance of both concretizing alliances (for example, by belonging to teams of *xq'atx qoya* or organizing through neighborhood affiliations) and the public enactment of membership locally and nationally. Unlike individuals and groups concerned with Pan-Mayanist efforts to supplant community and linguistic group affiliations with a broader Indian identity (Fisher 2001:116), migrants in Todos Santos after war have been interested in perpetuating the local from transnational locations. Both migrants and Pan-Mayanists have effectively claimed historical legitimacy and "authenticity"—claims endorsed, at least in theory, by the neoliberal state, which also seeks to perpetuate the nationally authentic. However, while the role of the Pan-Mayanists is well documented in crucial transitional issues related to culture and revitalization, the importance of migrants as *sociocultural* as well as economic actors has, at the time of this writing, been largely unexplored.

Wage Labor Migration: The *Longue Durée*

The tradition of wage-labor migration is a long one for most Maya, emanating from what David McCreery calls "the extended nineteenth century," a period from the 1760s to 1940 (1994:5). The expansion of capitalism on a world scale, and the consequent development of a new international economic order in Guatemala, brought unprecedented demands on rural indigenous populations for land and labor, as well as a dramatic increase in the integration of local production, markets, and populations into the world economy. By the mid-1930s, as a result of changes to tax laws implemented under General Jorge Ubico, many Maya paid their assessments with 100 to 150 days of labor (McCreery 1994). In the narratives about this era, men speak of their ancestors as connected to a larger project that, although exploitative, incorporated them into a nation and a national vision. Their labor, and their reputations as "good workers," were historically among the access points through which Maya were able to develop subjectivities that had a modicum of agentive possibility vis-à-vis the exploitative state. The recognition of a social identity that stressed their ability to work hard[9] affected Todosanteros' self-conceptions and their ability to act in vulnerable situations.[10] Indeed, the work ethic for which Todosanteros were known was thought to have lessened the blow of forced military inscription beginning in the late 1970s. Although villagers debated whether or not the law exempted them from military service if the town was categorized as "hardworking," all agreed that Todosanteros more than met this criteria and that they were "workers, respected, responsible" (fieldnotes, 2000).

La violencia caused utter turmoil in the labor possibilities and habits of many Maya. In Todos Santos, curfews were imposed, making it difficult to labor in the *milpa*, and fields were burned by the military. Mandatory service in civil patrols complicated labor migration patterns, as men who left were required to hire a replacement to fulfill their patrol duty. Others who had fled to Mexico or nearby cities in Guatemala accepted whatever work they could find, laboring primarily as porters and in restaurants (Carrescia 1989). While some traveled to the United States, by the mid-1980s, most families did not have the resources to pay *coyotes* (traffickers) or to find trustworthy ones. Some of the earliest Todosanteros to engage in wage-labor migration to the United States initially went to Florida, where they joined thousands of other refugees in competing for agricultural work, or to California, where they also worked in agriculture or for landscapers.

The Vice of Our People: Shifting Perceptions of Migration

Contemporary migration involves traveling long distances, multiple border crossings, danger, and financial expense. It also disrupts community life. No longer is attendance at the fiesta or at Semana Santa guaranteed, as it was through the 1970s. Instead, Todos Santos has become a transnational village, as defined by Peggy Levitt (2000:7). A large proportion of a relatively small community has left and resettled as migrant communities in the United States; many of those still in Todos Santos depend on remittances; and migrants and nonmigrants know each other well. Remittances, construction, shops, and new transport companies resulting from migration not only increase the quality of life for many in the home village, but also cement migrants' long-term connections to Todos Santos, although these are more difficult to negotiate when the border is closed between Mexico and the United States. Literally and metaphorically, the expanding center is concrete testimony to how migration has affected the physical landscape.[11]

The unintended costs of migration on the social landscape are subtler. Women effectively lead many households, a trend that began to occur in Todos Santos, albeit to a lesser degree, when the war left many women widowed. Migration exacerbated this trend in different ways. Data from the 2002 census indicates that thirty-six percent of urban households and twenty-four percent of rural households in Todos Santos are run by women. The majority of these households specify that a partner is living elsewhere, which almost surely indicates that men have migrated. These percentages are consistent with estimates that I made during my fieldwork. In rural areas, the majority of women who led their own households were at the time younger than forty, and in the urban center, they were younger than fifty. A peak in the number of widows between the ages of forty-five and fifty-nine was almost certainly related to deaths during *la violencia*.

Migration and shifts in household composition have brought about changes in the way men and women relate to each other in general; shifts in gendered divisions of labor, both in households and at the level of the municipality; and a gradual movement toward encompassing different

Gated house with minivan; part of the architecture of remittances in Todos Santos, 2006
(J. Burrell)

kinds of social situations and relations. The meaning of this change in
traditional family structure and family life historically central to social relations among the Maya will become increasingly clear as a generation
of children raised without fathers or without both parents reaches adult-
hood. A more recent shift, related to difficulties in migrating back and
forth across the U.S. border, has led to many families reuniting permanently in the United States.

In the 1990s, migrant women and men left their children with grandparents, sisters, or hired women, redefining the role of parenthood. The
fiesta was central to these changes, as parents would use it to condense
years' worth of shared experience into a few short weeks. Given the families' formidable spending power, each year, the fiesta boasted increasingly
larger and more expensive carnivals and video games, Ferris wheels, and
temporary movie halls whose volume echoed in surrounding hamlets.
For some migrant parents and their children, the activity they could most
comfortably share during those years was watching and discussing *Rambo*.
These children aspired to the life led by their parents, who often insisted
that they finish school first before making the journey to the United States.

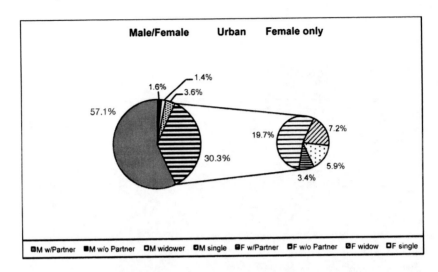

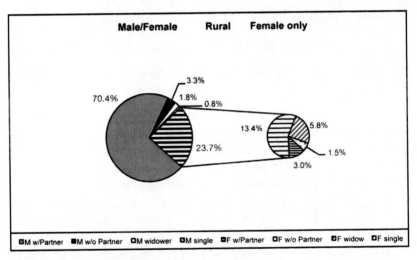

Leaders of households in Todos Santos in 2002

Occasionally, Todosanteros recounted the grueling journeys they took to reach the United States, the strategies that they employed to get through Mexico, and how they arrived at their intended destinations once in the United States. These tales were epic and frequently involved dangerous escapes from authorities, and grueling physical feats, both in rural Mexico and in the southwestern deserts of the United States. Occasionally, migration stories were punctuated with memories of kind acts by strangers or the coyotes, like offers of food, water, or medical assistance, but these were the exception. More often, coyotes demanded more money, threatening to turn them in if they didn't pay, or they were caught and sent back to Mexico. Once they arrived in the United States, family or community members arranged for transportation to their final destination (to Michigan, for example). What these tales would leave out was the brutality of life in the United States—the immigrants' severe marginalization in their new country, and the fact that their new lives were led in fear and under greatly reduced conditions. In short, in the early 2000s, the severe social and economic costs of migrating didn't make for good storytelling, so migrants emphasized the parts of their journeys that told of their overcoming obstacles and their eventual success.

Despite the positive gloss often included in migrant stories, and the contributions that remittances made to the local economy, not all Todosanteros saw migration as a positive development in their lives after war. Many noted that it became a way of avoiding local responsibilities, conflicts, and disputes. In a number of cases, men left behind pregnant women, refusing to acknowledge or support their children. Sometimes they had two (or more) families in different locations. Others "outsourced" responsibility for elderly family members to hired help, promising to send remittances to cover the costs of this help, or to support siblings left behind. Young men pursued conflicts transnationally and developed networks perceived as threatening to the community. In the aftermath of the April 2000 lynching of the Japanese tourist and his guide in Todos Santos, a number of men who were wanted for questioning immediately contracted coyotes and departed *elna* once they were announced as potential suspects. "Migration is now the vice of our people," recounted one community leader, expressing a growing concern with the conflicts and evasions resulting from migration. "Whenever people don't want to face their lives here, they just pick up and leave" (field notes, 1999).

The economic consequences of migration have likewise been challenging and sometimes devastating. While social and class differentiation has always existed, fiestas and other forms of community participation, like *cofradías*, acted as equalizers. The financial pressures on those who remained were of a different sort: land prices increased exponentially, the cost of building materials went up and workmen became expensive to hire, debt accrued, and liens on property to support migration and the possibility of foreclosure became a constant worry. All of this has produced new markers of class and difference and, sometimes, new kinds of relationships with the state, as community members negotiate things like deportation and the delivery of deceased migrant remains to Guatemala.

"Brain drain," migration's claim to many of the best educated and most productive members of the community, has likewise produced difference. Community pillars, including many members of a generation identified as future leaders, left Todos Santos in order to create opportunities for themselves and their children. By the mid-2000s, so many Mam-Spanish bilingual teachers had migrated that recent monolingual graduates from Huehuetenango taught classes. Teacher salaries have been an ongoing point of contention, inciting periodic strikes throughout the country. This shift in local leadership, and the cessation of back and forth movement that formerly characterized migration in Todos Santos, mean that only those from well-off families, or individuals who migrated early and returned, can afford to take up positions of authority.

The impossibility of imagining a future without migration, a decade after the Peace Accords were signed, is well demonstrated by the story of Pancho. He was a young community leader and teacher with abundant energy and infectious good will. Pancho and his parents owned land together. On it, they planted milpa and kept a donkey. During an argument between Pancho and his parents, the parents threatened to deed their share of the plots to the church. At this point, he realized how limited his options were: he could not afford land, nor could he finish the house he'd already built with his teacher's salary. He had recently become a parent and had additional worries about seeing to his child's education. His research into local options resulted in a series of dead ends. Relying on networks of in-laws, he traveled to Grand Rapids, where he planned to stay for a couple of years. Eventually, he sent for his wife and children, arranging their transportation with a trusted coyote. He now envisions settling permanently in the United States.

Idioms of Community: Social Networks and Relationships

As more people migrate to Grand Rapids, Oakland, San Francisco, or Boston, new conceptions of community increasingly emerge from their transnationalized experiences with other Todosanteros. Nostalgia, memories, social gatherings, and gossip become the common currency between people. In well-established communities in the United States, Mam is spoken and *traje* is worn for special occasions. These are powerful tools of the idiom of community and its meaningful persistence, especially as a climate of fear limits other kinds of relationships Todosanteros might build.

Todosanteros in the United States share many common experiences, including the difficulties of the migratory journey, settling into their new homes and finding work, and saving and sending remittances while maintaining contact with their families at home. They may form bonds with people they didn't know very well or had little to do with in Todos Santos. Shared experiences are fitted first into a context of particular local struggle and then into a wider field of conflicts—conflicts that provide the possibilities, idioms, and opportunities for local expression (Smith 1999: 206). Whenever they gather in Grand Rapids for soccer games, or send money and gifts home for the fiesta, migrants share a form of knowledge and a way of expressing it that comes from the extension of local experience—what Raymond Williams (1977) called "intimate culture"—to a wider, transnational field.

Even as the idioms of community are reinforced through contact with other Todosanteros in the United States, these communities have become additional forums for addressing intra-communal or intrafamilial disagreements, disputes, and struggles that are sustained in multisited and increasingly more complex ways. For example, one young man nearly lynched in Todos Santos in 1997 for, among other things, activities related to his alleged leadership in a so-called gang, was stabbed during a bar fight in Michigan. After recovering in a U.S. hospital, he returned to Todos Santos and resumed the type of behavior that had so angered community members in the first place.[12] His nemesis, allegedly the leader of a second gang operating out of Todos Santos, was deported from the United States after committing a petty crime. Some people speculated that he'd opted for a "free" trip back to Guatemala in order to continue his feud.

Migrants also continue to observe the many particulars of the lifestyle they lived in Todos Santos. If they aren't able to be physically present for celebrations, Todosanteros send decorations for their *txol* (neighborhoods), in addition to video cameras, videotapes, instamatics, and film for recording all the major events that their family members and friends participate in so that they can view these events in the United States. Families who nursed intergenerational disputes in Todos Santos continue to hold these grudges in the United States, and the feuders may settle in different communities. However, now living in multiple sites, migrants are united at least partially through shared interest in what goes on at home.

The fact that migrants do move back and forth across borders carrying various emotional, economic, legal, and physical baggage, and that the fiesta incorporates spaces for their participation, makes community something that continues to be relevant and central. Wage-labor migration, even if it lasted for a decade, was once considered temporary. "Todos

Santos is where I have my roots and my future," one man commented. "In my heart I always live there, even though sometimes I have to be in California." In discussing the diaspora of Todosanteros in the region and the world, villagers commented: "Todos Santos is everywhere. It's the only town that is everywhere." They concluded: "We are explorers." Given the prohibitive cost and danger associated with crossing the U.S. border, and the fact that many Todosanteros must now work toward permanent authorization in the United States, they may also see themselves as settlers.

Subversions, Critiques, and Authenticities in Fiesta Celebrations

Migrants experience nostalgia as a selective remembering of the past. This idealized past contributes to a present that is, in comparison, often hostile, and current living conditions that are difficult and circumscribed by fear. However, migrants are in a constant dialogue with their families and other people in their village who respond to them from a set of different recent experiences and histories, allowing migrants to continue with a sense of belonging.

The everyday quality of life in the factories of Oakland and Boston and the fields of Florida reinforce the ideas and expectations that migrants have about home, community, and belonging. Nostalgia involves memories of a shared past patterned with the exigencies of contemporary life. These memories compete and are contested in terms of their authenticity in the arena where ideas about inclusion and belonging are shaped and reshaped. In this arena, priorities are reordered and classifications are reworked in order to incorporate increasing social and economic differentiation and wider breadths of experience.

Migrants often find themselves embedded in conditions of severe structural violence and marginalization. These include isolating and strictly regimented work schedules and labor that is physically grueling and/or mind-numbingly boring. Todosanteros employed in meatpacking factories in Grand Rapids, for example, work nine hour shifts on production lines where they repeat the same motion all day. As the line speeds up, they must work faster. On-site injuries are frequent and are treated with Tylenol, but no vacation time for healing is offered. Anything that influences the market for meat, like news of mad cow disease, shortens their workweek and tightens their finances. These are risks that migrants incur, of course, when they are lucky enough to have work.

After work, the commute to and from work, and meal preparation, there is little time or energy left. The neighborhoods where migrants live are run-down, public transportation is sporadic, and resources for food and other shopping are often suboptimal and the ones that do exist are expensive. All of this contributes to nostalgia for the familiarity of everyday life in Todos Santos, for its social nature and its easy negotiation.

Across cultures, festive occasions provide opportunities to subvert the conditions of daily life. In Guatemala, dancing and other features of fiestas have historically provided a release from the daily petty humiliations, degradations, and domination implemented by the state, the church, and hierarchies of race, ethnicity, gender, and class, changing the typical order of social life.[13] During the fiesta, and integral to its central events, is a suspension of the hierarchies that people live with and struggle against: ironic fun is had at the expense of the plantation bosses, or a nightmare of Spanish conquerors on horses is relived with Todosanteros in the saddle. Migrants now embrace the everyday order that people formerly sought to escape through these fiesta subversions, because it is part of the shared and authentic past. When they do so, they revalorize an identity submerged by regimes of security and illegality in the United States.

Money and experiences of migration have changed the local cast of much of the petty economic domination, and the formerly stringent ethnic hierarchy that placed Maya at the bottom of the social ladder is less rigid in Todos Santos as a result of ladino flight during the war and other socioeconomic aspects like tourism and NGO funding that privilege indigenous over nonindigenous Todosanteros.[14] Many migrants are worldlier as a result of living within different systems of power and struggle and are wealthy by local standards. Nevertheless, because history is a common denominator and is considered to be authentic, it is powerful. There is efficacy in how the ancestors did things, even though contexts have changed. Certain practices and customs are understood as authentic. Therefore, these are of particular interest to migrants. Through migrants' participation in these customs, former subversions have shifted to authenticating moves, powerful not in terms of reversing what happens in the everyday but because they are a direct link to a shared past. As a result, certain customs and practices, like the *corrida* or the *Baile de los Conquistadores* (Dance of the Conquerors), become sites of contestation, especially with respect to material culture, because they are the most accessible forms in which migrants can intervene in terms of authenticity and memory.

Under these circumstances, everyday social relations, along with the networks of power in which they are embedded, become desirable and elusive for migrants. The pleasures of sitting down and eating with the family; drinking beers with buddies; wearing a new set of clothing a mother wove, while showing off new Nike sneakers or cowboy boots; and even buying eggs from the man blamed for injuring one's uncle in a drunken brawl all fulfill the migrant's yearning for the everyday experiences of the present and the past. Yet these are precisely the experiences that migrants can barely apprehend as guests on short visits: special meals are cooked for them every day by a rotating cast of neighbors, family members, and other visitors; they are obliged to spend and loan money; and in the constant whirlwind of activity, there is no opportunity to slip into the rhythm of quiet work in the *milpa*, convene with the ancestors in sacred sites, or listen quietly to a marimba.

If the nostalgia for everyday life is definitively out of reach for many migrants, the *corrida de caballos* and the *Baile de los Conquistadores* represent two arenas where authenticity is played out, where culture and transnationalism come together in ways that benefit a parallel (and yet, unallied) state agenda of perpetuating and demonstrating Mayaness.

Corrida de Caballos

The *corrida de caballos* (running of the horses)[15] is sometimes referred to as a re-creation of the arrival of the invading Spaniards—who were drunken and screaming, with boots on their feet, swords in their belts, and feathers in their hats—at the valley of Todos Santos. Local legend claims that the *corrida* has its roots in a game played by the Spaniards, where they would win a prize for successfully grabbing a hanging ring as they rode by. Todosanteros were not allowed to ride horses under the Spanish occupancy, but one day, an ancestor robbed a horse and went galloping off at top speed in order to escape from the Spaniards (Oakes 1951). The *corrida*, Todosanteros say, commemorates the brave act of this ancestor, and the purpose of the event is not for one individual to win a prize, but for all the participating men to show their bravery and courage while making the pueblo and the ancestors happy.

The horses rented for the *corrida* are from Chiantla, located at the foot of the Cuchumatanes range, just beyond the boarders of the municipality. On the afternoon of October 31, the horses arrive in Todos Santos after being driven up and across the *altiplano* and back down into the valley. After they reach the center of town, the men who will participate in the *corrida* arrive to claim the horses they will ride and to bring them to their houses. It is a festive moment and townspeople gather along the main street to watch.

The ladino owner of a horse ridden in the *corrida* is historically an honored figure in the fiesta pantheon. He and his family live with the rider and his family for at least two days and, as special guests at meals, are served the best cuts of meat and offered the highest quality drinks. On the night before the *corrida*, as the teams of *xq'atx qoya* (up to fourteen men) dance to marimba, drink, and smoke cigarettes while dressing and preparing to ride the following morning, the horse's owners may join them. Dressing for the *corrida* is done with great care. High levels of alcohol consumption can change it from an event of skill or showmanship to one of luck and chance. Under such circumstances, a recklessly handled machete can be the difference between life and death or a good experience and a negative one. A horse owner may be invited to help with this task, depending on the preference of the riders. The owners are offered special places from which to view the *corrida* and are escorted by the wives and families of riders. The relationship between owner and rider is one of great respect, derived from a number of historical imperatives. One is the ethnic hierarchy—now challenged—that long placed ladinos above Maya on a socioeconomic and racial scale. The carefully constructed relationship between *xq'atx qoya* and owners was largely for the purpose of thanking the ladinos for the rental of their valuable horses and for their participation, which added luster to the proceedings. Such constructions of social prestige were undergirded by serious economic considerations: a horse was a huge expense for an agricultural worker or day laborer that might not earn the equivalent in an entire year. Therefore, a social pact was at play: the ladino horse owner and his family were treated graciously and generously as honored guests in the hope that this would be taken into consideration if anything happened to the animal (or rider). The rider and his family incurred the risk of long-term debt repayment to the owner and his family if the horse died or was badly injured. If the horse survived and the rider died, his family would have difficulty paying for the rental without his labor.

Transnationalism, however, has decreased the power of some hierarchies, even as it has created others. Many migrant riders are well off by local standards and could purchase their own horses for the *corrida* if they desire. Nevertheless, the traditional relationship with the owner of the horse is prized. Although the economic basis for honoring the ladino owner may have passed, maintaining this custom means cultivating an active link to a shared past. It is perceived as an authentic act amidst a

Migrant rider on a horse, preparing for the *corrida*, 2003 (J. Burrell)

sea of change. By observing this relationship, a migrant who lives in the
United States full-time and has children who haven't learned his native
Mam language can feel as though he is having the same experience that
his great-grandfather had fifty years ago. The prestige of the past authen-
ticates the present.

Xq'atx qoya once received a spiritual calling to take part in the corrida.
Riders gathered with a captain in whose house meetings, preparations,
and festivities took place.[16] Although some riders still claim that a spiritual calling inspires their participation, when asked why they participate,
men are often more likely to answer: *"Por mi pueblo"* (for my commu-
nity/town).[17] Since many of the participants are migrants, interrogating
precisely what this means would seem to be related to a concern with
"transbordering": the continued development and maintenance of community across borders, experiences, and increasing social and economic
differentiation (Stephen 2007). *Corrida* teams have generally, although
not always, been composed of family members and/or people who live
in the same *cantón* or barrio, organized by kin groups or, more recently,
composed of men who have settled in the same community in the United
States, who may also be kin. Todosanteros meet in bars in Latino barrios

of U.S. cities, making *corrida* plans and sending money for the women who support them in their home community (wives, sisters, daughters) to begin preparations. Recently, if men cannot attend themselves, they have financed sons', brothers', or other relatives' participation.

Mesoamericanists have historically commented on the equalizing mechanism of these fiestas — that is, individuals can never get too far ahead economically before they are called upon to divert substantial resources to fiestas or other community celebrations or practices.[18] Migration distorts the meaning of these expenditures: the role of financial equalization is reduced, but expenditures are now more significant socially; migrant involvement may be seen as concrete proof of one's continued alliance with and desire to belong to the community, honoring a shared past while seeking to create building blocks for a common future.

As the table below shows, the costs for a *corrida* captain are significant. And yet, some migrants once performed this role year after year, citing that it was something they were able to do for their community and that it was within their financial means to do so.

The Baile de los Conquistadores

The *Baile de los Conquistadores* (Dance of the Conquerors) was historically performed during the two main days of the fiesta and one month later, in the beginning of December. Ideally, a team of twenty dance, including one woman and one girl. Although the dance is performed throughout Guatemala and more widely in Mesoamerica, a dog character distinguishes the Todos Santos version. The dance mocks and critiques the

Horse rental for one day	Q800 ($267)	Q1500 ($192)
Room and board for horse owner and family	Q300 ($100)	Q500 ($64)
Food, alcohol, wood, clothing, accessories, and other necessities for two days (Oct 31 and Nov. 1)	Q1,500 ($500)	Q16,000 ($2,051)[a]
Total Expenditures	Q3,000 ($1,200)	Q20,000 ($2,564)

[a]Average annual percent growth rate per year was 10%, a 130% increase over the course of nine years, or prices that are more than double. The price of the marimba reflects this almost exactly, but the changes in all other prices are either related to migrants' ability to pay or other factors.

Expenses for a team captain of the *Corrida de Caballos* for 1993 and 2002

plantation, or hacienda, system, and the hierarchy of owners, overseers, foremen, and their wives. It provides a pointed critique of ongoing structural violence by portraying how animals are often treated better than workers. The dancers wear elaborate costumes that represent the ornate clothing of Spanish invaders. They also use white, blue-eyed face masks with painted-on blond hair. White people in general as well as ladinos are ridiculed and made the butt of jokes. Hierarchies of plantation authority and race are reversed. Only during this dance could Todosanteros mock the systems of economic domination that otherwise imprisoned them. The dance took on a particularly wrenching significance during the years when many men had taken cash advances from plantation agents in order to celebrate the fiesta. They were loaded into trucks several days later to begin a grueling period of work from which they would bring home barely enough money to feed their families for the rest of the year and pay off their debts (Bossen 1984, Carrescia 1982).

Participating in the dance tied people to contemporary community and to the *antepasados* (ancestors) and their underworlds. Although the dance emphasized and mocked particular sets of labor relations, it was cosmovision in action—the manifestation of relationships between the past, present, and future as they intersected in domains that were material and spiritual. The dance no longer reflects the work experience of most Todosanteros, although it does reflect shared experiences of domination relative to a political economy of labor. In lieu of heading off to the coastal plantations to pick cotton or coffee, sometimes Todosanteros are more likely to arrange for a *coyote* to bring them to the United States, where they live under different forms of marginalization and vulnerability. However, although they no longer work on coastal plantations and are better compensated for their labor in the United States, some of the kinds of hierarchies mocked in the dance may still be prevalent in their working and migrant lives, albeit in different forms.

Another aspect of the dance is that it is a group activity that ideally spans a period of four to six months, including preparation, practice (especially of the complicated steps danced by some characters), traveling together to get the costumes, and so forth. This renders it a less attractive option to migrants. Women and children dance only two roles, so they cannot pick up the slack.

In 1997, the dance wasn't performed because no one wanted to take on the expense of costume rental. That year, people commented to me that the lack of a *baile* saddened them, as it was a poignant reminder of *la violencia*, when Todosanteros had neither the heart nor the money to perform.

Bailador in front of the church, dancing with visitors, 1996 (J. Burrell)

By 1999, a national cultural preservation organization donated costumes, and without the burden of rental, a revalidation of customs around costuming was sparked that hadn't been practiced in years. The *capitán* put on his costume and, accompanied by a marimba, visited the house of each dancer in turn. The dancers emerged from their houses fully attired and all present team members danced and drank. However, the act of participating in a team of dancers had lost much of its prior meaning in terms of being a sacred calling that people received and prepared for together throughout the year. One woman even commented that the local people that she worked with disapproved of her participation in the *baile* one year, as public drinking was involved. For these kinds of reasons, and with more money than time, migrants can get more mileage out of participation in the *corrida*.

The dance was performed during the fiestas of 2000 and 2001 as the project of a resident community leader interested in cultural revitalization. In 2002, he was a *xq'atx qoya*, and the dance was not performed again in 2003 because he had other responsibilities and no one else was willing to take on the expenses. Since then, the dance has been performed more often than not, but its continuation is never guaranteed. Removing the dangerous edge of multiculturalism (Hale 2002) by managing it from afar, combined with local disinterest in or the inability to continue to perform the dance—a custom that links the Todos Santos fiesta to other fiestas in Guatemala—demonstrates a potential political risk. Shifting responsibility to communities and to migrants allows them to choose what to perpetuate, and they decide according to local significance and meaning.

Fiesta and State

As post-war attempts are made to forge state-sponsored multiculturalism that includes substantial Mayan elements, like the common histories discussed in the previous chapter, fiestas become more important as cultural grounds on which a shared past can be expressed in the present. Indeed, public celebrations are arguably a necessary element in the state consolidation processes.[19] When seeking evidence of the impact of neoliberal order on the Monkey Dance performed at the fiesta in Momostenango, Guatemala, Thomas Offit and Garrett Cook (2010) expected to find that the dance would be abandoned due to expenses and tragedies befalling the dancers. Instead, they found a steadfast commitment to traditional Mayan culture and an extraordinary resiliency in the face of incredible obstacles. Cultural continuity, for multiple generations, constituted a firm base in a rapidly shifting world.

Community-based celebrations simultaneously capture the diversity and the commonality of Mayan culture—while versions of the *Baile de los Conquistadores* are danced throughout Guatemala and beyond, the *corrida* is unique to Todos Santos. Formerly, these local celebrations of cultural affiliation, important markers of identity based in communities, were left to community members. However, they are increasingly subject to state intervention in the form of monies for cultural revitalization, propaganda, and promotion on the part of Instituto Guatemalteco de Turismo (IN-GUAT; the national tourist agency). INGUAT is particularly aggressive in the promotion of a multicultural vision, especially one that is easily accessible to tourists. The stakes are high: while exports and remittances are the top two sources of foreign currency in Guatemala, tourism is third, generating just under 1.5 billion U.S. dollars per year;[20] and it is heavily dependent on Guatemala's ability to sell itself successfully not only as multicultural, but as a caretaker and promoter of community-based national diversity. After war, part of the ability to do this has hinged on distracting potential tourists from past and present violence and poverty—contexts of political conflict and danger—with the distinctiveness and sheer quantity of vivid local cultural possibilities. In this sense, fiesta practices also become a "cultural commodity in the modern global marketplace of tourism" (Babb 2004:553).

The festive terrain is among the only contemporary spaces where the influence of migration and migrants as new cultural actors meet with the Guatemalan nation-building project. While their remittances are recognized as crucial to the national economy, an additional source of respect and responsibility currently derive from migrant participation in the transnational cultural work of sustaining community and culture, and specifically, in preserving what is unique about Todos Santos.

Migration has had the paradoxical effect of bringing migrants into the nexus of the state and removing them from the national jurisdiction and other networks of state power. In order to begin the process of obtaining green cards to work legally in the United States, migrants must obtain passports and other paperwork largely unnecessary in daily life in Todos Santos. This aside, while acknowledging the crucial role that remittances play in the national economy, the state has virtually no other regular contact with migrants. Nevertheless, on the festive terrain, migrants and the state have a common agenda in supporting authenticity in relation to cultural customs. Both treasure the unificatory powers of the past in the creation of a common future and both search for methods of belonging. Migrants, in fact, fulfill a crucial neoliberal mission: they assume responsibility for some of the practices of material culture that the state would like to subsume, but the state doesn't have to take responsibility for their perpetuation.

Conclusions: the Local, the National, and the Transnational in the Fiesta

After war in Guatemala, culture has emerged as being valuable in relation to neoliberalism and multiculturalism. In this rationale, like history, it has become a commodity. Cultural practices, especially festivities, stand for the nation and privilege local histories and customs. Central to the substantive Accord on the Identity and Rights of Indigenous Peoples and the Accord on Socioeconomic Aspects and the Land has been the promotion of a "culture of peace" including cultural identity. The end result of this campaign is that the state ideally searches for "a culture," a series of practices to support or revitalize, or a set of practices that can be used to represent the whole of a multicultural nation. Migrants actively support a set of cultural practices around the fiesta, but do so to represent their own continued roles in their communities. Both migrants and the state, then, have vested interests in seeing to the perpetuation of local cultural practices, but act independently to achieve them. In this way, fiestas are one of the bases for what has become a key neoliberal strategy: political unity through the celebration of cultural distinction. Through them, new subject positions are made available to migrants, along with the possibility of forming alliances and collaborations that are *also* political.

By applying "thick" ethnographic description to the cultural practices of the transnational in the context of the Guatemalan after-war terrain, the dynamics of political economy and of repertoires of inclusion are made visible. As neoliberal states increasingly cut back on social benefits, cultural projects, and the interference of market forces, more people engage in wage-labor migration. These migrants fashion transnational lives, reworking households, families, and gender roles in attempts to concretize local identities. As they do so, they become actors who are as important socioculturally and politically as they are economically.

CHAPTER 5

After Lynching

Saison Tetsuo Yamahiro, a Japanese tourist, and Edgar Castellanos, a Guatemalan bus driver, were lynched by an angry mob during the Saturday market in Todos Santos on April 29, 2000. Rumors of an international satanic cult gathering in Huehuetenango had contributed to a panic fueled by local radio stations and word of mouth. In the tense atmosphere that resulted, villagers attacked and killed Yamahiro after he photographed and reached out to calm a crying child nestled on his mother's back. Castellanos, who ran when villagers boarded his bus to look for children they suspected were hidden there, was presumed guilty, caught on the far side of town, beaten, and burned.[1]

The death of a tourist attracted national and international attention to this lynching. Though I was not present for the incident, I was profoundly disturbed by media representations in the national and international press of Todosanteros as "backward" savages left behind by modernity—these were not the people I lived and worked with for years. With deep concern for the townspeople who had shared their lives and opened their homes and worlds to me, I returned several months later to make sense of the complex aftermath of this case. I also returned to address what was, critically, often absent from news and human rights accounts of the incident: I listened, as Robert Carmack (1988) and a generation of anthropologists had done during the war, to stories told by Todosanteros of what had happened and why it had happened. During my readings of articles and news reports, I had been consistently dismayed: rarely did anyone comment beyond superficial descriptions of Satanists and primitive cultural beliefs among an isolated tribe of exotic people. In the accounts that Todosanteros shared with me, I paid attention to the multiplicity of understandings that people brought to their explanations of the aftermath of the lynchings, to the connections they made to a rich history of long-term community conflicts, to their register in the present, and to how they imagined themselves in the future.[2]

In the weeks and months that followed the lynchings, I was told, Todosanteros engaged in a collective process of mourning Yamahiro and Castellanos. This included the construction of shrines at the sites of their deaths,[3] masses dedicated to the two men in the Catholic church, and a collection of money for Castellanos's widow and children.

At the same time, they struggled to make sense of the cooperation of some in state investigative procedures who directly implicated other community members. During this process, a host of past and present grievances that Todosanteros had with one another and with the state surfaced, taking new forms as they joined the forceful currents of transitional justice and neoliberal governance. The period immediately following the lynchings, they emphasized, was *"como el ochenta"* (like the eighties) in its arbitrariness and terror; villagers could never be sure whether they might be implicated and called upon by investigators and state functionaries searching for those responsible for the deaths. Referencing *el ochenta* recalled the worst period of the civil war, when neighbors and family members often found themselves on different sides of the conflict. "We were scared to leave our houses," people told me, speaking of the aftermath. After members of her family were implicated, one person commented: "I could never have imagined that my family would be involved in such a situation."

Lynching and other forms of vigilantism are among the forms of violence that have come to predominate after war in Guatemala. Their frequency represents a particular challenge to democratic rule of law and state power. In this context, lynching, as defined by MINUGUA, the UN peacekeeping mission in Guatemala, means to punish (not necessarily with death) one or more presumed criminal offenders by collective violence without due process of law.[4] A number of perspectives—barbarism, popular justice, and grassroots justice among them—attempt to account for the type of logic, ambiguity, criminality, and tensions associated with these forms of violence.[5] Lynching is also connected to specific histories of power and struggle in local communities, resurrecting competing versions of events and challenging dominant narratives that have come to inform how the war and the post-war period are understood. Lynching had been considered a potential means of settling internal conflicts since the end of the war, as well as during it, under the aegis of the PACs. While the lynchings of Yamahiro and Castellanos in Todos Santos are hardly representative of all lynchings in Guatemala, their aftermath provides a way of beginning to understand some of the connections between the discourses of transition; the realities of neoliberal governmentality; and local contradictions, experiences, and struggles. News accounts focused on the incident itself and generally ignored what occurred in Todos Santos afterward. In contrast, during my fieldwork, I considered the after-effects of the lynchings, including rumors, media accounts, and encounters between Todosanteros and the legal system. This instance of "popular justice," in which Todosanteros cooperated with the state in naming suspects of the lynchings, illuminates one community's encounter with what Rachel Sieder calls the top-down efforts of "rule of law construction [or strengthening]" in democracy building, an objective that animated the early after-war period in Guatemala (2007:68).

Lynching and the Guatemalan State After War

There were 580 incidents of lynching in Guatemala between 1996 and 2004, with over one thousand victims, of whom 255 died (MINUGUA 2004). These incidents often occurred in areas of the country that were hardest hit by the war, particularly the rural and indigenous western highlands where genocidal campaigns of the 1980s were followed by the paramilitarization of villages through the formation of civil patrols (see Kobrak 2013, Mendoza and Torres-Rivas 2003, Remijnse 2002, Snodgrass Godoy 2002). Incidents of lynchings were slowly but steadily decreasing by the mid-2000s but they surged again by the late 2000s.[6] These numbers must be understood within a larger context of post-war crime in Guatemala that includes the highest murder rate in Latin America and one of the highest in the world (Inter-American Commission on Human Rights 2005, Human Rights Watch 2011). While it is commonly argued that people are increasingly made desperate by the failures and shortfalls of the rule of law, there is an emerging understanding that this hopelessness is related to deep-rooted structural problems that keep the majority of the population in poverty, without basic services like water and power and without access to land (AVANCSO 2009, Burrell 2010, Nelson 2009). Crime in Guatemala has skyrocketed from already high levels, as the effects of the worldwide economic crisis, the slowdown in remittances, and the southward migration of violent Mexican cartels are felt throughout the country.

The idea of a "weak" and/or "failed" Guatemalan state is often proffered to account for the widespread occurrence of lynching. While this may very well be true, both lynching in general and the Todos Santos case in particular encourage nuanced and broad consideration in regard to this assumption. First, lynchings have occurred throughout Latin America, usually in marginalized places (urban and rural), and often in indigenous communities or areas that have majority indigenous populations.[7] In many Latin American countries, the terrain of justice is complicated by such factors as competing legal systems, indigenous forms of judicial administration, and the fact that rural populations often feel excluded or ignored by the state (Vilas 2003 and 2005). The Guatemalan state's presence throughout the nation is uneven, but this fact alone does not automatically equate to weakness. Veena Das and Deborah Poole (2004) write that the production of marginalization relative to the state is a mechanism of governance. Charles Hale (2005) has shown how this function of power operates relative to neoliberal multiculturalism in Guatemala, with very particular techniques of exclusion and inclusion. Intrinsic to it is the limited presence of cultural rights and the governmental institutionalization of racial ambiguity. As Maya work to build and sustain ongoing sociopolitical movements and economic stability, they are always vulnerable to being accused of "asking too much" or, as the media coverage of the lynchings case indicated, of being outside of modernity.

Equally important to consider is the fact that lynchings are not common regionally. While they have occurred in Mexico (Binford and Churchhill 2009, Fuentes Díaz 2004, Santamaria 2012), there have been few incidents in neighboring El Salvador, Honduras, and Nicaragua, where crime rates—and national dismay over the prevalence of crime—are similar.

"Failed" or "weak" states, then, may very well be likened to the "failed" development projects (Ferguson 1994, Escobar 1995) that produced unarticulated but desired goals, like roads and other infrastructure in formerly remote areas. While "failing" in one realm, the Guatemalan state may prosper in others: for instance, the opening of international markets, the privatizing of publicly owned concessions, increased remittances due to elevated rates of out-migration, and soaring wealth concentrated in fewer hands, all of which are consistent with the goals of neoliberalism and the production of neoliberal democracy.

Lynching is also analyzed in terms of "spectacular 'dramas of citizenship'" (Holston and Appadurai 1999:14 in Goldstein 2004:5), a means for those marginalized within national currents of politics and economics to thrust themselves violently onto the stage of civic life (Goldstein 2004:3). While this is undoubtedly the case for some lynchings in Guatemala, the lynchings of Yamahiro and Castellenos might be viewed in a different light, given the deeply intimate and "fratricidal" nature of their aftermath, as well as the discursive inconsistency of narratives that attempted to account for them. Lynching made clear the underlying grievances that nonetheless animated everyday life in the community: grievances with one another and with the state—both embedded within larger contexts of political and economic insecurity. This context contributes to what Ellen Moodie calls "democratic disenchantment, disillusionment with the state and with politics" (2010:145). In El Salvador, Moodie writes, this is often embodied in the sentiment that whatever is happening now is "worse than the war." This sentiment is explained in Guatemala, as in El Salvador and other places in Central America, by intolerable increases in crime. In Guatemala, however, fear of crime has produced a popular turn toward *mano dura* (iron fist), epitomized in the 2011 election of Otto Pérez Molina, a former army general linked to the genocide. The popularity of the "iron fist" approach is not seen elsewhere in the region to such a degree. Lynching is tied to this desire for security, as is vigilantism and the re-paramilitarization of community life.

Throughout Guatemala, there has been a contemporary resurgence of the ruptured social life experienced during *la violencia*—the blurred lines between perpetrators and victims; the refashioning of villages in the aftermath of severe fragmentation; and the erosion of the bases of community life, including trust, shared history and traditions, communal authority, and collective memory. It is, as Angelina Snodgrass Godoy has elegantly put it, not a story of villains and victims, but one of the "complex, confounding effects of violence on communities and the challenge of negotiating justice in a postgenocidal world where fear and repression persist" (2006:78). The turn to *mano dura* is part of the contemporary terrain upon which numerous local, national, and international processes are at play. While villagers carried out very specific interrogations of their conflicted histories with one another following the lynchings, a different kind of debate took place nationally, one that exposed some of the fault lines and shortcomings of post-war national unification and multiculturalism.

Neoliberal Legal Reform

The argument that lynching occurs where the rule of law has failed must be placed within the larger context of the neoliberal project of decentering law, currently promoted internationally as part of a transnational trend in rule of law construction. Sieder and others have pointed out that while this process has increased autonomy among some indigenous communities, it has simultaneously decreased state responsibility within the legal realm (2008:79). Compliance with the law, in this scenario, has fallen to communities that often possess few, if any, official resources. The Guatemalan Peace Accords, together with other national legislation and international treaties,[8] created mechanisms for reestablishing local forms of power and autonomy. The recuperation and strengthening of indigenous customary law, taking into account Mayan cosmovision, identity, and spirituality, became a linchpin of development and policy efforts relating to democratization and the construction of an inclusive legal system, one that recognized local indigenous authority. Among the goals of this project was to rebuild local political and economic relations destroyed by the war, and to recognize that many local institutions and structures of authority had been indelibly transformed by it, as they had by contemporary economic relations and migration.[9] But the mechanisms for achieving this were frequently what Jim Handy called "good governance as the new panacea," bringing "meaningful" government institutions to rural villages (2004:360).[10]

The Guatemalan state sought to decentralize power within this evolving legal terrain by placing more judicial responsibility at the level of towns, increasing the number of lower courts in rural areas, and providing court interpreters trained to work in indigenous languages (Sieder 2011). At first, without knowledge of bases of customary law or local worldviews, these authorities were frequently ineffective (Handy 2004:360). Sieder suggests that by the 2000s, "state justice officials were coordinating their efforts more with indigenous community justice systems in many areas of the highlands, tacitly recognizing the legitimacy—or at least the efficacy and de facto presence—of these local systems (2011:162). This situation, however, often serves to place indigenous authorities "in a state of permanent legal in-definition," never sure if their actions will be recognized as legitimate by the state or be subject to criminal prosecution (2011:174).[11] The end result is that many indigenous communities express profound skepticism most of the time toward the ability of the state justice system to address local problems.[12]

Regardless of how we view the state—as failed, weak, neoliberal, legally decentralized, and/or transitional—it arrived in Todos Santos in the form of mandates, laws and legalities, investigators, and visions of democracy following the lynchings of Yamahiro and Castellanos. In the latter instance, villagers did not necessarily turn away from it, run from it, or seek to undermine it. Rather, state presence was embraced by many for its potential to aid in addressing local conflicts that had remained unresolved at the village level, sometimes for decades. Although perpetrators of lynching often remain anonymous, escaping prosecution under conditions of widespread impunity, Todosanteros actively sought out and solicited the state's capacity to promote resolution. They did so because the state held emergent and unrealized power—in this early moment of after-war promise—to exercise forms of authority that Todosanteros envisioned as potentially beneficial.

This highlights the considerable ambiguity and the range of possibilities, promises, and disillusionments of the always in-process relations between the state and those it governs. The state in transition was, for some people in Todos Santos in particular and Guatemala more generally at the dawn of the new millennium, a state of waiting, promise, and potential as citizens came to project onto its imaginary a realm of new possibility and hope. For others, it was a tool that could effectively be used in the attempt to address contemporary or historic conflicts and tensions. The state had immediate and tangible meaning, but these meanings were various and disparate.

Conflict and the State

Tangled histories of intercommunal conflict reemerged, seething in new registers, in attempts to account for participation in the aftermath of the lynchings of Yamahiro and Castellanos. In one case, after she was accused of participating in the lynching with acts beyond her physical capacity, Doña Edna,[13] who was being pressured to sell a prime piece of land, was forced to unload her coveted *milpa* cheaply to pay for a lawyer. Wage-labor migrants to the United States linked to families who had been agitating for the land purchased it. In another case, Florencia accused Hernando of having participated in the lynchings. Florencia's father had been involved in a land dispute with the grandfather of Hernando, and Florencia claimed that Hernando later reported her husband to the army as a subversive in order to get even with her family on behalf of his grandfather. She therefore blamed her husband's death, at the hands of the military in 1982, on Hernando. After Florencia implicated Hernando in the lynchings, he was arrested and jailed, and he lost his state job, which he had trained years for. Hernando vowed to get revenge on Florencia, "even if it takes years." In a different case, a young man was jailed for allegedly providing the gasoline that was used to burn Castellanos. Rumors circulated that someone who had a long-standing grudge against the man's father had accused him. Another version of the story—corroborated by an independent Japanese tourist staying with the man's family—attested that this same man pulled Yamahiro's sister and father out of the mob and into the safety of his family's house. Undoubtedly, the past shapes the forms and textures of violence in the present. But as this case makes clear, the insertion of places into particular neoliberal and post-war contexts (in 2000, a transitional moment when the state held potential, the promise of economic reform began to dim, and rising numbers of young, wage-labor migrants to the United States created newly felt pressures for land) shaped the form and framing of violence and conflict in the present.

In these narratives, years and generations of (not always physical) violence that Todosanteros had committed against one another were linked to explain contemporary moments. "Even if it takes years" implies that these conflicts are given the time to develop a simmering life of their own that underlies everyday rhythms. Although some disputes may have been ongoing for generations, they became newly significant in response to contemporary forces in the post-Accords era and under neoliberal governance. Given this, in order to understand lynching and other forms of violence, we should look to the past and to the complexities and struggles of daily communal life and ask: "What forces in the present make the past immediately relevant?" In the encounter between Todosanteros and the transitional Guatemalan state in the aftermath of the lynchings, a history of conflicts with one another led individuals to name local names, which is important insofar that there were representatives of the state available to listen and to administer punishment.[14] While state intervention had not typically been sought or encouraged in local matters, individuals used its extraordinary presence, as opposed to its everyday formations, to resolve historic conflicts and antagonisms that they had with one another.

As a cascade of historical grievances animated actions within the municipality, Todosanteros venturing outside of the municipality were subject to an increasingly tense environment—one informed by the heated debates about lynching, location, and identity that swirled in the media. At the core of much of this was, as described by Raymond Williams (1973), a dialectic between the country and the city, and, by extension, between the largely ladino inhabitants of the capital and the Maya of the highlands, demarcating the profundity of the production of difference undergirding national discourses of multiculturalism. Revealed by their distinctive *traje*, Todosanteros were verbally and physically attacked—for imperiling the economic well-being of the nation as a whole, for being so backward and uneducated that they had lynched a tourist, and for attracting a stark international eye to the slippages and vicissitudes of the peace process.[15] Authorities and other inmates treated Todosanteros jailed in Huehuetenango dreadfully: when the first individuals were taken into custody, the warden called for backup, fearing an unruly reaction to their presence.

One woman recounted suffering verbal abuse and being called a murderer as she waited for the bus in Huehuetenango. She and other Todosanteros, people told her, were responsible for a drop in the national economy. It was their fault that people were unemployed in Guatemala. As another Todosantero woman remarked, life may have appeared peaceful in the town, but in the aftermath of the lynchings, other Guatemalans continued to think terribly of Todosanteros. She worried about the repercussions for Todosanteros living outside the community, among them, her children studying in distant cities.

By the time I arrived in July, these plentiful accounts were told by everyone, from students traveling to their universities, to mothers waiting in doctors' offices in the departmental capital, to teachers attending national meetings. Indeed, as I waited for a bus to Todos Santos on a street corner in Huehuetenango, I was asked why I wanted to go there, something that had never occurred in the many years and countless times I had made the journey. "They are not *buena gente*," (good people) I was told. In addition to these local and national preoccupations, as international media outlets like Univisión descended on the town center, villagers began to worry about national and even international retaliation, the cessation of aid, and the rupture of relationships built over many decades.

As tourists and *gringos* left Todos Santos following the lynchings, and tourism ceased, I returned. I distinctly remember exiting the bus on my return: an old man whom I had casually greeted in Mam nearly every day as I negotiated the lonely process of learning and improving my language skills came up and embraced me, saying: "Tey xuj tkyol" (the Mam-speaking woman), and thanked me for returning. He had, he told me in Mam, missed my stuttering but improving attempts at witty conversation; but mostly, he thought he might not see me again after what had happened. "Nyan ba'n tuj tnom," he told me, "Things are not good in town." I had never before shared such an encounter with him, and I was touched. I soon realized that my absence from Todos Santos during this incident was of value for Todosanteros in gauging the extent to which the lynchings and their aftermath potentially influenced long-standing relationships, especially with a wider international community. Old friends spent hours quizzing me: what did I think when I heard about the lynching? How did my family, friends, and colleagues from the United States and Europe, many of whom had visited over the years, react? What did they think of Todos Santos now that tourists had been lynched there? Was my family nervous that I had returned?

Igniting a State of Panic: Rumors and Post-War Governance

"Beware of those in whom the will to punish is strong."
NIETZSCHE[16]

"Panics" are often moral in nature and are combined with perceptions of ill-defined threats to society, as embodied in the "scapegoat."[17] Their mechanics mingle fear and rumor in an explosive mix. In this case, multiple processes of moral panicking and of scapegoating emerged, as villagers attempted to cope with swirling rumors, escalating fear, and the logic these produced, and were themselves subsequently scapegoated, becoming the targets of moral and media panic.[18]

Todosanteros repeatedly cited the circulation of rumors as central to what happened in the market on the morning of April 29. People feared the kidnapping of their children for ritual use by alleged visiting satanic cults and newspaper accounts claimed that teachers in Todos Santos had further fueled panic by closing schools.[19] Todosanteros, however, explained that bilingual teachers had been participating in an activity in a nearby town and other teachers had been attending a meeting in Huehuetenango: both meetings had been scheduled months earlier (Burrell 2000). The teachers' contribution to the climate that produced the lynchings was subsequently investigated and they were exonerated in August 2000.

Rumors circulate frequently in Guatemala, as they do elsewhere, but only at certain times and in certain places do they escalate from stories of the potential for violence into violence itself. Interrogating one of these moments provides a sense of the connection that rumors have to the workings of neoliberal power, politics, and governance. The Nietzsche epigraph that begins this section is from Roger Lancaster's guide to the inner workings of panic, which draws our attention to the connections between "false, exaggerated, or ill-defined moral threats" and the proposal to meet these via "punitive measures" (2008:45). When panic occurs, "moral entrepreneurs" cultivate acute senses of fear to persuade others that action against a designated scapegoat will "set things right" (2008:45–46).

In what context did the stories of satanic cultists, bizarre rites, and child sacrifice resonate and begin to feel immediately threatening to Todosanteros? Rumors of baby snatching, kidnapping, and organ harvesting have a long historical trajectory and circulate with frequency in Guatemala. Often, foreign, middle-aged women are implicated in them.[20] Because these rumors can generate an immediate response, one assumption is that they are easily manipulated—each time they surface they often correspond to credible calculations about why they gained credence. Generalizing across all cycles, however, ignores how rumor is specifically constituted in particular places and how historical experience makes them threatening. Following the signing of the Peace Accords, the children of wealthy and lower-class Guatemalans were kidnapped, rates of international adoption increased, and the legitimacy of some adoption agencies was questioned amidst growing allegations of child trafficking (UNICEF 2008). The increase in gangs claimed distressing numbers of young people, and girls continue to be murdered in a devastating and largely unexamined feminicide.[21] These methods of targeting children followed the abduction of boys for the army in the late 1970s and into the 1980s, and the earlier forced removal of children to work on large-scale plantations on the coast.

Rumor and gossip allow people "some measure of joint control over ambiguous, stressful situations" because they "affect the solidarity of a group, creating a public that can then participate in collective action" (Samper 2002). They are creative endeavors that allow people to negotiate meaning from common histories and experiences (Van Vleet 2003). About the tension in the marketplace in the minutes leading up to the lynching of Yamahiro, Todosanteros told how, due to the rumors and gossip that had circulated in the previous days, some individuals were alert for Satanists, wondering what they looked like and how to identify them. They debated potential colors of clothing and styles of hats, but no one had ever seen a Satanist before. They ultimately couldn't agree on how to identify one. Others warned that this conversation itself was dangerous and that pursuing it might result in action that could harm the tourists who had come by bus that morning for the market and were shopping, photographing, and wandering the streets. Rumors snowball and gain momentum that is difficult to stop. In their telling, people come to develop an understanding of themselves in relation to others and to forms of authority and governance. Rumors frequently develop in conjunction with confusion about, or vacuums of, power, at moments of uncertainty about who can and will act in relation to potentially explosive situations. If Satanists did arrive and snatch children, Todosanteros understood that they were on their own, without police assistance or intervention.

Todos Santos in 2000 was a community attempting to synthesize promises, potential, and the past with complicated new legal contexts and realities. It was difficult, as the lynchings of Yamahiro and Castellanos and the many others that occurred throughout Guatemala (and Latin America) indicate, to resist the urge to lynch when it became clear that under neoliberal governance, communities were expected to adminster justice without the provision of legal mechanisms or specific instruction. In this ambiguous terrain, panic, as Lancaster makes clear, was "ever more intricately woven into the basic structure of governance," and, in this place and time, rumor was its handmaiden (2008:47).

Todosanteros were asked why this particular cycle of rumors had such an impact when there were no previous incidents of such actions toward tourists. One woman, referring to the sway of these rumors in the department of Huehuetenango, replied: "If those who are educated were mistaken, then so are those of us who aren't educated and who don't speak Spanish well. If they were mistaken, so too are we" (Kobrak 2002). Rumors circulated, but people only acted on those embedded in a host of immediately meaningful contexts. As White notes: "The very act of talking about oneself or others, disciplines . . ." (White 2000:61, in Van Vleet 2003:499). In this sense, as people viewed themselves in relation to the state, to the region, and to local political and economic currents, the moral necessity of self-defense against the advancing (but unknown, and hence, hidden) enemy was reinforced through circulating rumors and gossip. As events unfolded, it became increasingly difficult to pinpoint who was scapegoating and who was scapegoated. Analogous to how the anonymity of the mob allegedly protected actual perpetrators of lynching, the swirl of rumors unsettled responsibility and problematized accountability, adding additional complexity to the criminal investigation.

Panic, Morality, and the Poor

The rise of moral panics and the popular grievances woven into them provide particular challenges for neoliberal democracy and good governance and underscore some of the shortcomings of these techniques and projects. At the very moment when Maya were encountering human rights education through post-war workshops and trainings about civic participation and governmental accountability, the "failure" of Todosanteros to absorb this knowledge became yet another poor grade on the "progress" report of the municipality and the state in the movement toward democracy. Writing about ordinary citizens who experienced moral panics during a transition in Malawi, Harri Englund explains how they were subjected to numerous governmental and NGO efforts to bring "democracy" and functioning governance to the country, including "inconsequential civic education" and "ineffective legal aid" (2006:171). In the absence of economic reform, these education efforts are overlaid upon poverty and meant to function in the everyday worlds of livelihood struggles. That poverty is a definitive reality for many people undergoing democratic transition is rarely recognized. Therefore, given the on-the-ground efforts by various programs to instigate peace, Englund points to how easy it becomes for "those who do not live under the conditions in which they emerge" to dismiss rumors as superstition (2006:170). The extent to which "popular" justice initiatives become politically problematic, especially during already fragile transitions, obscures what Englund refers to as "the legitimate grievances of the impoverished" (2006:182).

Introducing the explicitly economic—the concerns of poor people—into the equation of neoliberal democratic governance and transition sheds light on the interconnections between moral *panics* and the moral *economy*. Both are supported by norms, ideas about what is good or what is right at the cusp of difficult or monumental changes. Writing about eighteenth-century mob violence during the rapid expansion of capitalism and industrialism in rural England, E. P. Thompson pointed to the idea of a precapitalist "moral economy" in justifications of popular actions against merchants and traders thought to be unscrupulous (1971). James Scott has similarly shown the power of these ideas among Southeast Asian peasants as the Green Revolution produced vast changes in everyday life (1976). Underlying these challenges to ways of being is fear of the unknown (and fear of additional marginalization and humiliation) pushed to outer limits through panics and rumors.[22]

Collective, vigilante, and mob actions are viewed as politically problematic, but they often represent *political-economic* impasses that threaten livelihoods. Daniel Goldstein poses lynching as a kind of neoliberal violence, "produced by the scarcity and deficiencies of the privatizing state" and by the supersaturated tendencies of transnational capitalism (2005:239). The residents of Villa Pagador in Cochabamba, Bolivia, were quite clear that their turn to vigilantism and other forms of collective justice was an attempt to maintain an extraordinarily fragile level of subsistence. In repeated explanations to investigators, they emphasized that without the tiny amount of cooking gas stolen by the lynched thief, they could not feed their children. These profoundly basic needs are cast aside, in their view, in favor of the political rights and human rights accorded to and upheld for those who steal from them. Political imperatives trump the grueling daily grind of poverty in the framework of neoliberal democratic governance.

The concept of structural violence, defined by Paul Farmer as systematic, indirect, deeply historical, and economically driven, provides a theoretical intervention for making ethnographically visible the interconnections among poverty, morality, and rumor, and between moral economy and moral panic. Farmer writes that the acknowledgement of indirect participation in violence by all the people belonging to a certain social order provokes discomfort in "a moral economy geared to pinning praise or blame on individual actors" (2004: 307). For this reason, it has been politically difficult to move toward the recognition of oppression and the study of ongoing processes that construct inequalities. Benson and others make the point that while these conditions are true for all Guatemalans, "social, economic, and political conditions continue to be worse for Mayas than for ladinos" (2008:52). This shapes the contours and the interpretation of violence according to geography, race, and historical experience. "Most violent acts are not deviant" write Scheper-Hughes and Bourgois; instead, they are defined as moral in the service of conventional norms and material interests (2004:318). Lynching unsettles this assumption, requiring us to explore the erased and unexpected linkages between violence, suffering, and power.

For Todosanteros, the moral-political-economic landscape at the time of the lynchings was closely linked to eroding moral authority and an increased pressure for land, as migration shifted social and economic terrains. Former axes of power were under attack from a variety of new forces and the state was viewed as unresponsive to the desperate subsistence needs of the population. How the situation should be worked out and by whom were unclear, but for at least several years, newly emerging local forms of power were increasingly assertive in intervening to solve conflicts and address problems.

"Un Salvajismo Inaceptable": Violence and Neoliberal Indigenous Imaginaries in Media Coverage of Lynching

"GUATEMALANS KILL JAPANESE AND TOUR DRIVER"
GUATEMALA CITY, April 30—A mob in Guatemala killed a Japanese tourist and his tour's bus driver on Saturday, believing that the group had come to the village to steal children, the police said.

Tetsuo Yamahiro, 40, was beaten to death by a mob of 500 people
while visiting the popular tourist village of Todos Santos Cuchuma-
tan, 95 miles northwest of Guatemala City, near the Mexican border.
The mob, armed with sticks and stones, also beat to death the tour's bus
driver, Edgar Castellanos, 35.

Rumors have spread in the village that foreigners have come to the
area to steal children, said Faustino Sanchez, a spokesman for the Guatemala National Police.

NEW YORK TIMES

The press coverage of the lynchings in Todos Santos was a notable testament to the limits of multicultural inclusion and to continuing and per-
vasive racism and inequality within Guatemalan society and the state. A
deep-seated national divide between the rural and largely Mayan highlands and the city was set into stark relief in the news reports and debates.

This spatialized dichotomy is worthy of reflection because it conveys
particular kinds of conceptualizations of social, political, and cultural life
emblematic of deepening neoliberalism in Guatemala. In *The Country and
the City*, Raymond Williams draws our attention to the contrast between
these two antinomies as "one of the major forms in which we become conscious of a central part of our experience and of the crises of our society"
(1973:289). The urban and rural, in Williams's formulation, were inex-
tricably connected and often related to anxieties around social and economic changes. In 2000, less than four years after the signing of the Peace
Accords, Guatemala's economy was in the midst of substantial and ever-
intensifying turmoil. Coffee, an economic mainstay of the 1990s, was on
the verge of a period of sustained crisis as the world market flooded with
cheap beans from Vietnam.[23] The national economy was still recovering
from years of civil war, and the effects of structural adjustment, privatization, and increased financialization were newly felt. While remittances
were rising, they had not yet reached the stratospheric billions of dollars
that would pass through Guatemalan banks en route to home communities by the mid-2000s. Tensions between the country and the city, then,
demonstrated a plethora of national anxieties embedded in the social relationships and spatial articulations of state power.[24]

After lynching, Todosanteros were swept up in the discursive production of these emerging socioeconomic, legal, and political terrains. Because they are among the most photographed people in Guatemala for
their scenic mountain locale (called "a mountainous Shangri-la" in one
guidebook in the 1990s) and their colorful *traje*, some argued that the

paranoia leading up to the lynchings arose from the belief that taking photos robbed children of their souls. This curious belief was reported by Maud Oakes, and conveyed with authority by Monseñor Victor Hugo Martínez, interviewed by the press. It is unclear whether Monseñor Martínez ever set foot in Todos Santos, or whether he was aware of the growing transnational population then traveling back and forth between Guatemala and the United States. Indeed, as rumors circulated in the aftermath about the individuals responsible for the lynchings, several potential suspects left for the United States. This incongruent mix of antiquated cultural belief and neoliberal modernity was, in many ways, typified in the ensuing national debate prompted by the crime. Lines of deliberation were established, and various national positions were rendered stark in ways that were otherwise disguised by public discourses of unity and inclusion in the post-Accords multicultural milieu. Indeed, the way that various causes of the incident were constructed in the media highlighted competing ideological orientations in post-war Guatemala. At stake were the differences among and between people and cultures; various attempts to address them (or not); and questions of where economic, social, and cultural control would rest. In short, many of the anxieties circulating at the time lay at the heart of Guatemala's entrance into neoliberal democracy and the new millennium.

Coverage of the Todos Santos lynchings in newspaper and magazine articles, debates, and opinion pieces[25] became sites of cultural contestation and struggle. Anthropological approaches to the media most frequently hinge on the relationship between those who produce the news, "cultural producers," and those who consume it, "the audience." In their foundational critique of the "culture industry," the critics who became known as the Frankfurt School concluded that media produces and transmits cultural commodities that are entertaining and easily digestible. The more successful "cultural producers" are at constructing these bits, the more their message, emanating from dominant cultural ideologies, is absorbed (Adorno and Horkheimer 1947). British cultural studies later challenged this viewpoint, insisting that while the media may represent prevailing ideologies dominant in societies, it is always subject to various forms of counter-hegemonic contestation and challenge (Hall 1977). In this sense, then, analyzing media coverage of this incident provides access to specific voices and ears (Englund 2006) and allows for analysis of particular forms of contestation and struggle.

As the war came to an end in Guatemala, the Mayanist terrain and critiques of the burgeoning Pan-Mayanist Movement were intensively debated in Guatemalan newspapers. Kay Warren writes that political debates once fought in the confines of the university now entered the public realm and the pages of publications such as *Siglo Veintiuno*, *Prensa Libre*, and *Crónica* (1998:41). Although these were often the sites of critique of the movement, they also included Mayan voices and opinions. The rhetoric of inclusivity was occasionally present, later a "culture of peace" was nominally promulgated, and some healthy competition developed between major dailies in the mid-1990s. A number of important Mayan leaders—public intellectuals who were leading cultural nationalists as well as agents of globalization in Guatemala—wrote regular columns and often engaged in national debate. A few consistently figured in these debates, including Demetrio Cojtí (in *Siglo Veintiuno*), Estuardo Zapeta (in *Siglo Veintiuno* and *Prensa Libre*), Victor Montejo and Enrique Sam Colop (in *Prensa Libre*), and Irma Otzoy.[26] Given distance and language issues, Todosanteros did not make contributions to these exchanges.

In the coverage that erupted around the lynchings in Todos Santos, much about Guatemala, its past, and its future was subject to deliberation, filtered through neoliberal and post-war anxieties. Themes about the narration of history and violence that circulated in relation to the Rigoberta Menchú controversy in the early 2000s[27]—authenticity, legitimacy, the centrality of rumor—resonated once again, but in forms that reflected new circumstances. Economic incertitude and the question of whose narrative and version of history would prevail were central to this. The discourses that predominated were reductionist and oppositional, employing colonialist tropes that emphasized the abject savagery of provincial people: civilized vs. savage, sophisticated vs. simple, modern vs. primitive, friendly vs. fierce, and, ultimately, ladino vs. Maya. These pairings pointed to underlying ethnic hierarchies and racialized national constructions of inclusion and marginalization that simmered below the surface, not usually confronted as explicitly as they were in these accounts. Pointing to areas of tension and irresolvable conflicts, their primary axes tend toward the spatial, ethnic, and linguistic and disassociate ladino and Maya elite based in and near the capital from the rural poor. One effect of this project was to establish within the bourgeois public sphere (Habermas 1989) norms of identity deliberately exclusive of subaltern Mayan subjectivities then gaining ascendancy. These accounts assigned an identity to Maya, but attempted to elide the political subjectivity and power projected through it vis-à-vis the growing Mayan movement.

Monseñor Martínez blamed the Guatemalan Institute of Tourism (INGUAT) for its failure to protect visitors by warning them of local beliefs and customs—a Japanese tourist and his guide wouldn't have died at the hands of the hapless Maya if only they had been properly prepared. Juan Callejas, then-director of INGUAT, was puzzled, replying: "Children in Todos Santos are used to being photographed by tourists, because afterwards they ask for a *quetzal* [note]." Enrique Sam Colop, a prominent Mayan intellectual, responded in his column on May 2, 2000, by insisting that losing one's soul upon being photographed was the same kind of myth as turning wine to blood (in *Prensa Libre*, May 2, 2000), placing Monseñor Martínez's comment in the larger context of ladino Guatemalans' general ignorance about Mayan culture and society. Just as cases of lynching should be studied in order to better understand why they happen and to stop them, Colop opined, INGUAT should start educating Guatemalans about tourism and culture, because the country was bigger than the capital.

It took several days until an account that reflected conversations with Todosanteros and local officials in Huehuetenango was published, disrupting the cosmopolitan framing of the incident. Initial articles were full of authoritative commentary from Guatemala City: the president of the Guatemalan College of Lawyers and Notaries condemning the lynchings and lamenting such a start to the new millennium; a congress member from the National Action Party (PAN), which had just lost the previous election, saying lynching was the result of a climate of anarchy and ungovernability; the police spokesperson, commenting on how the twelve policemen stationed in Todos Santos at the time of the lynching were unable to stop the mob; representatives of the Japanese embassy indicating that diplomatic personnel had been dispatched to the area to get a clearer picture of what had happened; and Reina Batres, the wife of victim Edgar Castellanos, who presided over the burial of his body in Guatemala City, calling on President Portillo to insist on justice and to not permit impunity. Other than the interview with Batres, this early focus on "experts" in the capital to understand an incident in a rural town some eight hours away (where many had never been) underscored urban-rural tensions that were also about ethnicity: the vast majority of the population in the rural highlands was indigenous.[28]

A primary concern for many (including Todosanteros) was how the Japanese would respond to the lynching of a fellow citizen, especially one who had a family connection to the Japanese ambassador (*Prensa Libre*, April 30, 2000). Many noted that Japan was among the top three donors of foreign aid[29] to Guatemala, on occasion surpassing the United States. Although few Japanese tourists traveled annually to Guatemala (only about five thousand each year), the impact of this incident was judged potentially disastrous, pointing to Guatemala's increasing dependence on international assistance. In addition, approximately eighty-five percent of Japan's annual aid to Guatemala went to infrastructure, like road and bridge construction, often at the level of the municipality (*Siglo Veintiuno*, May 3, 2000). Loss of this funding would be devastating to local development efforts, potentially contributing to unruliness in the countryside.

For their part, the Japanese insisted that their priority was to conduct their own interviews in order to better understand what had happened in Todos Santos. In an opinion piece in *Siglo Veintiuno* on May 3, 2000, Gabriel Aguilera Peralta[30] commented:

> The Japanese are one of the most peaceful societies in the world. After the death of one of their citizens in such circumstances, Guatemala might have been portrayed in the Japanese media like one of those African countries submerged in perennial violence. But it wasn't like that. The major Japanese periodicals (*grandes rotativos nipones*) objectively analyzed the death of their compatriot.

The hierarchy of violence relative to regions of the world is particularly striking. That Africa is "worse off" than Guatemala or Central America is not supported statistically. The presumption effectively draws on the European imaginary of Africa as "an essentially violent 'darkness' that serves to define and emphasize a rational 'light,' an enlightenment" (Donham 2006:16). The dichotomy, grounded in the opposition between Europe and Africa, is similar in function to the many antinomies employed in this debate. Within a diplomatic geopolitics of violence and media reports about the violence, Peralta's seeming worry was that Guatemala might easily have been portrayed in Japanese newspapers in the same way that Maya were being portrayed in the Guatemalan press.

Considering the African case further, Donham (2011) suggests that post-war conflicts in Africa have been reported in a way that continues to construct Africa as an exception. "Senseless" violence erupts there because reason doesn't function. Analogous media accounts were employed in Guatemala to construct an indigenous Other without reason, and therefore unworthy of inclusion, during a critical moment in the construction of national identity. Todosanteros came to exemplify the hinterlands, collectively demonstrating the unworthiness of *all* Maya.

In the various admonitions against lynching and calls for studies to determine why they occur and how to stop them, most writers assumed that lynchings take place only in the indigenous highlands—in other words, that lynching was a particularly Mayan post-war social phenomenon, the "continuation of war by other means." Writing in *Prensa Libre*, journalist Mario Antonio Sandoval called for *"las organizaciones étnicas"* (the ethnic organizations) to do everything in their power to stamp out "these demonstrations of irrationality that directly impacted indigenous communities" (May 2, 2000). He highlighted how lynching, although it had reached crisis proportions, had not previously been viewed as particularly urgent because it was distant spatially and socially. Sam Colop pointed out, in the context of his larger argument about capital-centrism, that lynchings had also occurred in the capital and its immediate environs, including one on the campus of the University of San Carlos, the largest public university in Guatemala. By calling for the "ethnic organizations" to address this problem, Sandoval missed the failure of the state to address local issues, and the challenge this posed for democratic transition.

Various commentators noted a crisis of the justice system and a failure on the part of the ruling party to address rising crime and violence relative to the tourism sector. Violence, they noted, if not lynching, was something that happened to tourists the world over. One editorialist opined: "In some local sectors there's no consciousness of the economic transcendence of tourism and quite frequently, foreign visitors are intimidated, robbed and assaulted. What's really unacceptable and should be condemned are these types of mortal aggressions that make us seem like cave dwellers in the eyes of the world" (*Siglo Veintiuno*, May 2, 2000). Here, violence is ranked by what can be tolerated, a category that has grown wider in Guatemala. Colop responded by relating the rise in lynchings to the example provided by the army during the war. He called for investigation into the relationship between the two (*Prensa Libre*, May 3, 2000).

Todosanteros were accused of killing the (tourism) goose that lays the golden egg (Alonso, *Prensa Libre*, May 3, 2000). In lynching a tourist, they had unforgivably tampered with the image carefully spun to attract the thousands of tourists who visited each year.[31] This was demonstrated by the government's response, which seemed to be not so much about justice, as President Portillo claimed, but mostly about imagery. In the cases of the lynchings in Todos Santos and a few months later, on July 8, 2000, in Chichicastenango (where a market that is a key tourist destination is located), former President Portillo responded by promising to spend 615 million U.S. dollars to improve Guatemala's "violent image" and make the country an "obligatory destination" for international travelers (*Prensa Libre*, July 13, 2000).

Colop commented that while Maya were used by the state to attract tourists, very few were the direct beneficiaries of tourism. Profits from the sale of crafts were relatively low. Although some Maya might earn a living from tourists, the major beneficiaries were big hotels and INGUAT. Others suggested various plans for incorporating Mayan villagers into local tourism infrastructures (Zapeta, *Siglo Veintiuno*, May 5, 2000).

To return to Williams, if the city is an achievement, what is being produced there? For Williams, "actual and sustained social relationships" were generated by experience, including a sense of national belonging, which he saw as based more in the country than the city. By contrast, in the case of Guatemala in 2000, distancing processes were at work in fundamental ways in envisioning an after-war society. Themes that emerge repeatedly in the coverage of the Todos Santos lynchings, emphasized and utilized toward different ends, show how media representations are themselves the products of contemporary concerns and historical processes, of ongoing intellectual, social, and political debates and disputes in Guatemala. These portrayals contain the residue of earlier discussions and anxieties that resurface and collide with realities (and hopes) for the present.

"Nunca se pensó en Todos Santos," read one newspaper article summarizing an interview with MINUGUA representatives in charge of conducting antilynching workshops in the department of Huehuetenango. "We never thought about conducting these workshops in Todos Santos, because nothing like this had occurred there," said Arturo Soto Aguirre, Supreme Court magistrate (*Prensa Libre*, May 6, 2000).

Legalities and Imagining the Future

In April 2001, the trial for the first three defendants in the Todos Santos case commenced. The June 2001 acquittal of these defendants reflected a host of tensions in relation to democracy, law, and citizenship in the post-Accords era. In the face of pressure to convict, the court, presided over by Judge Josué Felipe Baquiax, concluded that there wasn't sufficient proof or testimony to establish that the defendants incited the mob to commit the lynching. "The state of justice in Guatemala is being consolidated," Judge Baquiax told reporters after the verdict was read (*Reuters*, June 26, 2001). "We simply couldn't condemn these people." Among factors that the judge cited in his decision was the issue of parents' fear for their children, declaring that the frightened screams of Catarina Pablo, the mother of the crying child Yamahiro reached toward to comfort, were a natural, suitable, and acceptable reaction for any mother who felt her child was in danger.

At the time, I read Baquiax's verdict as placing the Todos Santos case firmly within the national "good governance" project of the post-conflict Guatemalan state, pointing to the precarious nature of justice, citizenship, and the law at a critical moment. I viewed this as notable because of the particular characteristics of the state in transition and because of the dynamic nature of the notion of citizenship itself—a category with a social content that is contested and constantly subject to renegotiation and reinterpretation (cf. Sieder 2001:203). By its very nature, the after-war ("post-conflict") state is defined by what came before it—i.e., war or conflict—and this is used to ask citizens to exchange their immediate rights for rights in a theoretically democratic and hence better future. The combination of transition and the neoliberal outsourcing of legal responsibility and judicial administration has produced a peculiarly rightless citizen asked to bear with the challenges and hardships of the present as an investment in a better national future.

But the perspective of hindsight also shows that the Todos Santos lynchings case and its outcome were very much representative of what Sieder cites as popular expectation of justice versus recourse to courts: "the former demands immediate incarceration of the accused or public sanction and repentance," while the latter involves "the release of the accused for lack of evidence or on bail" (2008:83). It is, however, significant, regardless of the outcome, that a verdict was reached in this case at all within the national context where few cases are ever tried.

By the time Baquiax's verdict was announced, few Todosanteros seemed to have kept up with the process or knew what actually happened to the three defendants and the original group of nine who were taken into custody. Indeed, when I asked what was happening with these people just several months after the lynchings, answers were vague. I was told that six of the defendants had been able to buy their way out of jail. When I asked whether they would be standing trial in the future, most seemed to think they had bought their way out of the situation once and for all, an understanding consistent with their experiences with the justice system. Money, I was told, could resolve anything.

Todosanteros' disengagement with the law points to a profound sense of marginalization from legal processes of the state, one that by this point is felt by many if not most Guatemalans. However, marginalization, as Poole insists, is a powerful technique precisely because the margin is both a real place *and* a discursive and ideological position from which people learn how to speak about things like justice, to the state and among themselves (2004:36). It is in this space that the alternatives that people draw upon flourish. Certainly, these include lynchings, re-paramilitarization of villages (Burrell 2010), the increase of rural and urban gangs (Manz 2005, Burrell 2009 and 2010, Levenson 2013), and debt migration (Rus and Rus 2008, Stoll 2010 and 2012). But also present are Mayan community strengthening efforts, including the revitalization and recuperation of various aspects of indigenous and customary law and, with them, the possibility for a future in which these are the primary methodologies by which people negotiate everyday life and legalities.

At the time of this writing, legal and extralegal options, state-related possibilities, and other alternatives are weighed in relation to individual cases. In an incident in January 2011, several individuals, including a teacher and her accomplices, were clandestinely removed from Todos Santos as an unruly crowd clamored for justice for a scam the individuals had allegedly perpetrated against teachers in the town (cf. Sharp 2012). The mayor was asked by Salvadoran journalist Daniel Valencia Caravantes why the teachers did not seek the help of the police and justices of the peace stationed in Todos Santos. He answered: "Because no one believes in these authorities." Do you agree with the lynchings, he was asked? "Of course not! We wish that what happened to the Japanese tourist never occurred. Especially because it was a misunderstanding, a misunderstanding born of confusion." "Why couldn't you stop the mob that almost lynched the scammers?" "We tried, but the judge refused to take part in the affair. What did the judge do? He packed his bags and said that he couldn't hear the case. People see these things, and then they act. Once this happens, it's difficult to control" (Valencia Caravantes 2011). The past and the present continue to intermingle as individuals and communities weigh options based on after-war experiences and against a backdrop of ongoing impunity.

CHAPTER 6

Life and Death of a Rural *Marero*:
Generations in Conflict

On October 28, 2003, during the final days leading up to the annual All Saints' Day fiesta, Alfonso,[1] a young man in his early thirties, was killed by two members of the National Civil Police (PNC), the force charged with keeping order and guarding citizen safety after the signing of the Peace Accords. The police fired eight shots into the man's back, claiming afterward that he was a gang member, or "marero," and a dangerous criminal. He died shortly after. Following his death, Mayor Julián Mendoza Bautista requested that the police leave Todos Santos, citing concerns for their safety during the most important days of the All Saints' Day fiesta, when drunkenness is common and every broken beer bottle becomes a potential weapon. The military arrived the following day to keep order until new police officers were assigned.

Alfonso's murder, like the rise of *maras* (gangs), was the object of local contention and has had an ongoing and polarizing effect in Todos Santos. At the crux of the conflict are community anxieties regarding rising rates of local crime attributed to gangs and chronic insecurity, and intergenerational struggles over local power. Elders decry the nearly intolerable disrespect of contemporary youth, while young men stress the absence of meaningful local roles or work that take into account new experiences, like migration, that they have had.

The conflict over *maras* and, by extension, youth culture has become central to indigenous community experiences of the after-war epoch. While intergenerational struggles are a general feature of social life likely to divide people (Holland and Lave 2001:17), age cuts across the social and economic processes of Guatemala's after-war terrain in particular ways, separating those who experienced genocidal violence and "scorched earth" policies carried out by the army from those who were born or came of age afterward. Long-term struggles for social justice and dignity on the part of older generations are frequently overlooked or underestimated by the youths. The spaces of mutual betrayal or forced complicity that many Maya negotiated during the war remain fundamentally misunderstood, in the shadows manufactured by ongoing violence and impunity.

Generation has come to take on new resonance after war, creating different types of divisions even as it exacerbates preexisting ones. *Maras* have become a catchall, in many ways, for these anxieties and differences. Actions once viewed with dismay in Mayan communities but acknowledged as rites of passage join an expanding notion of what it means to be a *marero*, ranging from those connected to groups like Mara Salvatrucha, or MS-13,[2] to young men drinking on the street. Equally important to consider is why there has been such a concerted effort to repress these conflicts in increasingly violent ways that sometimes culminated in murder.

Security and the Criminalization of Conflict

After war in Guatemala, the legal culture in indigenous communities consisted of "a hybrid mixture of local adaptation and practices and elements of universalist or national legal norms" (Sieder 1998:107). As expectations and hopes have been disappointed by reality, surprising alliances have formed in the name of suppressing community youth rebellion, conceptualized as *maras*, in Todos Santos. Former civil patrollers and guerillas have mobilized under the umbrella of community security to combat a perceived gang problem, utilizing the older form of *comité de seguridad* (security committees), commonly shortened to *seguridad*. In the past, civil patrols served as a form of local power and a secure connection to the state for rural village men. When *seguridad* first commenced their activites in Todos Santos in the early 2000s, they were subject to repeated legal censure from regional and national authorities and human rights organizations, and Todosanteros defended their need for them as an antigang measure. Security committes are now considered so successful that similar forms are being implemented throughout the country, and there are national attempts to regulate them (*Prensa Libre*, March 12, 2007).

Mara activity, such as it is in Todos Santos, represents a choice for interceding in community processes, made by both returning migrants and the young people who are influenced by them. Through their participation in *maras*, some young men channeled their education, experience, money, and time into less socially accepted activities—activities that appealed to desires among young people to consume, look, and act in certain ways. Gangs in Todos Santos hung out in the street until late at night, hassled one another and drunks, grew their hair long, drank to excess, occasionally stole from other community members, and were rumored to take drugs. No one would claim that these activities never took place in the town before, but before, they were isolated or associated with fiestas. By the late 1990s, they were part of the daily lives of many young people.

Alfonso, for example, grew his hair almost to his waist—a source of great consternation among men and much amusement and admiration among women, who sought him out for his hair-care secrets. His muscles grew larger and his shirts, at least during hot summer days, became smaller (much to Todosanteras' delight) as he lifted weights like the car mechanics he had lived among in Michigan. Another public privilege that Alfonso enjoyed is that while most other men were working in schools, local government offices, or fields, he practiced his English with captivated *turistas*, adding to his already sizeable prestige among young men.

The seamless managing of these styles and behaviors in relation to transnational experiences, whether young men had personally migrated or not, provided them distinct advantages in negotiating other domains that were economically and politically important in the community, particularly tourism and NGOs. Speaking English, wearing baseball caps and sweatshirts from cities around the United States that served as reference points for starting conversations, and hanging out in local bars provided them with opportunities to share and receive valuable information that other Todosanteros could not access as easily. Embodied in this activity, and coupled with their economic success, was a substantial threat to older community members, particularly if young border crossers were able to parlay this social capital into meaningful and legitimate local political power.

Life cycles and age-related hierarchies have always been central to contemporary Mayan social life (Brintnall 1979, Carlsen 1997, Cancian 1965, Falla 1978, Watanabe 1992, Wilson 1998). These are frequently noted as sources of local conflict or the potential for it. Another generational focus of Mayan culture has been the close relationship to the ancestors, *antepasados*, who guide and watch over the living. There is yet another trajectory of the contemporary conflicts between generations: how ongoing inequality and structural violence have led to the posing of generational conflict itself as a threat amidst the waiting that defines after war.

Thinking through the production of this reconfigured vector of conflict, it is tempting to suggest that violence begets more violence; that is, following genocide and ongoing impunity, more violence is natural, what we might or should expect. And yet, this notion fails to account for the sustained, systematic campaign that has slowly shifted the parameters of social and political life in Todos Santos in ways that are now expanding throughout Guatemala. The latest face of conflict between young men and their elders is firmly embedded in the complex nexus of local culture, contemporary political economy, and democracy as they play out in Central America.

Historical and Contemporary Perspectives on *Maras*

Gangs contribute to post-war anxiety throughout Central America, and gang culture is arguably the source of one of the most visible and brutal, but least understood, forms of violence following the end of armed conflict in the region. By the mid-2000s, *maras*, or *pandillas* as they are known more generally in Spanish, were seemingly everywhere—in major cities where they had formerly held sway, in the countryside and deep into the rural and largely indigenous highlands in Guatemala, and along international borders in the region. Gang members filled entire wings of prison complexes, corrupted the youths, lowered the country's overall life expectancy, and allegedly controlled drug trafficking and migrant pathways to the United States, as memorably depicted in the 2009 film *Sin Nombre*.

Ordinary citizens became increasingly nervous about gangs as the multitude of crimes for which they were supposedly responsible expanded exponentially (Moodie 2009, Zilberg 2011, Thomas et al. 2011). U.S.-based zero-tolerance policies, antigang laws, and the expansion of the prison-industrial complex encouraged the wholesale targeting of those who looked like gang members. Tattoos, piercings, a shaved head, a baseball cap worn backward or other kinds of head coverings or hair dye were all considered markers for males. Gangs consequently adapted, wearing neatly pressed khaki Dockers pants, loafers, and collared shirts, and carrying messenger bags, and have allegedly graduated from relatively minor robberies to large-scale extortion, prostitution, car theft, and kidnapping (Associated Press 2007).[3] Under the guise of antigang measures, social cleansing and feminicide has flourished. Police assigned to cases of women's murders in Guatemala automatically characterize those with piercings, tattoos, or sometimes, absurdly, even sandals as involved in gangs and/or prostitution, making their cases unworthy of further investigation (Sanford 2009). As a result, the region has now become one of the most dangerous in the world.[4]

Maras first came to public attention in Guatemala in September 1985, when they joined students from a Guatemala City high school to demonstrate against an increase in public bus fares. Over the course of several days, as thousands of teenagers rioted throughout the city, burned buses, and looted stores, the police came to call these groups "*maras.*" This name was embraced by the general public, and over the next several years, some sixty *maras* were formed (Levenson 2013, AVANCSO 1988). Police associated these groups with drugs, prostitution, and other forms of organized crime, in effect criminalizing urban popular protest, which had long been a tradition among Guatemala City youths (AVANCSO 1988). Jorge Ramón Ponciano González (2013) argues that this form of criminalization was crucial in the discursive movement from "the Indian problem" to the "youth problem," a strategic neoliberal change that targets the younger generation, especially the poorer and more marginalized among them, as a "problem" rather than the possessors of "a fundamental social energy for the construction of a nation's future."

Early urban *mareros* talked about their *maras* as fictive kinship groups and networks that often provided support that was missing elsewhere in their lives. The extent of their criminal activity was limited: they stole trendy clothing, sunglasses, and shoes from stores or from other kids. On the basis of long-term work with urban *maras* in Guatemala City, Levenson (2013) marks their urban trajectory from groups of young people with communal vision and ideologies of social justice—when she first interviewed them in the 1980s (AVANCSO 1988), to victims of state-sponsored clandestine social cleansing, to killers preoccupied with death, the end product of state necropolitics (Mbembe 2003) and the military's "absolute negation of life as the job of power" (Levenson, 2013).[5]

What is clear is that in the political imaginary of the after-war period, *maras* came to embody a worst-case scenario. They effectively became the scapegoats for all that was intolerable, uncontrollable, and threatening, a phenomenon that Thomas et al. refer to as "a new common sense that involves blaming gangs and other unsavory elements of the population for danger and insecurity" (2011:2). This sentiment migrated to the countryside, where it took on a life of its own, differently configured for the conflicts and struggles of indigenous communities after war.

Targets After War

While regional urban gangs and urban gang violence are relatively well documented,[6] the emergence of rural groups throughout Guatemala is a growing phenomena, often ocurring in villages that were formerly free of violent crime. Beatriz Manz (2004), for example, writes that drunkenness, drugs, stealing, burglaries, rapes, and taunting fellow villagers have all become more frequent in Santa Maria Tzejá. Controversies in Tecpán, where *mareros* serve as scapegoats for preoccupations over rising crime (Benson et al. 2008), and Nahualá have been noted (Edvalson 2008). Gang activity is often seen as related to military downsizing, which left many ex-combatants jobless and large numbers armed. While some rural groups have allegedly become involved in drug trafficking and weapons running, what is happening in Todos Santos and in many other rural Mayan communities is a kind of activity distinct from urban gang crime.

"*Mara*," though, is often used as a blanket term to describe very different kinds of activities, levels of criminality, and modes of participation, with only occasional distinctions made between "urban" and "rural." This at least partially accounts for the hold that fear of gangs carries in many places. As young Todosanteros noted after the death of Alfonso, using the same word to describe the activities of Mara Salvatrucha and the locally based antagonisms between two groups of young men in one village is not only misleading, but may in fact have shaped their activities. Put simply, the extreme local reaction to these groups of youth may have pushed them toward behavior that was more troublesome.

Eric Wolf warned that "by turning names into things we create false models of reality . . . Names thus become things, and things marked with X can be targets of war" (1982:6–7). *Mareros*, in this case, became the new targets after war, and *maras* became a category so universally maligned that use of it, despite its numerous local forms, came to justify virtually any kind of zero-tolerance effort and the gradual remilitarization of rural communities.

Unlike their urban counterparts, who originally attracted poor, marginalized, and disenfranchised youth, some of whom were concerned with community well-being and social justice (Levenson 2013, Rodgers 2008), the young *mareros* of Todos Santos were often well-off by local standards. They came from respected local families, attended secondary school outside of the town, and had fathers who were educated, ran businesses, were teachers, and were sometimes involved in local politics.[7] Necessity, poverty, or escapes from violent families were not factors for these young men. In short, the original leaders of the two *maras* in Todos Santos—the Cholos and the Rockeros—were young men who had had every conceivable local opportunity to advance themselves, as did those who were associated with them. Both were well-spoken and generally considered intelligent, at least until they started engaging in *mara* behavior and badly influencing others. In most cases, the labor of these young men, as agriculturalists or elsewhere, was not vital to the livelihood of their families. In other words, being a member of a gang, which was not a lucrative endeavor in Todos Santos, implied both resources and leisure time. The sons of poor or more economically marginal families could not afford to belong to a *mara*.

The use and circulation of the word *mara*, which originally came from the Brazilian movie *Marabunta* (about the struggle between humans and red ants who devoured everything in their path),[8] has led to a gradual, locally sanctioned escalation in the violence used to deal with these groups. In Todos Santos, this includes the imposition of curfews, attempted lynchings, the (re)activation of security committees that closely resemble in both character and range of power the civil patrols of the war years, and, ultimately, murder.[9] These measures are ostensibly invoked to protect citizens, who support these community-level impositions, and are the local manifestation of national and regional preoccupations with increasing crime, gangs, and antigang legislation. Taken as long-term processes, they constitute the context for what Álvarez Castañeda (2007) refers to as "the social construction of *seguridad*."

Generational Conflict and Family Perspectives

There is no denying the role of structural violence and the sustained lack of decently paying jobs for young people in Todos Santos and throughout Guatemala and the way that this circumscribes futures, dreams, and desires even for the most well-off in local terms. These ongoing conditions are symptoms of the lack of redistributive peace that Todosanteros noted when they linked peace to work during the official end of the war.

A number of recent works approach generational conflict among Maya from different perspectives. These include Warren's (1998 and 2001) work on indigenous activism, in which she suggests that the social relations of generational change are a central mediator of political struggle; Green's (2003) and Goldin's (2009) studies of Mayan youth and *maquilas* in Chimaltenango, Guatemala; and Foxen's (2007) observations on generational differences in transnational Mayan migration. One commonality among them is the stress on how political and structural violence have contributed to shaping new kinds of generational relations. Foxen notes how age shapes different "identity strategies" by participants in the transnational project (2007:181). Green and Goldin both analyze how work experiences in the tax free factory zones contribute to the desire for new consumer goods and new patterns of consumption, which can often be indulged if the entirety of a young person's wages are not required for household subsistence.

Leisure time and the availability of different kinds of spaces for social interaction also impinge on traditional forms of Mayan social life, contributing to tensions in households. Whatever the local factors influencing the particular cast of generational conflicts and struggles, increased spatial, economic, and social mobility also contribute to these processes. Another trajectory of contemporary generational conflict is the question of how ongoing inequality and structural violence have led to posing generational conflict itself as a threat.

Generations are generally defined through life cycles or historical moments. In Guatemala, traditional civil-religious hierarchies that once ordered lives in terms of phases have broken down in many places, contributing to murkiness in terms of age-grade and what one ought to be doing at a particular point in life, roles that were once sharply delineated. Instead, current generations are defined by the historical moments that have shaped their lives: war and counterinsurgency for parents and postwar/post-Accords for their sons and daughters.

The generation of young adults to which the *mareros* belong is the first generation to come of age since *la violencia*. One of the consequences is that while they are "familiar with the local legacies of repressive violence, they have little firsthand knowledge of their parents' struggles for social justice and dignity" (Green 2003:63). The sense of social collectivity once experienced in many highland Mayan towns has been precipitously eroded, although Todosanteros engage in the maintenance and strengthening of community in other ways.

The disruption of family ties and personal security that animated childhoods continues to shape the experiences of individuals and community members. Mayan constructions of kinship, which structure family authority around cyclical generations, have a number of intragenerational concerns that have been central to Mayan social life and more recently are complicated by war and migration. For example, the eldest and youngest sons are important family markers of generation (Bunzel 1952). The eldest holds authority and becomes almost a father figure in the family. He is consulted by younger siblings and by parents for advice. The youngest brother is often indulged by his parents and inherits the responsibility for their care and the family homestead at the end of their lives. The older brother inherits the land (Ibid.). Frequently, eldest or youngest sons have passed away or are now living in the United States, where their social influence is restricted or diminished. Youngest sons may be unable to take on the responsibilities associated with their roles back home, or may miss out on the indulgences that once would have been part of their upbringing. As Reynolds (1997) notes in the case of South Africa, high mobility during the worst of the violence in that country made it difficult for adults to establish families in accord with traditional norms. These kinds of situations have profound implications for the formation of identity.

Generational Anxieties

Intergenerational strife may be exacerbated in times of conflict, when scarce resources are battled over under conditions of severe inequality. Anxieties concerning gangs and violence have swept through much of Latin America, where many countries have recently experienced transitions to democracy or the onslaught of hardships imposed by neoliberal economics and structural adjustment. In South Africa in the early 1980s and into the 1990s, severe "intergenerational tensions" stoked civil strife and African parents "complained stridently" of a "breakdown of respect" for adults. Older men especially voiced "outrage at the failure to accord them the status and authority they [deserved]" (Campbell 1998, in Carton 2000:142).[10]

Frustration at the lack of respect and desperation to recover it are often felt by parents who may feel powerless in the face of some of the choices made by their children. Youthful rebellion is universally feared among parents, but perhaps particularly among the Maya because age and kin relations have been central to social life and the construction of local identity. These anxieties are reflected in oral traditions, particularly in legends and prayers. In the prayers used by both *costumbristas* and *cofradía* members, one theme is the possibility that younger generations might ignore their elders on the path of life, dismissing them as models of moral action (Warren 2001:75, Oakes 1951, Watanabe 1992, Green 2002). Warren quotes one prayer: "Perhaps, the elders will be forced to ask God to punish the youths, to call for their time" (2001:75). She also notes that some Catholic Action parents had nightmares that their children would learn martial arts and beat them (2001:76). Bunzel's extraordinary account of family conflict in Chichicastenango, which she calls "the break-up of family," speaks to the centrality of *envidia* (envy) over status and inheritance rights within families (1952:132). Supporting her description of family feuds with extensive evidence from the texts of religious rituals, Bunzel emphasizes how everything in individual life and social institutions paves the way for familial conflict:

> the exalted position assigned to the father, his absolute authority over his children, and his secret fear of them; the strong identifications which children of both sexes make with their fathers, the ambiguous position of the young married man in the parental household, the stern morality and rebelliousness against it expressed in small thefts of money to spend on drink and prostitutes; the desire when a young man has children of his own, to be a father to them with all that word has come to mean, coupled with the realization that with property institutions being what they are the only way he can become a father to his children is to oust his own father from his sacred heritage. (1952:142)

These traditional roles, already problematic, have been complicated and altered by recent experiences of war, after war, and migration in terms of generation and respect and in terms of gender. Land tenure and agriculture production have been radically reconfigured in response to ever-increasing pressures. These include the inability to meet subsistence needs with smaller plots, escalating prices for land exacerbated by large-scale migration, and regional free trade agreements, such as CAFTA-DR, which make it more difficult for agriculturalists to access emerging markets. The reconfiguration of families resulting from war and migration has meant that traditional gender roles, working lives, and property ownership mechanisms among the Maya are challenged and reworked.

Others affirmed the older fear that their children would pass as ladinos outside of indigenous communities to get ahead on their own (Warren 2001:75). Many Mayan municipalities in Guatemala, including Todos Santos, have their own version of the story in which an older parent goes to visit her son/daughter at school and is ignored or finds out later that she was explained away as the servant. Clearly, having entered into oral histories, certain forms of generational anxieties have been consistent. In

Todos Santos, where both men and women wear *traje*, these stories often have to do with young men refusing to continue this practice.

Currently, youth strain against patriarchal control that is itself severely diminished after years of war and structural violence. The lives of the current generation of Todosanteros who are now between twenty-five and forty-five are further bounded by ongoing impunity that has both structural effects—crime may and often does go unpunished—and psychological ones. Edelman, Kordon, and Lagos (1998) have noted impunity as a new traumatic factor in their work with the children of survivors of the political repression in Argentina. Little or nothing has been done to achieve the symbolic reparation offered by justice, and impunity is accompanied by the periodic reappearance of the same types of campaigns that caused trauma in the first place (Edelman et al. 1998:451). Impunity is processual: the normalization of violence and forgetting coexists with governmental and societal refusal or inability to acknowledge the ongoing production of inequalities.

Similar to gang members in the Chimaltenango area of Guatemala, *mareros* in Todos Santos gained access to "a modicum of local power and authority—features of earlier 'traditional' cofradía . . ." (Green 2003:67). However, while Chimaltenango gang members brutalize "their neighbors and kin with the same counter-insurgency tactics utilized by the army—violence, kidnapping and extortion" (2003:67), in Todos Santos, it is the community and authorities who enact these tactics to save themselves from the "dangerous *maras*," the out-of-control youth among them. Critically exploring such variations of power is vital to understanding the elaborate and growing forms of repression enacted under the umbrella of the gang problem and the growing desire for *seguridad* in Guatemala.

From Bad Boys to *Mareros*

Prior to 1996, people gossiped about groups of young men who would drink and get rowdy late at night and on Saturdays after the market. I would occasionally hear of a stolen radio or a missing *huipil*, considered among the worst things a thief could steal because of the huge amount of time it took to weave. During the initial stages of my fieldwork, this pattern of local male behavior didn't seem unusual. Indeed, it fit with the observations I made of the annual fiesta and everyday life during my prior trips and with local conceptions of gendered identities. As a cultural activist father put it, "Women have more freedom [*libertad*] to sit with their daughters, but men [and boys] always spend a lot of time in the street" (field notes, January 2000). "*En la calle*" (in the street) was a euphemism for visiting the cantina, but drunkenness wasn't usually noticeable other than on Saturdays and occasional holidays. At these times, it was likely that groups of men would spill out of cantinas, and brawls would often erupt on the street. I recall being told to tread carefully during those days, and to avoid walking past cantinas whenever I could.

Starting in mid-1996, when I moved to Todos Santos to begin field-work, I began to hear about *maras* and my field notes from that time are sprinkled with notations about them. Mentions of *mara* activity and what they allegedly did or didn't do were always rather indefinite and circulated as rumors, even (or perhaps especially) by family members of the so-called *mareros*. This had *not* been a feature of accounts of youth delinquency that I had heard between 1993 and 1995.[11]

I found the talk of gangs disturbing. From my perspective, these groups and their activities didn't fit with anything I thought or read about gangs. I wondered why they were labeled as such and what was at stake. I talked quite a lot with Alfonso during this time. In a conversation in early 1997, I brought up the *maras* and asked him about his alleged leadership of one of the groups. While he denied being the leader of a gang, he did acknowledge being a leader, commenting that some kids respected him and that there was nothing wrong with that. I have come to understand that Alfonso's struggle was to define alternatives in the curious space of local post-war politics delineated by waiting and uncertainty, and to insist that transnational migration was producing something new in Todos Santos that demanded political and social acknowledgement. I noted in particular how he stressed the importance of protecting both his position as a leader and his reputation so that he could constructively parlay these into future community roles.

The label *mara*, in his case, seemed to reinforce the most negative aspects of what otherwise might have been understood as youthful rebellion or the legitimate questioning of formations of community-based power that no longer reflected contemporary needs and experiences. In a particular local sense, youths came to justify the use of the label in ways that made it practical to utilize the reputation of established and renowned transnational gangs to generate mystique. One strategy Alfonso used was to tell newly arrived tourists, especially those setting up businesses or planning to stay in Todos Santos for the long term, that he was a member of a gang in Los Angeles. He had never lived in L.A. And he did not use his alleged gang connection to extort bribes, ask for protection money, or insist on free drinks, which were common practices among the police assigned to Todos Santos. By invoking the connection, he situated himself in relation to an internationally known quantity of the category into which he claimed to feel forced. Through his manipulation of this category and the assumptions about identity that accompanied it, he gained at the very least recognition, and perhaps even respect (at least among fifteen-year-old Todosanteros) for his role. As a social actor labeled in a particular way, he skewed and manipulated the category to his individual needs. Such strategies, and other more serious risks or displays of bravado, contribute to "a sense of masculinity defined by the power of violence" (Levenson 2011:45). An example of what Roger Lancaster refers to as "the essence of machismo's ideal of manhood" (1992:195), these actions contributed to the construction of Alfonso's "outlaw" identity. After war in Todos Santos, they were part of the bid for the recognition of alternative forms of masculinity, leadership, and ways of life that remained unacknowledged in community pantheons of politics and power.

The *mareros'* behavior was initially more youthful rebellion than dangerous criminality. But their influence on youth was vast and was indexed by many community members as a growing and intolerable lack of respect for the elders and for established forms of municipal and community based authority. Villagers commented that the youth no longer maintained particular customs or celebrations because of the influence of the *maras*. The historical existence of these kinds of conflicts seems constant. When Victor Perera traveled to Todos Santos in the late 1980s, he related the following anecdote about Don Francisco Matías, a former leader of the *cofradía*:

> [He] harangued us in a loud crackling voice about the loss of respect for the ancient laws, which had led to venality, theft and rampant violence. Bellowing with his craggy face thrust six inches below my nose, Don Francisco scoffed at the contentiousness in the community . . . (1993:139)

Given the persistence of conflicts, the reaction to current crimes would seem to be less about the actual criminality and more about what is at stake or at risk at this historical juncture. The "crime" of disrespect for culture, and its potential resulting loss, is also commented upon in the following:

Nowadays, people decide what to do based on the least amount of work for them. This is how changes happen. There's a rich culture, but by now, every time, every year, every day it's changing. There are always new forms of life and sometimes they don't turn out to be so good. Or people don't share. Some people now, like young people, [they] don't appreciate our customs. Nor do the [evangelicals]. Because people who have respect are the ones who believe in the culture, in the beliefs, in all of that. And now with these new religions, there are many who don't care about these things. Then, all of the culture that has value isn't valued anymore. (interview with a man in his thirties, February 27, 2000)

As local social life is increasingly differentiated, particularly due to religion and to migration, the thing that potentially binds people together or unites them in the project of envisioning common futures is shared cultural practice, now under threat by young people and evangelicals.

Escalations of Violence: Bad Things Happen to Bad People

A focus on history and violence invites thinking about process, thereby moving away from static notions of culture and society and from reading particular forms as received or natural. The violence toward Alfonso, and his increasingly punitive actions, illustrate how *maras* in Todos Santos shifted from a relatively nebulous catchall category to one that was associated with a very specific set of occurrences.

By late December 1997, just before Christmas, it was hard to ignore the polarizing effect that the *maras* were having on the town. At the Saturday market on December 20, Alfonso was nearly lynched in the town square by a mob that was urged on by the mayor after a public confrontation between the him and Alfonso. The mayor had called Alfonso and two other alleged gang members thieves and menaces, commenting that long hair was bad and set a terrible example for boys in the town. Some people took this as license to attack Alfonso and threw punches at him; when his younger brother tried to pull them off, they beat him, too. As the crowds surged around the altercation and more people joined in beating him, Alfonso was dragged from the park to the town hall, where people threw banana crates emptied on the spot, rotten fruit, and stones at him. Shortly after, he broke free and managed to run the hundred feet or so to the weaving cooperative, where his father was president.

Cooperative associates quickly closed the door and bolted it shut while an unruly crowd gathered. As the mob grew increasingly menacing, rumors circulated that they planned to gather gasoline, burn the wooden building, and force Alfonso out to the street. Some villagers placed calls to MINUGUA and two community leaders caught rides to the departmental capital to seek police assistance to calm the crowds and safely remove Alfonso.

While this was happening, a friend and teacher walked past me with his child and commented, "Bad things happen to bad people." Shocked by his passive advocacy of what was happening, I turned away and my eye caught a few bloody quetzal notes on the cobblestones. They must have slipped out of Alfonso's pocket when he was dragged through the streets. Just then, another man directed his young son to pick up the bills. As midday approached, the buses rolled through town to take people back to their hamlets. The crowds dispersed somewhat, but some people remained in front of the co-op, calling for Alfonso to exit, for his father to open the door.

All afternoon, small groups gathered throughout the village, discussing the incident and the ongoing standoff, supportive of the mayor's actions or strongly against them. One woman referred to the mayor's stupidity and his penchant for speaking unwisely and incautiously. "One day," she said, "he'll get somebody killed." Others felt that Alfonso needed to be reprimanded, perhaps even publicly, if not quite in this fashion. Continuing to take advantage of the crowds still gathered on market day, the mayor allegedly issued a petition during the afternoon in an effort to collect 10,001 signatures or fingerprints (approximately fifty percent of the population, plus one) in order to lynch Alfonso.

At nine p.m. that evening, a truck full of police arrived from Huehuetenango to remove Alfonso from the cooperative and transport him to the hospital in the departmental capital. The next day, people flooded into town from the hamlets, perhaps to sign the petition, or alternatively, to finish their holiday errands. Although a town meeting was called for, it never happened. Later, the petition was dropped, although no one claimed to know why. Gossip and rumor reflected community divisions. Most prominent among the various analyses was that the attempt to lynch Alfonso was caused by people from the hamlets (like the mayor) and not from the urban center, where residents were less likely to engage in such activity. I immediately thought of the bloody quetzal notes, remembering tacit approval and the lack of intervention.

Alfonso returned to Todos Santos to recover from his injuries and

Alfonso at the picnic with *cascarones* confetti in his hair, 1998 (J. Burrell)

stayed out of sight. After six weeks, there was an incident that raised the ire of the community and diminished any sympathy that existed after the lynching attempt. On carnival Tuesday each year, children from the Urbana primary school and their teachers held a picnic in a high alpine meadow. Everyone was invited to join the festivities. For weeks, children prepared *cascarones* (hollowed eggshells filled with confetti) to break over one another's heads, and socks filled with lime or chalk. Buses and trucks were hired to convey the children to the picnic site, where they played, sang, and ate their lunches.

Alfonso and a few friends arrived in their own pickup truck with several cases of beer. Several hours into the event, they got into an altercation with some of the teachers, which resulted in a fistfight. One teacher was injured and his glasses were broken in the fight. The children panicked and scattered, running toward the road. Terrified, some hid under bushes and behind rocks. In the ensuing chaos, several were left behind in the mountains and were not found until the following morning. During the rushed return to the municipal center, Alfonso and his friends drunkenly threw beer bottles into the open trucks carrying the children. Once they arrived in town, various teachers and parents ran to the town hall to report what had happened and file complaints. At one point, an older ladino man I'd never seen before walked into the street and fired a gun into the air, adding to the sense of confusion. Alfonso returned to the United States shortly after this incident. Several months later, he was in a hospital in Michigan, following a knife fight with another Todosantero at a bar in Grand Rapids.

These three discrete moments—an attempted lynching, a ruined carnival celebration, and a bar fight in Grand Rapids—link specific instances in the escalation of violence and the shift in the meaning and therefore "targetable" quality of the *marero*. Bad things might happen to bad people in random ways, but a process was now underway in Todos Santos to prioritize security. It involved methods that illustrated contradictions and continuities of the after-war period.

Community Responses and the Rise of *Seguridad*

Prior to the war, community policing in Todos Santos had been carried out by municipal authorities appointed to their positions via local political hierarchies (Bossen 1982, Oakes 1951). These patterns were interrupted during the war by the imposition of the civil patrols. When the patrols were dissolved in 1996, many places in Guatemala waited a number of years for the introduction of police forces at the local level. In 1999, several National Civil Police (PNC) agents were assigned to Todos Santos, and residents were happy to receive them. Although some local business owners complained about the *multas* (fines or bribes) they were constantly required to offer to these underpaid state employees, most Todosanteros gladly welcomed their presence and anticipated assistance in their campaign against the gangs. This outcome failed to materialize, and the police themselves eventually became highly problematic and polarizing in their own way. Recognizing a continuing vacuum of power, community members soon turned to organizing patrols in which service of all adult males was required.

In late February and early March 2003, Mayor Julián Mendoza was called to the departmental capital to meet with a supreme court judge regarding the illegal actions of the *comités de seguridad* (*Prensa Libre*, February 20, 22 and March 4, 2003). "*Seguridad*," as the patrols came to be called, operated much as the civil patrols did during the 1980s and 1990s and, not surprisingly, involved much of the same leadership. They imposed and enforced a local curfew (*toque de queda*) and were, in the specific instance for which Mayor Mendoza was ordered to the court in Huehuetenango, clandestinely imprisoning their captives, holding people for up to several days with no legal recourse or rights. Some of their prisoners were held in outhouses. Mayor Mendoza claimed that *seguridad* was necessary because of the forty gang leaders operating in the municipality (although Todos Santos would be hard-pressed to produce forty gang *members*). The reporter writing about the initial incident mentioned "how curious" it was that these *comités* operated in much the same way as the old civil patrols but without guns. Instead, they carried *lazos* and *látigos* (ropes and whips).

Nevertheless, Todosanteros generally supported the formation of *seguridad*, seeing it as proactive and necessary in the community's ongoing fight to combat petty crime committed (mostly against each other) by teenage boys and young men. *Seguridad* also addressed the absence of municipality-level, centralized policing that many had expected from the PNC. Todos Santos was not the only municipality to struggle with the stark difference between expectations of policing and the reality of underfunded and poorly trained forces sent to Mayan communities, unaware of cultural norms and practices and unable to speak local languages.

As *seguridad* expanded the nexus of its power, human rights organizations reported a death threat issued to a judge appointed to the community when the leadership of the security committee disagreed with one of his decisions. The judge reported that he feared for his life following the threat, and consequently thereafter cleared all of his verdicts with the committee leadership before making them public (Guatemala Human Rights report, May 2003). Step by step, *seguridad* went about concretizing local power and political influence, using the ever-present threat of *maras* to justify increasingly repressive actions. At the end of this trajectory of escalating repression is the murder of Alfonso.

Slowly but surely, *seguridad* and the vision of generational conflict and control that its power rested upon came to dominate the political spectrum in Todos Santos, influencing everyday life in ways that were felt by all residents. *Seguridad* implemented curfews, excercised influence over the local judiciary, publically humiliated community members by dunking them in the fountain; and in short, brought back the kinds of "forcivoluntary" paramilitarized forms that characterized the war years (McAllister and Nelson 2013). Also, cantinas were closed and the public sale of alcohol was prohibited in Todos Santos.

Mareros, in the case of Todos Santos, were the *raison d'etre* of these local structures of power, and the reason for their continued authority. This is a central conundrum for the incorporation of future generations into hierarchies of power and politics. It is also a mechanism so successful at crime control that it is increasingly being adopted throughout the county.

Revolts and Rebellions: Generational Conflict Through a Historical Perspective

It is widely acknowledged that young people join gangs in response to a multiplicity of social, economic, and cultural factors, finding in a gang what they cannot find elsewhere, or perceiving that they have no other choice. In Todos Santos, *mareros* had choices, and they became adept at utilizing the unexpected and even the shocking to grab the attention of their community. In challenging existing power structures, in refusing to pay respect to authority figures and to elders so important to the Mayan conception of community, they developed a critique and challenged a way of life at a moment of flux, one where the recent past of the war years and the revitalization of forms central to community life prior to the war mixed in uneasy tension. In this context, what might *mareros* have hoped to achieve through the kinds of actions that grated against the rhythms of daily life? A critique of parents' actions during the war? Quick access to power without time-consuming movement through established hierarchies? The acknowledgement of increasingly complex lives and experiences that recognize transnationality? The answers to these questions are embedded in a rich and well-documented history of generational relationships coalescing around local power. This history clarifies how the emergence of *maras* and *mareros* and the conflict embodied within their rise are at once a contemporary problem and part of an endemic set of practices and reactions against those practices that has deep roots in notions of Mayan identity, community, and family.

Mayan communities and Mayan family dynamics have historically been structured around various types of hierarchies. Early Mayan society had been organized around ranked lineages in which kinship, generation, and regionality (Carmack 1981, Orellana 1984, Hill and Monaghan 1987) were key elements in the construction of identity. The later imposition of colonial Catholicism stressed community-specific saint societies and the Mayan practices of *costumbre* emphasized mountain shrines and sacred geography. Both colonial Catholicism and *costumbre* contributed to a heightened awareness of the local and an increasingly rooted notion of community. As communities became more insular, neighboring villages were viewed with hostility and envy, regional rivalries were remembered through an increasingly historical perspective, and conflicts over formerly shared resources intensified (Watanabe 1992). The mechanisms of local economic and bureaucratic power that ensured continuing differences between indigenous communities and ladinos were resisted through the elaboration of parallel religious and jural institutions (Warren 2001:66). Power structures and hierarchies such as plantation life, the authority of Mayan elders, and parents' authority over children were subverted and mocked at community festivals and critiqued in moral narratives.

Within Mayan communities are different sets of family dynamics that structure how social relations and patrilocal kinship ideologies constitute individual experiences and are transformed in the actual unfolding of lives (Warren 2001:64). Many students of the Maya have pointed to the great emphasis on collective leadership, consensus making, and the tolerance of different rationales for action in the face of the diversity of individual reasoning and intentions (Warren 2001, Green 1999, Watanabe 1992). Families formerly turned to *chimanes* and *costumbristas* to unmask hidden truth. Misfortunes caused individuals and communities to seek shamanic assistance to interpret and redress wrongs and to grant material blessings (Warren 2001:69). This network has largely disappeared or changed in Todos Santos.

Typically, after marriage, young men were drafted to join the civil-religious hierarchy—uniquely town-focused Mayan organizations of rotating administrative and religious office—by holding a series of ranked positions, or cargoes. Young men would be inducted to the lowest positions of the *cofradías* or saint societies, or function as messengers for town authorities. In Todos Santos, these positions included *fiscales, ixcueles, regidores,* and *mayores.* There were approximately sixty to seventy people associated with the civil hierarchy and called *mayores* (elders), a global term (Oakes 1951). One Todosantero commented on what he perceived as the wisdom of this process: young men were allowed to burn up their excess energy before committing to the more serious work of family and community leadership (field notes, January 2000).

Over time, an adult male (and very occasionally in Todos Santos a woman) could work his way to a higher position in the moral and civil administration of the community by moving through an elaborate ascending scale of offices, during the course of his life, to gain authority and finally become a community elder. These offices included engaging in service, sometimes voluntary and sometimes obligatory, that often entailed heavy expenditures to host or participate in community events. Expectations were often embedded in a discourse of spirituality: one received spiritual callings that shaped and directed participation in, for example, the running of the horses or the dance of the *conquistadores.* These kinds of arrangements gave a localized shape to the relationships between generations. Elders became the leaders of saint societies and learned the role of ritual guides and *chimanes,* thereby becoming living archives of religious knowledge and speaking at rituals and marriage negotiations. These elders, according to Oakes (1951), joined boards of overseers, or *principales,* that administered moral community, drafted new officials, and settled interpersonal disputes between indigenous community members (but not between Maya and ladinos). Through this extensive and elaborate age-grade system, *costumbre* ensured that indigenous municipal authorities were the oldest and most spiritually orthodox of community members.

Although Mayan communities had nominally converted to Catholicism, the advent of Maryknoll missionaries and the explicit training of and investment in young catechists presented new challenges to local hierarchies and claims to authority. The young men and women catechists, in their role, could speak out on morality, though their frame of reference, as Warren points out, was rooted in contemporary institutionalized Catholicism rather than the local community (2001:72–74). The politics of Catholic Action were also attractive to younger people who were beginning to question traditional authority. Originally part of a Cold War–era project introduced by Archbishop Rossell y Arellana in the 1940s and 1950s to address elite fears regarding the specter of communism, Catholic Action was meant to depoliticize impoverished indigenous populations who might balk at poorly paid and grueling plantation labor (Warren 1992). However, the local conflicts that erupted at the time of conversions had unforeseen consequences, including the frequent alliance between *costumbristas* and ladinos and, ultimately, how people aligned during the war.

Sometimes the skills and knowledge of the younger generation were acknowledged to be vital. Then younger, more aggressive Mayan men could rise to community prominence through their ability to speak Spanish and, as a result, better defend the community against increasing encroachments (Watanabe 1990:192). Early Catholic Action converts, the youthful rebels in revolt against the elders *and* the ancestors, tended to have significant connections to the cash economy and local commerce (Brintnall 1979, Falla 1978). Through these connections, they were able to circumvent some of the ways in which *costumbre* had perpetuated age hierarchies, for example, through the inheritance of land: traditionally, one paid respect to one's father and to the *antepasados* in order to inherit land. If disrespected, ancestors would inflict declining productivity and poor family health. Once other sources of livelihood were available, however, people did not have to worry so much about offending their fathers by participating in Catholic Action.

Outside of this religious conflict, the ethnographic literature on the Maya is littered with a wider variety of almost constant intergenerational turmoil around power, land, work ethics, and the like. Referring to a young man who held the office of Principal in the local municipality in Chupol in the 1930s, Sol Tax related: "His getting the office is a sign of recent breakdown: a few years ago such an upstart would have gone to jail" (1947:341, in McAllister 2003:219). As a history of generational struggle and anxieties makes clear, these conflicts tend to surge at times of rapid and widespread cultural change and may often be brutal in nature. Throughout the Guatemalan highlands, for example, *costumbristas* violently defended churches and public spaces that were being usurped by catechists, in one case confronting a priest in a church and threatening him: "We'll fuck you up now and if you come back, we'll kill you" (Falla 1978:446, in McAllister 2003:178).

After war, generational conflict is expressed through the criminalization of youth rebellion and the subsequent remilitarization that quells it. These forms are substantiated and granted legitimacy because they are familiar methods and techniques that function in contexts of widespread and continued impunity.

Rebellion and Appeals to Nostalgia

In his meditation on rebellion and revolution, Albert Camus (1953) writes: "Every act of rebellion expresses a nostalgia for innocence and an appeal to the essence of being." Throughout this chapter, I have juxtaposed the kind of behavior that now falls under the aegis of the gang problem with what used to be considered normal youthful rebellion. According to friends and family, by the time of his death, Alfonso had reached the markers that formerly signaled maturity and a man's willingness to settle down, to take responsibility for himself, his family, and his community. He had a Todo-santera wife, and she had given birth to their child. He was apparently in the process of constructing a house on a plot of land he owned amidst the homes of other family members. Friends and family indicated that he had been engaged in discussions about viable alternatives for funneling and/ or obtaining more legitimate local authority and had been considering the possibility of running for local office. In lamenting the lack of local oppor-tunities for young people, he had been thinking about spearheading the organization of an often talked about but never realized plan for a youth center. In short, he was doing exactly what might have been expected of him in taking on meaningful roles as a community member. In pursuing these paths, he was also fulfilling the potential that community authori-ties may have feared all along: successfully maneuvering his transnational social capital into legitimate local power.

For Alfonso, there was no way out. Associated with years of defiance and insolence, and widely considered to have caused or contributed to problems that caused the community despair, he was powerless to stop the mechanisms that had been mobilized against him. He had been made the object, the target of after war, the pariah, *and* the golden boy migrant through a steady process that had lasted years, and in many ways, he had mocked this process. Eventually the "war" became bigger than the threat he embodied. It was, in the end, too late for Alfonso to do the "right thing."

Power and Nostalgia

One rainy Sunday afternoon in February 2000, middle-aged and older Todosanteros, now at a time in their lives when they might have taken on increased civic responsibilities, earning respect from younger villagers, discussed hierarchies of power once active in the town. I was surprised by the bittersweet nostalgia for former structures of authority—the very forms that many of these individuals contested when they were youth, sometimes violently. Within this group was a range of historical paths and experiences. Some had joined Catholic Action as a way to address generational inequality and the tyranny of gerontocracy in the 1950s and 1960s. Others became cultural activists, or settled land in distant parts of the country. Still others followed highly untraditional and nonconformist paths through the war years, braving gossip, criticism, and *envidia* to shape lives for which there were no precedents.

Despite the economic costs and the strict hierarchies enforced through these age-grade systems, and some of their consequences, there was a distinctive yearning for the idealized kinds of individual and community identities that emerged from the roles they promoted, especially in terms of social recognition, public initiation, and local sovereignty. The idea of respect as an important factor for the growing responsibilities that came with movement through successive rankings repeatedly circulated, along with a nostalgia for the sense of interconnection that this promoted among and between the various offices, responsibilities, and cargoes of community. At one time the youthful rabble-rousers of their day, these Todosanteros were now wistful about the very past that they had once worked to dismantle, or at least to escape.

Nostalgia functions in ways that aren't always straightforward. The past is idealized and the present can never fully reach the same glory, orderliness, or security. In theorizing the desire for democracy and community in post-war El Salvador, Ellen Moodie characterizes nostalgia in terms of an idealized state, as something we wish for so fervently that we imagine that we have experienced it (2010:157). The people involved in the aforementioned discussion were community leaders and were acknowledged as such by many people. Their yearning for forms of power that they could access through service and experience involved projecting idealism onto a system so fraught with problems that conflicts concerning the costs of belonging to it led to its eventual demise.

The dynamics of relationships privileging generation and age, where respect was accorded for experience, service, and local knowledge, pervaded the social relations of the history workshops, the reason that we had all gathered that day. While people of various ages met together, there was clearly a great amount of respect among the participants, and younger participants deferred to older ones. This did not mean that younger Todosanteros were silenced or did not participate, but the space of the workshops privileged the older Todosanteros' knowledge and experience. Indeed,

Oakes's book, according to participants, indicated to them a kinder and gentler past vis-à-vis generational concerns. One man commented how, by reading Oakes's ethnography, "We come to realize how our ancestors lived. How our people lived at that time. There was more respect and more unity. Everyone was eventually a [respected elder]." The path used to be clear. If one followed it, one garnered respect. In a rapidly shifting milieu, where nothing is secure or certain, how does one earn and keep respect? This is not an idle question, as the past decades have shown. Individuals will risk their lives or kill for it.

Shaping the Future

Generational struggles, as I have illustrated, are not anything new, particularly among Maya, where they are consistently cast among contemporary worries. However, in their latest incarnation, they have taken a curious turn that is concretely based in regional and national anxieties and realities as well as local ones. In the case of *maras* and *mareros* in Todos Santos, multiple kinds of violence have simultaneously shaped subjectivities: the political violence of the war and its legacies, the structural violence of everyday life and the lack of local work or livelihood opportunities, and the violence of larger national and regional attitudes of anxiety over youth violence.

I began this chapter with the death of Alfonso. He died as he lived the last years of his life—amidst controversy and polarization. His death was a productive moment in that regardless of what individuals felt about him, his actions, or appropriate punitive measures, it represented an opportunity to contemplate the past and strategize for the future. In the kind of irony that characterizes after-war periods, Todos Santos–style security committees have now been formed throughout Guatemala, and the success they have had with gang control in particular has prompted national and departmental attempts to regulate them (*Prensa Libre*, March 12, 2007). A number of them registered with the PNC, which is notable as they are often a main source of authority in many rural locations, especially where the police have been removed, often due to corruption. According to the *Prensa Libre*, Guatemala's daily newspaper, a large number were known to exist in Todos Santos but mostly remained unregistered. Few police were stationed in Todos Santos, and then, only intermittently (Sharp 2008 and 2012). One Todosantero who preferred to speak anonymously explained that the townspeople distrusted the police, believing that they worked in conjunction with delinquents whom they permitted to rob and extort in exchange for a percentage of their takings (*Prensa Libre*, 2007).

Security committees were empowered to patrol by foot, with machetes and nightsticks as weapons, and to capture criminals and bring them to the PNC for booking and prosecution. Abuses have been rampant. The Todos Santos mayor claimed that these abuses were related to the creation of the committees (*Prensa Libre*, 2007a), but in the community, they fall firmly under the category of actions that have been ongoing since at least 2002. In other words, while Todos Santos may register a committee or two (with many more remaining unregistered) it remains to be seen whether they will actually change their practices given that the success they have achieved is now emulated nationally.

Among the kinds of conflicts that arise in communities throughout Guatemala after war, generational conflict and increasing repression invoked to handle it may be the struggle that will have the most devastating long-term effects for communities. While Alfonso would surely not have enjoyed living under the ever-expanding security regime in Todos Santos (or its parallel in the United States, which ultimately targets all migrants, regardless of legal status), I suspect he might have appreciated that it had formed in response to a long-term process in which he was a lead protagonist.

Waiting after War

In Todos Santos on December 29, 1996, the recent past and shared complicity in the shape and form of local violence hovered over the town's celebration of war's end, a reflection of how the war had influenced Todosanteros' lives in unalterable ways and continued to do so. Although the celebration was meant to be a triumphant festivity, acknowledging the official end of armed warfare naturally emphasized the fact of the war itself—and with it, the violence, local conflicts, and differences that were set into motion and continued to reverberate in new forms. Pressing one's inked thumb onto a "peace document" did little to ameliorate the effects of this shared history of violence. It was quite notable that so many rural community leaders, and members of all generations, saw peace as fleeting, ambiguous, and problematic, and many made a direct link between the impossibility of peace vis-à-vis the political and economic situation in Guatemala and the nightmare of the past, to paraphrase Marx.

The artist Laurie Anderson evoked this dialectical relationship perfectly in her 2004 performance *The End of the Moon* with a series of vignettes meant to challenge the audience on the nature of dichotomies. In one of these, an editor walks into his office in St. Petersburg in 1868, unwraps a brown paper parcel sent to him by Tolstoy, has a look at the title page of an exceedingly thick manuscript, and thinks: "So, it *is* possible to consider war and peace together." With this quick scene, Anderson conjures a vision in which each—war and peace—is part of the other, conveying what Todosanteros expressed in the church square that December. We cannot separate war and peace just as we cannot separate the political from the economic, the lofty ideals from the everyday realities. Yet we try to.

Conflicts, with their historicity, their reassuring ordinariness, and their continuity, provide a possibility for bridging this illusory gap, a way of recognizing the enduring nature of the past in the present. They index resilience in what are often profoundly unfavorable conditions. They enable us to track how power and politics work. The theorist in me is reassured. But recognizing the new faces of these conflicts is often challenging and deeply disturbing. Understanding the processes that lead to some present-day realities can be terrifying. I know that I am not alone in feeling this way among those of us who work on issues of war and violence in Guatemala, or anywhere else, when I write this.

The commonplace regularity of conflict and its relevance for following pathways of power also definitively problematizes "the community," especially "the local community," as a space of homogeneity and unity. To convey the impression of cohesiveness is itself the outcome of internal dispute and political process: who gets to perform this and what do they earn from it? Why are some performers chosen over others? What are the stakes in presenting a public veneer of unity, and how do people arrive at a consensus for achieving this? This is not to say that communities cannot choose the idea of collectivity or cohesiveness to promote themselves and their projects, but when they do so, it is simply one strategy that won over competing possibilities.

In constructing a compendium of the disputes and struggles that consume Todosanteros after war, I have been attentive to the conditions of their formation across local and national, and sometimes international, contexts. The more slippery analytical space involves accounting for what is particularly neoliberal, or arising from neoliberalization, in the formations of power and relationships. To address this issue, I have emphasized a number of key concepts, showing the characteristics that they evince at different moments. The domains of culture, violence, security, and governance are among them. There is one more concept, however, that has been echoing throughout this book, perhaps produced through particular contexts of neoliberalism, but definitely connected to the after-war epoch: waiting.

After war is defined by waiting. This is particularly true in relation to the uncertainty and insecurity that characterize these periods. The act of waiting and what it promotes are key elements of the functioning of power after war. Citizens are asked to cede liberties, authority, or guns in the short term for something better in the long term; or to live with impunity and escalating crime while waiting for the trickle-down effects of the market or the promised glories of democracy. All Guatemalans wait for desired outcomes to manifest, for returns on their investments of hope.

Pierre Bourdieu has theorized waiting as one way in which the effects of power are felt. Waiting is intimately intertwined with hope; a key element of the mechanics of its function as a form of power is to delay—without destroying—hope (2000:228). It involves, like hegemony, a delicate balance that can be easily toppled, and "adjourning without totally disappointing" is integral. Waiting is a form of power that remains unexplored and under-theorized in the research of after war. We take waiting for granted. And yet, it produces something important for post-war analyses: a crucial structure of feeling (Williams 1977), a particular lived experience and quality of life at a given time and place. The array of sentiment about the transition from war to after war, from "things are better now" and "things have improved" (Benson et al. 2008), to "worse than the war" (Moodie 2009, Levenson 2013) point to the continuum across which this can be experienced.

Waiting can produce particular kinds of subjectivities, especially relative to states. In his work on Malawi, Englund indicates that post-conflict citizens are kept docile and submissive by the mechanisms and the education of the post-conflict state and the human rights and development regimes that uphold it. To be a "good" Malawian means to uphold the national virtues of "discipline" and "order," objectives that were introduced by the organizations that worked for peace (2006:168–169).

In his work theorizing the waiting done by poor people in the welfare offices of Buenos Aires, Javier Auyero writes that experiences of waiting persuade the destitute that they need to be patient. This excessive waiting produces compliant clients rather than proactive citizens—although this compliance is very different from passivity. Power is exercised over people's time in the forms of "adjourning, deferring, delaying, raising false hopes, or conversely rushing, taking by surprise" (2011:6). People wait, especially after war, in states of expectation, hope, anxiety, powerlessness, discouragement, and despair. They may also assert agency and find empowerment in the refusal to wait. For example, Todosanteros' refusal to wait for economic benefits resulted in massive wage-labor migration, a pattern that was echoed throughout the country as remittances grew precipitously from 1996 to 2007. Likewise, they took security into their own hands after waiting for potential resolutions that never came. In some domains, the uncertain, confusing, arbitrary nature of waiting was no longer tolerable.

The power evinced through waiting suggests another way of thinking about conflicts. The refusal to wait may be a powerful counter-hegemonic subjectivity relative to the state. Seen this way, it earns Todosanteros the right to negotiate and to refuse further state overtures without repercussion. Repeatedly censured for instituting security committees and clandestinely imprisoning captives, the municipality has consistently refused to wait for the state to deliver alternatives (although it does take advantage of the intermittent presence of the state). This subjectivity spills over into other aspects of political life, as Todosanteros negotiate legal terrain and the continuing evolution of a "vigilante justice" movement.

Viewed in this way—one of many possible interpretations of how waiting might function as a mode of power after war—there is hope and the permanent presence of alternatives. Nevertheless, I am cautious. In an interview included in *Resources of Hope*, Raymond Williams urges: "We must speak for hope, as long as it doesn't mean suppressing the nature of the danger" (1989:322). It is the danger that concerns me.

Notes

Introduction

1. The triangle of Guatemala, Honduras, and El Salvador was recently named "the deadliest zone in the world" aside from Afghanistan and Iraq, due in large part to the estimated six billion dollars in drug money that is laundered there (*Time* magazine online, June 22, 2011). In a decade, well over one hundred thousand people were murdered, more than the toll of El Salvador's twelve-year civil war. See "The Deadliest Zone: Hilary Clinton Visits Central America's Narco-Nightmare," in *Time* magazine online, June 22, 2011.

2. Anthropologists have long noted conflict as a particularly fruitful domain of analysis. This line of inquiry arguably reached a disciplinary and ethnographic apotheosis in the mid-twentieth century with the work of Max Gluckman and his colleagues at Manchester University. Gluckman's interests, once focused on social process, gradually coalesced around the idea of contradiction, on "people cooperating and disputing within the limits of an established system of relations and cultures" (1958:35, in Frankenberg 1982). Contradictions eventually *became* conflicts, and conflicts were constitutive of social and political order. Indeed, Gluckman came to believe that conflict was necessary to uphold society (1954 and 1963). This analytical stance in turn influenced the Manchester School of anthropology as well as French post-structuralist political anthropologists, among them Bourdieu (1977), Clastres, and Althusser.

3. The names, of course, are pseudonyms unless otherwise noted, and some of the details are changed so that this precise conflict is not traceable to particular individuals. This vignette is a composite of several different histories, representative of the kinds of conflicts, and their mechanisms, that move from the past to prevail in the present. That these strategies are embraced by Mayan storytellers has been a point of contention, particularly during the Menchú affair (Stoll 1998, Arias 2001).

4. The quest to maintain both the generalities of typology and the specificity and embeddedness of ethnography has been at the center of long-running methodological debates. Burawoy (1991, 2000, 2009), Narotzky (2010), and Smith and

Narotzky (2007) argue for such an approach toward political-economic research on a variety of scales.

5. As a discipline, anthropology has recently been concerned with increasing its public visibility and engagement in the wider world, devoting considerable debate to the ethics, politics, and dilemmas of doing so. As Checker argues in *American Anthropologist* (2009), we are on the threshold of a new era, in which knowledge can be swiftly disseminated through new technology and forms of media. Disciplinary insights are rapidly spread and incorporated in new ways. A number of articles and notable collections that explore new forms of involvement and commitment, and corresponding dilemmas, include Alvarez et al. 2011, Fox and Field 2007, Kirsch 2002, Low and Merry et al. 2010, Hale 2006, Rappaport 2008, Sanford and Angel-Ajani 2006, Smith 1999, and Speed 2006, among others.

6. A range of conflicts documented among the Maya include land and agrarian conflicts (Bunzel 1952, Grandin 2000 and 2005, McCreery 1994, Watanabe 1992, Lovell 1988, Webre 1988, Handy 1996); the struggle between *costumbristas* (traditional religious practitioners) and Catholic Action, the social-justice-based movement of the Catholic Church (Brintnall 1979, Calder 1976, Falla 1988, Harvey 1998, Warren 1989); religious recuperation and revitalization (Adams 2009); involvement in development and economic schemes (Little 2004, Fischer and Benson 2006, DeHart 2010); and conflicts regarding migration (Foxen 2007).

7. Javier Auyero's (2011 and 2012) sensitive research on waiting as a political tool of the Argentine state captures this dynamic of political power. Through waiting, Auyero suggests, the poor learn the opposite of citizenship; that is, that they are patients of the state.

8. See Goldin 2009, 2011 and Green 2003 for a discussion of the maquilas, Fischer and Benson 2006 for an in-depth discussion on export agriculture, and Robinson 2001 on the development of entrepreneurialism in Guatemala.

9. Harvey (2005) contends that the arts and culture flourish at moments of financial hardship, often producing new and innovative forms. As financial processes implemented in New York and connected to structural adjustment policies underway in the global south took hold, the city recovered from its own devastating bankruptcy awash in a definitive creative moment.

10. The concept of "securityscape" extends Appadurai's (1996) notion of a series of hybridized cultural flows and global connections and disjunctions (defined as "scapes"). It first appeared in Hugh Gusterson's work on the military complex, in a discussion and analysis of "asymmetrical distributions of weaponry, military force, and military-scientific resources among nation-states and the local and global imaginaries of identity, power, and vulnerability that accompany these distributions" (2004:166). The idea has since been taken up, expanded, and refined by Zilberg (2011), Albro et al. (2011), and many other scholars engaging in new research.

11. This quote appeared in the *Report of the Special Rapporteur on Extrajudicial, Summary or Arbitrary Executions* in 2007, authored by Philip Alston.

12. Reports from *Prensa Libre* (August 25, 2011), and various other sources suggest that for the country as a whole, the murder rate in the first half of 2011 was about ninety-eight people per week. In comparison, 490 people were killed in New York

City in 2011 (through December 18, 2011) and 519 in 2010 (through December 19), according to the *New York Times City Room* (blog), December 22, http://cityroom .blogs.nytimes.com/2011/12/22/a-flat-year-overall-for-crime-in-new-york/.

13. As Donham (2006), Scheper-Hughes and Bourgois (2004), Binford (2002), and others have similarly noted, the "after-the-factness about narratives of violence is not sufficiently problematized" (Donham 2006:27). Long-term field-work that blends history and ethnography provides an important corrective to what Daniel (1996:4) calls a "pornography of violence"—a crisis in our ability to accurately represent violent acts—and shows the cultural and political processes that contribute to particular events and outcomes.

14. I use it in this book when they have done so; for example, in describing the aftermath of lynching in Chapter 6.

15. There were no courses or field schools for learning Mam, as there are for other Mayan languages. The relevant books that were available were a dictionary, a bible translation sponsored by the Summer Institute of Linguistics, and a manual for studying Mam grammar. While these helped me learn how to write, they weren't of much use in speaking. I finally asked friends, neighbors, and teachers to stop speaking Spanish with me, which was lonely and isolating, but efficient.

16. By emphasizing what I've referred to as "inclusive" methodologies, I do not suggest that there was any sort of consensus among Todosanteros with regard to my presence or cooperation with anthropologists in general. Instead, there was always debate about whether to participate in workshops or discussions, or to allow one's children to participate in after-school projects, even (or especially) when these were promoted or supported by other community members.

Chapter One

1. The CEH was an innovative commission for transitional justice; it married human rights scholarship and activism on the ground in ways that have shaped how truth commissions and transitional justice initiatives deal with questions of genocide (Garrard-Burnett 2010, Grandin 2000, Sanford 2003).

2. Both of these emerged from the Armed Rebel Forces (FAR). To a lesser extent, the urban working-class-based Guatemalan Worker's Party (PGT) followed suit (Ball, Kobrak, and Spirer 1999).

3. Among the victims were employees of the Spanish embassy, CUC members, and university students from the Robin García Revolutionary Student Front (FERG). Ambassador Cajal López and *campesino* (peasant) Gregorio Yula survived, although, two days later, Yula was abducted from the hospital by a group of heavily armed civilians and his body was thrown from a car in front of the rectory of San Carlos University, with the message "Tried as a traitor, the Spanish ambassador will run the same risk" (OAS 1981). Vicente Menchú, father of Rigoberta Menchú Tum, winner of the 1992 Nobel Peace Prize, died in this incident. The massacre is discussed at length in Menchú's influential testimony, *I, Rigoberta Menchú: An Indian Woman in Guataemala* (1983, with Elisabeth Burgos-Debray). See Grandin 2006 and IACHR *Report on the Situation of Human Rights in Guate-*

mala, October 13, 1981, http://www.cidh.oas.org/countryrep/Guatemala81eng /chap.2.htm; See also *Organizing and Repression in the University of San Carlos, Guatemala, 1944–1996,* American Academy for the Advancement of Sciences, http://shr.aaas.org/guatemala/ciidh/org_rep/english/part2_9.htm.

4. Approximately six thousand people were part of the Ixcán Communities in Resistance. See *Interamerican Commission of Human Rights Country Report on Guatemala,* 1993, http://www.cidh.org/countryrep/Guatemala93eng/chapter8 .htm.

5. Bossen reports that sixty-three percent of the urban Todosanteras she surveyed in 1975, and twenty percent of the rural women, already earned a cash income from selling their weaving, either in the town, through a middleperson, or through the weaving cooperative (1984:67). Interviews I conducted in 1994 with the president and members, and with others who had once been part of the cooperative, revealed this history of tensions.

6. The congregation of the only evangelical church in Todos Santos in 1974 consisted of about one hundred members (Bossen 1984:105).

7. This account of *la violencia* in Todos Santos was constructed from a variety of sources, including the CEH reports of human rights violations in Todos Santos, Victor Perera's *Unfinished Conquest: A Guatemalan Tragedy* (1995), Olivia Carrescia's *Todos Santos: The Survivors* (1989), Mitsuho Ikeda's "The Cultural Involution of Violence: A Guatemalan Highland Community and Global Economy" (1999), and stories told to me over the years by Todosanteros and others who were living in the community during these years.

8. These rocks were whitewashed in the mid-1990s, prior to the dissolution of the civil patrol. Occasionally, well-intentioned tourists have attempted to organize projects to paint them, oblivious to their history and meaning.

9. Mitsuho Ikeda details the torture: "Each man's fingers were cut off with a knife, his stomach ripped open, penis cut off, head cracked with a machete, the skin on the back of his legs taken off, and then [he was] finally shot and killed. In other cases, they were killed by being drenched in oil and burned. About 140 men met death in such ways. The final ten men, said to be the most important ten guerillas, were made to walk the road to S (name of a nearby town on the other side of the mountain, about a five-hour walk through the mountains). Over the course of the route the soldiers sliced the men's ears, cut off their toes, made them continue walking, and did everything they could to torture them so that they died an agonizingly painful death" (1999:9).

10. Some still live in that area, occasionally returning to Todos Santos for the fiesta and other occasions. Because the Ixcán was thought to be guerilla territory, reintegration back into Todos Santos has been difficult for many people. Until the 1990s, their visits with their families were under close surveillance by the paramilitary civil patrol, who were fearful that they might precipitate violence in the community (Perera 1993).

11. Eyewitnesses recalled their return as a solemn affair: they were malnourished, beaten, and prematurely aged (author interview, 1998).

12. Davis writes: "If we assume that an Indian male could earn 2.25 quetzales a day by selling his labor, each man was contributing, through his participation

in the civil patrols, approximately 101.25 to 112.50 quetzales a year to the state in the form of an indirect 'labor tax.' With the per-family monetary income in rural Guatemala between three hundred and five hundred quetzales a year, this 'labor tax' was an enormous financial drain on the peasant household economy as well as on the cash flow in the local, regional, and national economies" (1988:29).

13. "Don Gaspar" is a pseudonym, also used by Perera (1993).

14. One civil patroller from elsewhere in the country complained: "The problem is there are spies everywhere. You can't trust anybody. The army has successfully made one distrustful of one's neighbors. The Civil Patrol as well: they are always ready to denounce anybody as a collaborator [with the guerillas]" (CEI-DEC, quoted in Arias 1988:189 and Schirmer 1998:93).

15. I have constructed this account from the CERIGUA report and from accounts shared by Todosanteros and others living in Todos Santos at the time.

Chapter Two

1. This is a significant improvement since I first traveled there in 1993. In that year, there were few buses and they originated in ladino towns further up the valley. This meant that by the time the bus arrived in Todos Santos, there were rarely seats, and many people would have to stand for several hours while the bus bounced over precipitous and challenging dirt roads. Since the late 1990s, roads have been built, improved, and paved, and there are new bus companies and minivans owned by Todosanteros who migrated or made money by selling coffee during the boom. Expanded service makes it easier for Todosanteros to make trips for studying, shopping, and medical appointments in Huehuetenango, the departmental capital.

2. 26,118 people, according to the 2002 census, with 2,980 of them living in the town center.

3. Cosmovision, a word that has emanated from Mesoamerica, implies a particular understanding of the world, and of time and space in relation to the *antepasados* (ancestors) and to ritualized forms of representation. Although cosmovision is usually used in ways that privilege the spiritual over the economic and political, suggesting the antithesis of neoliberal processes of identity formation, these three domains are intimately linked for Maya in the post-war period in Guatemala. Through the integration of cosmovision as a key component in a national project of neoliberal multiculturalism and the revitalization of indigenous culture, worldviews, and practices, the spiritual and the everyday have now become deeply political for Maya. Indeed, cosmovision, for those of us inclined to a more materialist analysis of identity formation, is a crucial element in defining a Mayan "structure of feeling" for the generation of the new millennium. While Williams (1977) developed this concept to emphasize the lived experience and quality of life at a particular time and place, he simultaneously resisted idealistic notions of "the spirit of an age." Instead, "structures of feeling" root us in the specificity of what people do every day.

4. This sociocultural turn toward understanding space has been embraced by

geographers and anthropologists alike. A (by no means exhaustive) list of authors and their works includes Massey 1984 and 1994, Ferguson and Gupta 1997, Gordillo 2004, Pred 1994, Watts 1992, and Harvey 1997.

5. This workshop was cotaught with Francine Pickup, a Cambridge University student conducting fieldwork for her senior thesis.

6. Thanks to Rob Hamrick for pointing this out based on his observations of the 2002 census in Santa Catarina Palopó.

7. By 1994, a low-key tourism was beginning to flourish in Todos Santos once again, and there were a number of *turista* residents. The nearest military garrison was located in Chiantla, and although it controlled, on and off, access to the *altiplano*, it wasn't part of the everyday life of Todosanteros. Additonally, the school that taught Spanish and Mam to tourists was now attracting a reliable trickle of students. Because many tourists eventually worked on local projects to benefit the community (a library, health centers, the procurement of an ambulance and a tree nursery for a reforestation project, among them), one more person with a project was hardly unusual.

8. The curriculum in the Todos Santos middle school in 1994 did not make the slightest pretense to include local knowledge and experiences. For example, a middle school music class was entirely focused on European classical music, but there was no phonograph or cassette player, nor records or tapes of this music, only a chapter in a textbook. In the meantime, the local music was extraordinarily rich and complicated, full of instruments and rhythms that Todosanteros could use to tell the stories of people's lives. This music was ignored in the classroom and and is slowly dying out.

9. Although photographs were taken, unlike Wood's (2003) professional images of *campesino* maps, they were, lamentably, not of reproducible quality.

Chapter Three

1. Christian Tomuschat, coordinator of the CEH, detailed the formation, work, and reporting in "Clarification Commission in Guatemala," *Human Rights Quarterly*, 2001.

2. See Bickford, "Unofficial Truth Projects," in *Human Rights Quarterly*, 2007, especially 1010–1011.

3. The Oficina de Derechos Humanos del Arzobispado (ODHA; Archbishop's Office of Human Rights of Guatemala) was established and is still in existence, providing assistance to victims of human rights violations. REMHI enabled the CEH to provide data far beyond what it would have been able to generate under its own mandate to reach its conclusions. The fact that many of REMHI's human rights workers were indigenous meant that they were able to reach into many rural communities.

4. For a comprehensive and compelling account of the murder and the labyrinth of politics surrounding it, see Francisco Goldman's *The Art of the Political Murder*, 2007.

5. See E. Oglesby and A. Ross, "Guatemala's Genocide Determination and the Spatial Politics of Justice," in *Space & Polity*, 13 (1).

6. Filed in 1999 by Rigoberta Menchú and other survivors, the case charges eight senior Guatemalan government officials, including three former heads of state, Efraín Ríos Montt, Fernando Romeo Lucas García, and Óscar Humberto Mejía Victores, with responsibility for genocide, state terrorism, torture, and other crimes against humanity. In April 2011, Judge Santiago Pedraz, of the Spanish National Court, issued an arrest warrant and extradition request for Jorge Sosa Orantes, for his participation in the Dos Erres massacre of 1982, in which more than two hundred people were killed. See http://www.gwu.edu/~nsarchiv/guate mala/genocide/round1.htm and http://www.cja.org/section.php?id=83.

7. David Tolbert, president of the International Center for Transitional Justice, has commented on the historic and hopeful nature of this undertaking for the Guatemalan justice system. He says: "The crime of genocide is rarely tried in a national court; not only are the investigations very complex, but the political will is often lacking to bring such serious charges against the powerful." See http://ictj .org/news/guatemala-genocide-case-vital-step-end-decades-impunity.

8. Frank Taylor, a North American who lived in Todos Santos during the 1970s, told me that he had to barter work in the owner's fields for borrowing the book a certain number of hours every day to read it. In 1994, several copies of the ethnography were prominently displayed in a tourist handicraft store in Antigua, Guatemala, run by a family of Todosanteros. Their grandmother had been Oakes's servant, a fact that the family was very proud of. The prestige and status of the ethnography as object is also related to the fact that a few Todosanteros who had worked closely with Oakes during her residence in Todos Santos in 1947–1948 (especially her house servant, Simona, and her neighbor and handyman, Domingo) were beneficiaries of her largesse and had gone on to do relatively well in their lives.

9. This understanding of space and the way that people refer to it is consistent with William Hanks's explanation of Mayan systems of diexis as bounded wholes in a square shape formed by the four cardinal directions plus the square's center. "The center is where God and the face of the earth, or cosmology and practice, meet" (Hanks 1990:300–301). More colloquially, as one friend commented, the number four is a part of everything: marimbistas play songs in sets of four, young men pass by the homes of the girls they are courting four times before clarifying their intentions, fiesta dancers emerge in their costumes and assemble their teams to dance to four songs. "Anything that you take on [you must try] four times in your life," commented one community leader.

10. Oakes begins her monograph with a story of the two crosses. To briefly paraphrase, she is told by the chief prayer maker that before he took on his role, there was only one cross in front of the church and another at the ruins. The ladino intendente ordered that the tall wooden cross in front of the church be pulled down and replaced with a stone one. The chief prayer maker begged him not to take the wooden cross down, as it was the cross of the ancestors, but the intendente's orders were carried out and both crosses were cast aside among a pile of old wood. Soon afterward, a wind came up and never stopped, followed by the worst cold front in years. Livestock died from lack of food, crops dried up, and women had to walk long distances for water. The prayer makers asked for advice from the spirits of the mountain and the head chiman performed a ceremony asking for rain. The spirits who inhabited the mountaintops told the Todosanteros:

"You have cast down the big cross, the cross that was born long ago when *Santo Mundo* was born, the big cross that came with the creation of the world. For this you have done you are now being punished. God has sent this, our *Santo Mundo* has given you this drought. Put the big cross up again in the same place. Otherwise all the people and the animals will die" (1951:24).

At the church, a group gathered and reinstated the old cross. Another ladino *intendente* asked what they were doing, insisting that they were committing a crime by using the wood and would be thrown into jail. After explaining that the spirits had demanded that the cross be put back, the members of the group asked to be put into jail in Huehuetenango (the departmental capital), claiming that it was better there. "If you imprison us, you will win and we will win. Send us to prison; we have no fear" (1951:25). The *intendente* finally understood that they were serious and said nothing while they put the cross back up. In a short time, the rains commenced again. The big ancient cross directed Todosanteros to restore the small one at the ruins. The stone crosses were left where they were, however, and that is why there are two.

11. This third cross was placed in the plaza in front of the church, and the date likely reflects its placement at this location.

12. They were knocked over in 1997 by broccoli trucks using the plaza for parking, but were replaced again later that year. I mention this because it demonstrates how the two crosses were central to such a variety of processes in the town, including, eventually, increasing traffic (to the point that a bypass was constructed to divert traffic from the center of town) and changing commercial interests.

13. Parents may place *fiadores* (literally, "sponsors" or "guarantors," used to describe special stones closely connected to an individual and symbolizing her or his connection to the environment) at these sites for their children, in order to foster their spiritual connection to the *twi' witz*.

14. The earliest payment record is from 1603. The contents of the Caja Real became more widely known and available in 1995, when a group of Danish researchers agreed to pay what was by local standards an exorbitant fee to the keeper of the box. They photographed and transcribed (from the handwritten documents "translated" by paleographers) the original documents and presented a copy of its contents to the local library.

15. Two caretakers oversaw the cleaning and maintenance of the church, rang church bells, and assisted visiting priests; six elders (*mayores*) and thirty trainees/ younger volunteers (*escuelix*) were responsible for the care of the church and other church-related duties; there was one drummer and one flutist; six *principales*; and three officials carried out ceremonies under the aegis of the calendar priest (Oakes 1951:55–56).

16. These were instituted in the 1880s to provide a steady source of Indian labor for vast coastal coffee plantations (McCreery 1994).

17. Because of her focus on the absence of change and the centrality of Mayan religion, it's possible that Oakes may have missed political shifts already underway or occurring in other locations. Or perhaps revolutionary changes had not yet been experienced in Todos Santos.

18. This priest was part of an earlier movement of Maryknoll expansion in

the department of Huehuetenango, which was initiated in 1943 and grew significantly after 1954, following the counterrevolution (Calder 1970:47–59, in Watanabe 1992:196–197, Behrens 2004).

19. A Maryknoll film (1960) melodramatically documents the process of one young man coming to realize that Catholicism is his true faith. Tensions between local beliefs, practices, and generational expectations are weighed against progress and modernity as represented by the Maryknoll priest and the Catholic Church.

20. Liberation theology's roots trace back to a sector of the Roman Catholic Church in Latin America in the 1950s and 1960s that arose as a moral project that addressed the poverty and huge social and economic inequalities that characterized the region. Theologians and clergy who espoused the doctrine of liberation theology often found themselves at odds with a more conservative church hierarchy, and the movement was often characterized in the press and more broadly as "an exotic brew of Marxism and Christianity" or as "a movement of rebel priests bent on challenging church authority" (Berryman 1987:4). As Philip Berryman makes clear, the controversies surrounding it were not "purely an internal church matter," as it "played a major role in the Reagan administration's efforts to justify its Central America policy" (1987:3).

21. See Neil Harvey, *The Chiapas Rebellion: The Struggle for Land and Democracy*, for a discussion of this dynamic in Chiapas.

22. Personal communication with Frank Taylor, who lived in Todos Santos in the 1970s and corresponded with Oakes during that time.

23. One Church gatekeeping mechanism that is regularly exercised is the two week course for people hoping to receive a sacrament or to participate in one, for example, as godparents. The *cursillo* is conducted in Mam and is held five or six evenings per week for at least three hours per meeting. Individuals must participate in a new *cursillo* each time they participate in a church activity.

24. This took place from March to November of 1999. All three had studied English in the United States—two of them in high school (one as an exchange student) and the other at a community college for a semester. At the time, one worked in Guatemala City, another in Quetzaltenango, and the third had recently returned to Todos Santos after studying in France. None had previous experience as a translator, but all felt strongly that Todosanteros should work to translate the ethnography. "It's like a Bible for us," one said, "and no one else feels the same way about it that we do." Another said, "If a Mam [Maya] translates Shakespeare [to Spanish] it's not ethical." Knowing nothing about Shakespeare's world, the translator's words could not make Shakespeare come alive for readers. A translation of *The Two Crosses* produced by anyone other than a Todosantero, he argued, would be lacking in "*sentido*"—that is, a sense of genuineness and authenticity that could only be conferred by someone who believed in the profound importance of the book, the way these young people and some community members did.

25. The Cultural Office of the U.S. embassy in Guatemala generously donated copying services under the aegis of my Fulbright fellowship.

26. Attendance at the workshop generally fluctuated, although a core group came regularly. At one point, one constant participant imagined the workshop as an intensive university course with homework (reading the ethnography) that he needed to complete each week.

27. From the beginning, individual men commented to me that they weren't interested in what so-and-so's grandmother was doing when she narrated a history; they were tired of hearing about it. Why couldn't she just tell the story?

28. Some people would occasionally confuse how many crosses were in the title, inserting a random number. Other Todosanteros would immediately correct them.

29. Recent surveys indicate that thirty to thirty-five percent of Guatemalans now belong to one or more evangelical congregations. This shift in the religious landscape began between 1976 and 1983, a period during which Guatemala experienced a devastating earthquake followed by the worst violence of the civil war (Stoll 1994:100, Philpot-Munson 2009).

30. Note, for example, the observations of Benito Ramírez, teacher and community leader, after he visited New York at the invitation of filmmaker Olivia Carrescia in 1989:

"We have many problems in Guatemala. The violence has turned neighbor against neighbor, and the army continues to control us through the civil defense patrols. Our *costumbres* are dying, and we are forgetting the wisdom of our ancestors. But after visiting New York, I realize that our Mayan communities have more culture than I had thought. In spite of the city's great wealth and high technology, I found poor and broken people everywhere, most of whom did not appear to have a home. North American evangelicals come to tell us what to believe in, but their own people do not know what to believe in. Their anthropologists come to study our customs but don't seem to pay any attention to the homeless people in their own cities. North Americans should work to save their own culture before they come down to Guatemala to pretend to save ours." (Perera 1993:151)

Chapter Four

1. UNDP indicates that as of 2006, 11.7% of the population was living on less than a dollar per day, including 14.6% of employed people. The poorest quintile's share in national income and consumption was 3.4%.

2. *Assessment of Development Results, Guatemala*, UNDP, 2008, http://www .undp.org/execbrd/pdf/ADR-Guatemala.pdf.

3. "Hispanics of Guatemalan Origin in the United States, 2009," http://pew hispanic.org/files/factsheets/76.pdf. Seventy-three percent arrived in the United States in 1990 or later and sixty-eight percent are born outside the United States (compared with thirty-seven percent of Hispanics and thirteen percent of the U.S. population overall). Guatemalans comprised 2.2% of the U.S.'s Hispanic population. For comparison, the largest group of Hispanics in the United States is Mexican, comprised of 31.7 million people, or 65.5% of the U.S. Hispanic population.

4. Banco de Guatemala, Ingresos de Divisas por Remesas Familiares, Años 2008–2011, http://www.banguat.gob.gt/inc/ver.asp?id=/estaeco/remesas/remfam 2012.htm&e=98870. See also the report *Central America's Economic Diaspora*, Center for Strategic and International Studies, February 24, 2011, http://csis.org /blog/central-americas-economic-diaspora.

5. I've arrived at this approximation (about six thousand to seven thousand people in the mid-1990s, and now closer to eight thousand with a corresponding population increase) through a combination of an informal household survey and census data.

6. While those who are undocumented are particularly vulnerable under this regime, all foreigners, particularly those who are Mexican and Central American, are ultimately caught up in its sweep.

7. The role of alcohol consumption in fueling some of this cannot be underestimated and is common in festival participation in general and Mesoamerican fiestas in particular. See Sharp 2012, Perez 2000, Kearney 2004, Rosenbaum 1993, Eber 1995, and Taylor 1979.

8. Ethnographers have documented a range of results, including ghost towns and interlinked transnational villages. See Binford 1998, Cohen 2004, DeHart 2010, Foxen 2007, Loucky and Moors 2000, and Stoll 2012.

9. Todosanteros engaged in decades of wage-labor migration to coastal plantations to pick coffee beans and cotton. By the 1940s, according to Oakes, Todosanteros had already been working on the coast for decades and were still doing so in the 1980s. (Carrescia 1982 and 1989.) Oakes notes that *finca* (plantation) agents roamed the streets during the fiesta she attended in 1947, looking for drunken victims to sign up for work (1951:209). Bossen writes that in the 1970s, villagers told her that seasonal migration was so widespread that the whole population was present only in late October, for the harvest and the fiesta, and at Easter time (1984:66). Data collected by Bossen in the mid-1970s supports the fact that seasonal wage migration at that time was nearly as prevalent as migration to the United States by the mid-2000s, with twenty-eight percent of rural women, fifty percent of rural men, and twenty-three percent of urban women and men traveling to plantations each year (1984:68).

10. Gomberg Muñoz (2010) develops this concept in relation to a cohort of undocumented Mexican migrants working in Chicago, claiming that it serves to bolster dignity and self-esteem.

11. Data from the national census conducted in 2002 indicates that between 1994 and 2002, the number of houses (+42%) increased more quickly than the population (+36%), most notably in the rural areas. There has been a tremendous increase (+65%) in uninhabited houses in rural areas—with only a thirteen percent increase in abandoned houses—which is a strong indicator that migrants were constructing houses they and their families don't currently inhabit.

12. National civil police killed this young man during the fiesta in 2003. The police entered his sister's house and shot him and his brother-in-law, who survived. The circumstances surrounding these actions remain unclear. See Burrell 2010 and 2013.

13. Anthropologists and other social scientists have long been fascinated with celebrations, festive occasions, and fiestas as key moments for analyzing societies and communities. Classic studies range from van Gennep's (1960) theories of rites of passage, to Turner's (1969 and 1974) performativity studies, with their emphasis on communitas, or relationships derived from shared ritual experience, to Creed's (2011) exploration of Bulgarian fertility rituals that challenge standard orthodoxies of postsocialism. An extensive Mesoamerican literature on fiestas and

fiesta systems (to narrow the vast contributions from Latin America) has concentrated on such themes as reciprocity (Wolf 1968, Monaghan 1990 and 1996), value and cost (Brandes 1981 and 1988), behavior (W. Smith 1983), ritual humor (Bricker 1973), drinking (Perez 2000), the role of migration and migrants (Kearney 2004), and patron saint adoration (Lastra et al. 2009).

14. Many businesses and buildings along the main street, almost entirely owned by ladinos prior to the 1980s, are now owned by indigenous families.

15. It was formerly referred to as *corrida de gallos*, or the rooster race. Toward the end of the day, riders would grab on to a rooster to break its neck (Oakes 1951).

16. See Oakes 1951:214–215.

17. The sense of danger, however, is also ever-present, and for this reason, some teachers told me they would not participate in the *corrida*. They perceived their roles in the community as too valuable to take on such a risk.

18. An extensive area literature is available on cargo and fiesta systems in Mesoamerica, from historical times to the present. The literature has concentrated on the development and economic components of these practices, as well as their relationship to forms of local leadership and authority. See Cancian 1965 and 1992, Wolf 1966, Nash 1966, Brintnall 1979, W. Smith 1977, Kearney 1970, Wasserstrom 1983, Vogt 1976, Stephen 1991, Rosenbaum 1993, and Eber 1995.

19. Hobsbawm understood public celebration to be one of three "invented traditions" essential to the elaboration of new secular states. The other two were public education and public monuments (Hobsbawm 1983:271, in Guss 2000:175).

20. The World Travel and Tourism Council estimates that tourism accounts for just over three percent of Guatemala's GDP. See the Travel and Tourism Competitiveness report for Guatemala, 2008, produced by the World Economic Forum, https://members.weforum.org/pdf/TTCR08/Guatemala.pdf.

Chapter Five

1. This description is composed from interviews with Todosanteros and their descriptions of what happened as related to me in July and August of 2000, from eyewitness accounts offered in the press, from television segments, and from other sources that reported on the incident.

2. As Englund stresses with regard to his work in Malawi, the purpose of the project here is less to give a voice to the voiceless than to provide ears to the earless, a metaphor that I find helpful in unsettling the often paternalistic currents of power involved in anthropological reporting (2006:171).

3. For the Maya, the soil upon which blood is spilled is sacred and should be accorded the same respect as physical remains.

4. There are numerous definitions for lynching. Mendoza (2003) remarks that this may not be the most useful for analysis (he prefers a definition of those incidents that end in death), but given the history of lynching in Todos Santos, it is appropriate for this case.

5. See Mendoza and Torres-Rivas, eds., *Linchamientos: ¿barbarie o "justicia popular"?*, 2003; Snodgrass Godoy, "Lynching and the Democratization of Terror in Postwar Guatemala: Implications for Human Rights," *Human Rights Quarterly*

24 (3) and *Popular Injustice: Violence, Community and Law in Latin America*, 2006; Handy 2006; Kobrak 2003; Kobrak and Gonzalez 2003. The blog "Linchamientos en Guatemela" (http://linchamientos.blogspot.com) by Carlos Mendoza is an exhaustive compendium of debate and thought on lynchings in Guatemala and elsewhere.

6. In a December 2009 report, Grupo de Apoyo Mutuo (GAM) provided statistics from the Guatemalan Supreme Court: in 2009, by the beginning of December, there were forty-four deaths and 151 injured by lynching in 2009; in 2008, eight deaths were reported and 102 injured. Data compiled by Carlos Mendoza from the Ministerio de Gobernación. La Unidad de Información Pública from Policía Nacional Civil (PNC) statistics indicate forty-nine deaths by lynching, one percent of a total of 6,498 violent deaths in Guatemala in 2009. The departments with the highest number of lynchings were Huehuetenango, with fourteen incidents (six in the departmental capital), and Guatemala with eleven incidents.

7. Vilas (2003), Fuentes Díaz (2004), García (2002), and Goldstein (2004, 2005, and 2012) are among those who have written about lynching in Mexico, Bolivia, and Ecuador.

8. The most influential implementation in terms of addressing the value of local knowledge and judicial mechanisms relative to the national legal system was the Accord on the Identity and Rights of Indigenous People, signed in March 1995. This accord recognized a Mayan worldview based on culture and land and acknowledged the presence of traditional juridical systems that were essential elements of social regulation and daily life in indigenous communities, part of the maintenance of their cohesion (IDIES 1999:x). On customary law, the convention reads: "In applying national laws and regulations to the peoples concerned, due regard shall be paid to their customs or customary laws. These people shall have the right to retain their own customs and institutions, where these are not incompatible with fundamental rights defined by the national legal system and with internationally recognized human rights . . . The methods customarily practiced by the peoples concerned for dealing with offenses committed by their members shall be respected" (Article 8).

9. In the attempt to implement and recuperate indigenous forms of law and authority, local indigenous leaders have been encouraged to experiment with new forms that can be implemented locally. The vast bulk of this work is performed through linkages with international and national NGOs. See Sieder 2008 and Kalny 2010.

10. Handy (2004) further argues that this violated the letter and spirit of the Accords.

11. Deborah Poole's (2004) work in Ayacucho, Peru, refers to this conundrum as being "between guarantee and threat," a liminal zone for indigenous authorities.

12. This, however, is not to imply a wholesale rejection at all levels of the legal/judiciary system: human rights training and democracy-building initiatives have had some influence on the local level, and indigenous groups increasingly turn to courts to defend collective rights and human rights. For different perspectives on this, see Sieder 2008 and 2011 and Ekern 2008.

13. The details have been changed in these accounts to protect the anonymity of those involved.

14. I draw upon a literature that refers to the state as a domain that becomes knowable through everyday contact with state institutions and representatives. These include outposts like schools, health clinics, and post offices, which impart nationally mandated order and discipline — particular ways of doing and knowing that constitute techniques of governing and complicate the conflicting pulls upon modern states that come from demands for good governance and increasing securitization. See Abrams 1988, Corrigan and Sayer 1985, Gilbert and Nugent 1994, Foucault 1975, Trouillot 2001, Roseberry 1994, Scott 1998, and Nugent 2010.

15. This is particularly because this peace process had been labeled such a success and one to emulate. "Guatemala is our big success story" (Attaché to the U.S. embassy in Caracas in Nelson 2009:xviii).

16. Friedrich Nietzsche, *Thus Spake Zarathustra* (in Lancaster 2008). In the formulation of this section, I am heavily indebted to Lancaster's impressive work on contemporary sex panic and suburbia in the United States (2008 and 2011).

17. Lancaster draws attention to the deliberate attempt to reshape social relations often at the center of moral panics, which relates them to "social revitalization movements" that similarly seek to address "some real or perceived condition of moral decline and social disrepair" (2008:45).

18. See Thomas Shevory 2004 (also, in Lancaster 2008:46) on the role of the media in fomenting and deepening panic in contemporary U.S. society.

19. Teachers are a key political group in Todos Santos, and several recent mayors have risen from their ranks. The accusations leveled against them for fomenting panic and fear also represented a way of challenging the local power that they hold.

20. This was particularly true in the period leading up to and immediately following war's end. Women of this demographic were often in positions of leadership and power in effecting the changes and the development and policy work of this period. Rumors served to undermine their authority by placing them under suspicion. In 1994, two women were attacked by angry mobs, in the highlands and on the coast, respectively (cf. Adams 1999).

21. See Sanford 2008, Torres and Carey 2010, and Chazaro and Casey 2006. The volume *Terrorizing Women: Feminicide in the Américas* (2010), edited by R. Fregoso and C. Bejerano, provides an excellent regional overview.

22. Fisher and Benson document the blend of morality, fear, and desire among indigenous export crop farmers in the Tecpán region of Guatemala in *Broccoli and Desire* (2006).

23. Lyon (2010) and Scott (2012) provide an in-depth discussion of this moment and its effect on local producers.

24. See *Securing the City: Neoliberalism, Space and Insecurity in Postwar Guatemala* (2011), edited by Kevin Lewis O'Neill and Kedron Thomas, for a thoughtful analysis of and theoretical foundation for many of these tensions.

25. I limit my analysis to these forms because they were shared throughout the country and were the most widespread. Although there were various television reports in both Guatemala and the United States (on Univisión, in particular) most people did not have access to these and therefore had a limited role in these debates.

26. Pan-Mayanist activism in Guatemala includes a variety of expressions

ranging from religion to language to politics. A number of books written in English and Spanish capture the diversity of issues and stances that have risen from this dynamic sector. In English, see Victor Montejo's *Mayan Intellectual Renaissance: Identity, Representation and Leadership* (2005); Kay Warren's *Indigenous Movements and Their Critics: Pan-Maya Activism in Guatemala* (1998); and *Maya Cultural Activism in Guatemala* (1996), edited by Edward F. Fischer and R. McKenna Brown. See, in Spanish, Demetrio Cojti Cuxil's *Politicas para la reivindicación de los Mayas de hoy: Fundamento de los derechos específicos de pueblo Maya* (1994) and *El movimiento Maya (en Guatemala): Ri Maya' moloj pa Iximulew* (1995).

27. David Stoll's *Rigoberta Menchú and the The Story of All Poor Guatemalans* (1999) raised questions about the veracity of Menchú's influential testimony, which focused world attention on Guatemala and led to her being awarded the Nobel Peace Prize in 1992 (Stoll 1999, Arias et al. 2001, Grandin 1999), and being the target of claims of duplicity (Nelson 2001).

28. Ethnicity in Guatemala is primarily a matter of social identity without phenotypic characteristics of race. Ladinos and Maya may often look exactly alike, and passing from Maya to ladino can be a matter of moving to the capital and renouncing language, community connections, and *traje*.

29. In 1999, the year before the Todos Santos lynchings occurred, Japanese aid was ninety million U.S. dollars, plus an additional fifty million dollars in soft loans repayable over forty years (*Siglo XXI*, May 3, 2000).

30. Peralta was a lawyer, notary public, and social scientist who served (as of February 2000) as Foreign Ministry Advisor in Defense and Security issues and as a member of the Belize Commission. He was Vice Minister of Foreign Affairs from 1996 to 2000.

31. The World Travel and Tourism Council (WTTC) estimated the direct contribution of travel and tourism to Guatemala's GDP to be GTQ10.8bn (3.1% of total GDP) in 2011, and expected it to rise by 3.5% pa to GTQ15.1bn (3.1%) in 2021 (in constant 2011 prices). http://www.wttc.org/research/economic-impact-research/country-reports/g/guatemala/

Chapter Six

1. This narrative is derived from human rights reports, newspaper articles, and accounts by Alfonso's family and community members who called me to report Alfonso's death (see Burrell 2010 and 2013a).

2. Mara Salvatrucha arrived in Guatemala City in 1995. Also known as MS-13, the gang assembled in Los Angeles during the 1970s to fight the many preexisting gangs hostile to Central Americans (Zilberg 2011).

3. The rise of the Zetas (a criminal organization once associated with the Sinaloa cartel in Mexico but now counting among its membership a growing percentage of former Guatemalan military, including former members of the elite *Kaibiles* force) represents a new frontier in this terrain.

4. UN Development Programme (UNDP) Informe sobre desarrollo humano para América Central 2009–2010, http://www.idhac-abrirespaciosalaseguridad.org/inicio.php.

5. Achille Mbembe (2003) describes necropolitics as the subjugation of life to the power of death. The authority to kill is no longer controlled by the state but is distributed throughout society.

6. See AVANCSO 1988; Rodgers 2008; Zilberg 2011c; Valenzuela Arve 2008; and J. A. Nateras Dominguez and R. Reguilo Cruz 2008. See also "Las Maras: Identidades Juveniles al Limite," Washington Office on Latin America (WOLA), 2006, and *Youth Gangs in Central America: A WOLA Special Report*, Washington Office on Latin America, November, http://www.wola.org/media/gangs_report_final _nov_06.pdf.

7. Through personal correspondence, Rob Hamrick told me that this was also the case for young men involved in similar activities around Lake Atitlán during his fieldwork in the late 1990s. John Edvalson and Winston Scott (2012) describe a similar situation in Nahualá and Senahú, respectively (2008).

8. Levenson (2013a:182–183) was offered this explanation of "*Maras*" by the spokesperson for Public Relations for the Guatemalan National Police: a teenager who hung out with his friends at Plaza Vivar, a run-down mall on Sexta Avenida in the city's dingy downtown, remembered that "the guys from the press and the cops said, 'Here comes the *Marabunta*!' and that's how it came to us and we started the Mara Plaza Vivar Capitol."

9. Manz (2004) and others have reported the murder of alleged gang members in communities throughout Guatemala.

10. One older South African man captured some the frustrations inherent in these kinds of generational conflicts: "I grew up understanding the word father as meaning he is the only head of the house with the final word and decision-making power. This is no longer the case. [The youths] are all disobedience and contempt toward their elders. Sometimes I wish I could ask the government to send officials to my house and pick up all these children and beat them heavily, and having got that lesson, bring them back" (Campbell 2000:142).

11. The account below is typical of my notes from the time:

There are many rumors of *maras* in the different hamlets. According to [a young woman], the murder on Sunday night is probably related to the gangs. The latest gossip indicates that [her younger brother] is in a gang in [undisclosed location] with [another friend]. One night, they heard that his ear was severed in a gang fight. They were relieved to discover he only had a small cut behind his ear, but they worried because things seemed to be escalating. When he married [shortly after], they hoped this would have a calming influence, that he would stay home with his wife and not go out to drink and get into fights every night. Last time he went to [visit his in-laws], two men, allegedly from another *mara*, followed him, but nothing happened. Everyone is happy that [he migrated] and escaped from this. (field notes, April 1997)

Bibliography

Abrahams, Ray. 1998. *Vigilante Citizens*. Cambridge: Polity Press.

Abrams, Philip. 1988. "Notes on the Difficulty of Studying the State." *Journal of Historical Sociology*, 1 (1), 1–18.

"Acciones ilegales: Medidas de seguridad en Todos Santos están al margen de la ley." 2003. *Prensa Libre*, February 20.

Adams, Abigail. 1998. "Gringas, Ghouls, and Guatemala: the 1994 attacks on North American women accused of body organ trafficking." *Journal of Latin American Anthropology*, 4 (1).

Adams, Abigail. 2009. In Walter E. Little and Timothy J. Smith, eds., *Mayas in Postwar Guatemala: Harvest of Violence Revisited*. Tuscaloosa: University of Alabama Press.

Adams, Richard. 1970. *Crucifixion by Power: Essays on Guatemalan National Social Structure, 1944–1966*. Austin: University of Texas Press.

Adams, Richard, and Santiago Bastos. 2003. *Las relaciones étnicas en Guatemala, 1944–2000*. Antigua, Guatemala: CIRMA (Centro de Investigaciones Regionales de Mesoamérica).

Adorno, Theodor W., and Max Horkheimer. 1997 [1947]. *Dialectic of Enlightenment*. New York: Verso.

Albro, Robert et al., eds. 2011. *Anthropologists in the SecurityScape*. Walnut Creek, CA: Left Coast Press.

Alonso, Ana. 1997. *Thread of Blood*. Tucson: University of Arizona Press.

Alonso, Conrado. 2000. "Contrastes: Por todos los diablos." *Prensa Libre*, May 3.

Alston, Phillip. 2007. *United Nations Report of the Special Rapporteur on Extrajudicial, Summary or Arbitrary Executions in 2007*.

Álvarez Castañeda, Andrés. 2007. "*La construccion social de la seguridad en Guatemala*." Tésis de Maestría en Sciencias Sociales. Quito, Ecuador: FLACSO (Facultad Latinoamericana de Ciencias Sociales).

"Amedrentados como en el conflicto armado: Todos Santos Cuchumatán se halla bajo medidas ilegales de resguardo." 2003. *Prensa Libre*, February 20.

Amnesty International. 2002. *Guatemala's Lethal Legacy: Past Impunity and Recent Human Rights Violations*. London: Amnesty International.

Anderson, Benedict. 1983. *Imagined Communities: Reflections on the origin and spread of nationalism*. London: Verso.

Anderson, Laurie. 2005. *The End of the Moon*. Visual performance.

Annis, Sheldon. 1987. *God and Production in a Guatemalan Town*. Austin: University of Texas Press.

Appadurai, Arjun. 1981. "The Past as Scarce Resource." *Man*, 16, 201–219.

Appadurai, Arjun. 1996. *Modernity at Large: Cultural Dimensions of Globalization*. Minneapolis: University of Minnesota Press.

Arias, Arturo, ed. 2001. *The Rigoberta Menchú Controversy*. Minneapolis: University of Minnesota Press.

Auyero, Javier. 2011. "Patients of the State: An Ethnographic Account of Poor People's Waiting." *Latin American Research Review*, 46 (1), 5–29.

Auyero, Javier. 2012. *Patients of the State: The Politics of Waiting in Argentina*. Durham, NC: Duke University Press.

AVANCSO (Asociación para el Avance de las Ciencias Sociales en Guatemala). 1988. *Por Si Mismos: Un estudio preliminar de las maras en la Ciudad de Guatemala*. Guatemala City: AVANCSO.

AVANCSO (Asociación para el Avance de las Ciencias Sociales en Guatemala). 1998. *Homogeneous images of a country with different faces*. Guatemala City: AVANCSO.

Babb, Florence. 2004. "Recycled Sandalistas: From Revolution to Resorts in the New Nicaragua." *American Anthropologist*, 106 (3), 541–555.

Bakhtin, Mikhail. 1984. *Rabelais and His World*. Bloomington: Indiana University Press.

Ball, Patrick, Paul Kobrak, and Herbert Spirer. 1999. *State Violence in Guatemala, 1960–1966: a quantitative reflection*. Washington, DC: AAAS.

Banco de Guatemala. 2011. *Ingreso de Divisas por Remesas Familiares Años 2008–2011*. Retrieved July 7, 2011, from http://www.banguat.gob.gt/inc/main.asp?aud=1&id=33190&lang=1.

Barrera Nuñez, Oscar. 2009. "Desires and Imagination: The Economy of Humanitarianism in Guatemala." In Little, Walter and Timothy J. Smith, eds., *Mayas in Postwar Guatemala: Harvest of Violence Revisited*. Tuscaloosa: University of Alabama Press.

Basch, Linda, Nina Glick Schiller, and Christina Szanton Blanc. 1994. *Nations Unbound: Transnational Projects, Postcolonial Predicaments and Deterritorialized Nation States*. Amsterdam: Gordon & Breach.

Becker, David, and Margarita Diaz. 1998. "The Social Process and the Transgenerational Transmission of Trauma in Chile." In Yael Danieli, ed., *International Handbook of Multigenerational Legacies of Trauma*. New York & London: Plenum Press.

Behrens, Susan F. 2007. "Confronting Colonialism: Maryknoll Catholic Missionaries in Peru and Guatemala." *Helen Kellogg Institute for International Studies, Working Paper 338*.

Benjamin, Walter. 1940 [1968]. *Thesis on the Philosophy of History*. New York: Harcourt Brace Jovanovich.

Benson, Peter, Edward F. Fischer, and Kedron Thomas. 2008. *Resocializing Suffer-*

ing: Neoliberalism, Accusation, and the Sociopolitical Context of Guatemala's New Violence. Latin American Perspectives, *35* (5): 38–58.

Berryman, Philip. 1985. *Liberation Theology: Essential Facts About the Revolutionary Movement in Latin America and Beyond.* Philadelphia: Temple University Press.

Bickford, Andrew. 2007. "Unofficial Truth Projects." *Human Rights Quarterly, 29* (4), 994–1035.

Binford, Leigh. 1998. "Accelerated Migration between Puebla, Mexico and New York." *Conference on Mexican Migration to New York.* New York: Barnard College, Columbia University, and The New School for Social Research.

Binford, Leigh, and Nancy Churchill. 2009. "Lynching and States of Fear in Urban Mexico." *Anthropologica, 51* (2), 1–12.

Black, Jeremy. 1997. *Maps and Politics.* Chicago: University of Chicago Press.

Boehm, Deborah A. 2011. "US-Mexico Mixed Migration in an Age of Deportation: An Inquiry into the Transnational Circulation of Violence." *Refugee Survey Quarterly, 30* (1): 1–21.

Bossen, Laurel. 1984. *The Redivision of Labor: Women and Economic Choice in Four Guatemalan Communities.* Albany, NY: SUNY Press.

Bourdieu, Pierre. 1977. *Outline of a Theory of Practice.* Cambridge & New York: Cambridge University Press.

Bourdieu, Pierre. 1998. *Practical Reason: On Theory of Action.* Palo Alto, CA: Stanford University Press.

Bourdieu, Pierre. 2000. *Pascalian Meditations.* New York: Polity Press.

Brintnall, Douglas. 1979. *Revolt Against the Dead: The Modernization of a Maya Community in the Highlands of Guatemala.* New York: Gordon & Breach.

Brosnan, Greg. 2001. "Mayans Acquitted of Lynching Japanese Tourist." *Reuters,* June 26.

Bunzel, Ruth. 1952. *Chichicastenango.* Locust Valley, NY: J. J. Augustin Publishers.

Burawoy, Michael. 2004. "Public Sociologies: Contradictions, Dilemmas and Possibilities." *Social Forces, 82* (4), 1602–1618.

Burawoy, Michael et al. 1991. *Ethnography Unbound: Power and Resistance in the Modern Metropolis.* Berkeley: University of California Press.

Burawoy, Michael et al. 2000. *Global Ethnography: Forces, Connections and Imaginations in a Postmodern World.* Berkeley: University of California Press.

Burgos-Debray, Elisabeth. 1983. *I, Rigoberta Menchú: An Indian Woman in Guatemala,* trans. A. Wright. London & New York: Verso.

Burgos-Debray, Elisabeth. 2001. "Memoria, transmisión e imagen del cuerpo." In Mario Roberto Morales, ed., *Stoll-Menchú: La invención de la memoria,* 19–86. Guatemala City: Consucultura.

Burrell, Jennifer L. 2000. "The Aftermath of Lynching in Todos Santos." *Report on Guatemala, 21* (4), 12–15.

Burrell, Jennifer L. 2005. "Migration and the Transnationalization of Fiesta Customs in Todos Santos Cuchumatán." *Latin American Perspectives, 32* (5), 12–32.

Burrell, Jennifer L. 2009. "Intergenerational Conflict After War." In Little, Walter E., and Timothy J. Smith, eds., *Mayas in Postwar Guatemala: Harvest of Violence Revisited,* 96–109. Tuscaloosa: University of Alabama Press.

Burrell, Jennifer L. 2010. "In and Out of Rights: Security, Migration and Human

Rights Talk in Postwar Guatemala." *Journal of Latin American and Caribbean Anthropology*, 15 (1), 90–115.

Burrell, Jennifer L. 2013a. "Ephemeral Rights and Securitized Lives: Migration, 'Mareros' and Power in Millennial Guatemala." In *Central America in the New Millennium: Living Transition and Reimagining Democracy*. New York & London: Berghahn Press.

Burrell, Jennifer L. 2013b. "After Lynching." In Nelson, Diane, and Carlota McAllister, eds., *Aftermath: War by Other Means in Post-Genocide Guatemala*. Durham, NC: Duke University Press.

Burrell, Jennifer L., and Ellen Moodie. 2013. "Introduction: Ethnographic Visions of Millennial Central America." In *Central America in the New Millennium: Living Transition and Reimagining Democracy*. New York & London: Berghahn Press.

Burrell, Jennifer L., and Gavin Weston. 2007. "Lynching and Post-War Complexities in Guatemala." In Pratten, David, and Atreyee Sen, eds., *Global Vigilantes*, 371–392. London: Hurst & Company.

Caldeira, Teresa. 2001. *City of Walls: Crime, Segregation, and Citizenship in São Paulo*. Berkeley: University of California Press.

Caldeira, Teresa, and James Holsten. 1999. "Democracy and Violence in Brazil." *Comparative Studies in Society and History*, 41 (4), 691–729.

Calder, Bruce. 1970. *Crecimiento y Cambio de la Iglesia Católica Guatemalteca 1944–1966*. Guatemala: Editorial Jose de Pineda Ibarra.

Calder, Bruce. 1992. *The Catholic Church in the Context of Guatemalan Politics, Society and Culture from 1940 to the Present*. Paper delivered at the XVII International Congress of the Latin American Studies Association, Los Angeles, California, September 24.

Calder, Bruce. 1995. "The Catholic Church and the Guatemalan Maya, 1940–1969: Building a Base for the 1990s." Annual Meeting of the American Academy of Religion. Philadelphia.

Camus, Albert. 1949 [1992]. *The Rebel: An Essay on Man in Revolt*. New York: Vintage Press.

Camus, Manuela. 2012. "Fronteras, comunidades indígenas y acumulación de violencias." *Descatos*, 38 (enero–abril), 73–94.

Cancian, Frank. 1965. *Economics and Prestige in a Maya Community: The Religious Cargo System in Zinacantán*. Palo Alto, CA: Stanford University Press.

Cancian, Frank. 1992. *The Decline of Community in Zinacantán Economy: Public Life and Social Stratification, 1960–1987*. Palo Alto, CA: Stanford University Press.

Carey, David. 2001. *Our Elders Teach Us: Maya-Kaqchikel Historical Perspectives*. Tuscaloosa: University of Alabama Press.

Carlsen, Robert. 1997. *The War for the Heart and Soul of a Highland Maya Town*. Austin: University of Texas Press.

Carmack, Robert. 1981. *Quiche Maya of Utatlán: The Evolution of a Highland Guatemala Kingdom*. Norman: University of Oklahoma Press.

Carmack, Robert. 1988. "Preface to the First Edition." In Robert Carmack, ed., *Harvest of Violence: The Mayan Indians and the Guatemalan Crisis*, 39–69. Norman: University of Oklahoma Press.

Carmack, Robert, ed. 1988. *Harvest of Violence: The Mayan Indians and the Guatemalan Crisis*. Norman: University of Oklahoma Press.

Carrescia, Olivia. 1982. *Todos Santos Cuchumatán*. New York: Icarus Films. Motion picture.

Carrescia, Olivia. 1989. *Todos Santos: The Survivors*. New York: Icarus Films. Motion picture.

Carrescia, Olivia. 1994. *Mayan Voices, American Lives*. New York: Icarus Films. Motion picture.

Carrescia, Olivia. 2008. *Sacred Soil*. New York: Icarus Films. Motion picture.

Carrescia, Olivia. 2011. *A Better Life*. New York: Icarus Films. Motion picture.

Carter, Paul. 1987. *The Road to Botany Bay: An Exploration of Landscape and History*. Chicago: University of Chicago Press.

Carton, Benedict. 2000. *Blood from Your Children: The Colonial Origins of Generational Conflict in South Africa*. Charlottesville & London: University of Virginia Press.

Casaus Arzú, Marta. 1995. *Linaje y racismo*. San José, Costa Rica: FLACSO (Facultad Latinoamericana de Ciencias Sociales).

CEH (Comisión para el Esclarecimiento Histórico). 1999. *Guatemala: Memoria del silencio*. Guatemala City: United Nations Operating Projects Services.

CEH (Comisión para el Esclarecimiento Histórico). 2005. *Guatemala: Memory of Silence*. Retrieved July 12, 2011, from http://shr.aaas.org/guatemala/ceh/report/english/toc.html.

CEH (Comisión para el Esclarecimiento Histórico). 2009. English translation of sections of the genocide argument in the final report of the Guatemalan Commission for Historical Clarification, *Guatemala: Memory of Silence*. In Etelle Higonnet, ed., *Quiet Genocide: Guatemala 1981–1983*, 17–155, trans. Marcy Mersky. Piscataway, NJ: Transaction Publishers.

Centro de Reportes Informativos de Guatemala (CERIGUA). 1993. "Refugees Plan Return to Occupied Site." *Weekly Brief*, December 2.

Chazaro, Angelica, and Jennifer Casey. 2006. "Getting Away with Murder: Guatemala's Failure to Protect Women and Rodi Alvarado's Quest for Safety." In *Hastings Women's Law Journal, 141*.

Checker, Melissa. 2009. "Anthropology in the Public Sphere: Emerging Trends and Significant Impacts." *American Anthropologist*, 162–169, *111* (2).

Chomsky, Noam. 2006. *Failed States: The Abuse of Power and the Assault on Democracy*. New York: Metropolitan Books.

Christian Science Monitor. 2000. "Lynch-Mob Justice," December 12.

Cifuentes Herrera, and Juan Fernando. 1998. *Historia moderna de la etnicidad en Guatemala. La visión hegemónica: rebeliones y otros incidentes indígenas en el siglo XX*. Guatemala City: Universidad de Rafael Landívar, Instituto de Investigaciones Económicas y Sociales.

Clark, Kim. 2002. "The Language of Contention in Liberal Ecuador." In Leach, Belinda, and Winnie Lem, eds., *Culture, Economy, Power: Anthropology as Critique, Anthropology as Praxis*. Albany, NY: SUNY Press.

Cole, John, and Eric Wolf. 1974. *The Hidden Frontier: Ecology and Ethnicity in an Alpine Valley*. New York: Academic Press.

Colloredo-Mansfeld, Rudi. 1999. *The Native Leisure Class: Consumption and Cultural Creativity in the Andes*. Chicago: University of Chicago Press.

Colloredo-Mansfeld, Rudi. 2007. "The Power of Ecuador's Indigenous Communities in an Era of Cultural Pluralism." *Social Text*, 51 (2), 86–106.

Colop, Sam. 2000. "Ucha'xik: Todos Santos." *Prensa Libre*, May 3.

"¿Cómo era Todos Santos Cuchumatán hace 50 años? Nueve horas a caballo." 2001. *Prensa Libre*, January 23.

Corrigan, Philip, and Derek Sayer. 1985. *The Great Arch: English State Formation as Cultural Revolution*. Oxford: Basil Blackwell.

Creed, Gerald. 2004. "Constituted Through Conflict: Images of Community (and Nation) in Bulgarian Rural Ritual." *American Anthropologist*, 106 (1), 56–70.

Creed, Gerald. 2011. *Masquerade and Postsocialism: Ritual and Cultural Dispossession in Bulgaria (New Anthologies of Europe)*. Bloomington: Indiana University Press.

Crehan, Kate. 2002. *Gramsci, Culture and Anthropology*. Berkeley: University of California Press.

Daniel, E. Valentine. 1996. *Charred Lullabies: Chapters in an Anthropology of Violence*. Princeton: Princeton University Press.

Danieli, Yael, ed. 1998. *International Handbook of Multigenerational Legacies of Trauma*. New York & London: Plenum Press.

Dary Fuentes, Claudia. 2012. "Acknowledging Racism and State Transformation in Post-War Guatemalan Society." In Burrell, Jennifer L., and Ellen Moodie, eds., *Central America in the New Millennium: Living Transition and Regaining Democracy*. New York: Berghahn.

Das, Veena, and Deborah Poole, eds. 2004. *Anthropology in the Margins of the State*. Santa Fe, NM: School of American Research Press.

Das, Veena, Arthur Kleinman, Mamphela Ramphele, and Pamela Reynolds, eds. 2000. *Violence and Subjectivity*. Berkeley: University of California Press.

Davis, Shelton. 1988. "Introduction: Sowing the Seeds of Violence." In Carmack, Robert, ed., *Harvest of Violence*. Norman: University of Oklahoma Press.

Davis, Shelton. 1997. *La Tierra de Nuestros Antepasados: Estudio de la Herencia y la Tenencia de la tierra en el altiplano de Guatemala*. Antigua, Guatemala: CIRMA (Centro de Investigaciones Regionales de Mesoamérica).

DeHart, Monica. 2009. "Fried Chicken of Pop? Redefining Development and Ethnicity in Totonicapán." In Little, Walter, and Timothy J. Smith, eds., *Mayas in Postwar Guatemala: Harvest of Violence Revisited*. Tuscaloosa: University of Alabama Press.

DeHart, Monica. 2010. *Ethnic Entrepreneurs: Identity and Development Politics in Latin America*. Palo Alto, CA: Stanford University Press.

De la Cadena, Marisol. 1995. "Women are More Indian: Ethnicity and Gender in a Community Near Cuzco." In Larson, Brooke, and Olivia Harris, eds., *Ethnicity, Markets and Migration in the Andes: At the Crossroads of History and Anthropology*. Durham, NC: Duke University Press.

Donham, Donald L. 2006. "Staring at Suffering: Violence as Subject." In Bay, Edna G., and Donald L. Donham, eds., *States of Violence: Politics, Youth, and Memory in Contemporary Africa*, 16–33. Charlottesville & London: University of Virginia Press.

Donham, Donald L. 2011. *Violence in a Time of Liberation: Murder and Ethnicity at a South African Gold Mine, 1994*. Durham, NC: Duke University Press.

Doyle, Kate. 2012. "Notes from the Evidence Project: Guatemalan Government to Dismantle its 'Archives of Peace.'" Published in *Unredacted: The National Security Archive Unedited and Uncensored* (blog), June 1. Retrieved June 14, 2012, from http://nsarchive.wordpress.com/2012/06/01/guatemalan-government-closes-peace-archives/.

DuBois, Lindsay. 2005. *The Politics of the Past in an Argentine Working Class Neighborhood*. Toronto: University of Toronto Press.

Dym, Jordana, and Karl Offen, eds. 2011. *Mapping Latin America: A Cartographic Reader*. Chicago: University of Chicago Press.

EAAF (Equipo Argentino De Anthropología Forense). 2003. Annual Reports: 2000–2003.

Edelman, Lucila, Diana Kordon, and Dario Lagos. 1988. "Transmission of Trauma: The Argentine Case." In Danieli, Yael, ed., *International Handbook of Multigenerational Legacies of Trauma*. New York & London: Plenum Press.

"Editorial: Peligroso vacío de autoridad." 2000. *Siglo XXI*, May 2.

Edvalson, John. 2008. *They Have No Respect*. M.A. thesis, Department of Anthropology, University at Albany–SUNY.

Ekern, Steiner. 2008. "Are Human Rights Destroying the Natural Balance of Things? The Difficult Encounter between International Law and Community Law in Mayan Guatemala." In Pitarch, Pedro, Shannon Speed, and Xochitl Leyva-Solano, eds., *Human Rights in the Maya Region. Global Politics, Cultural Contentions and Moral Engagements*. Durham, NC: Duke University Press.

Englund, Harri. 2006. *Prisoners of Freedom: Human Rights and the African Poor*. Berkeley: University of California Press.

Escobar, Arturo. 1995. *Encountering Development: The Making and Unmaking of the Third World*. Princeton: Princeton University Press.

Escobar, Arturo, and Sonia Alvarez, eds. 1992. *The Making of Social Movements in Latin America: Identity, Strategy and Democracy*. Boulder, CO: Westview Press.

Fabian, Johannes. 2011. *Anthropology With an Attitude: Critical Essays*. Palo Alto, CA: Stanford University Press.

Fabri, Antonella. 1994. *(Re)composing the Nation: Politics of Memory and Displacement in Maya Testimonies from Guatemala*. Ph.D. dissertation, University at Albany–SUNY, Department of Anthropology.

Falla, Ricardo. 1978. *Quiché rebelde: estudio de un movimiento de conversión religiosa, rebelde a las creencias tradicionales, en San Antonio Ilotenango, Quiché (1948–1970)*. Guatemala City: Editorial Universitaria de Guatemala.

Falla, Ricardo. 1994. *Massacres in the Jungle: Ixcán, Guatemala, 1975–1982*. Boulder, CO: Westview Press.

Farmer, Paul. 2003. *Pathologies of Power: Health, Human Rights and the New War on the Poor*. Berkeley: University of California Press.

Ferguson, James. 1994. *The Anti-Politics Machine: Development, Depoliticization, and Bureaucratic Power in Lesotho*. Minneapolis: University of Minnesota Press.

Ferguson, James. 1999. *Expectations of Modernity: Myths and Meanings of Urban Life on the Zambian Copperbelt*. Berkeley: University of California Press.

Ferguson, James, and Akhil Gupta. 2002. "Spatializing States: Toward an Ethnography of Neoliberal Governmentality." *American Ethnologist*, *29* (4), 981–1002.

Ferme, Mariane. 2001. *The Underneath of Things: Violence, History, and the Everyday in Sierra Leone*. Berkeley: University of California Press.

Fernandes, Sujatha. 2010. "Urbanizing the San Juan Fiesta: Civil Society and Cultural Identity in the Barrios of Caracas." In Greenhouse, Carol ed., *Ethnographies of Neoliberalism*, 96–111. Philadelphia: University of Pennsylvania Press.

Fernández García, María Cristina. 2004. *Lynching in Guatemala: Legacy of War and Impunity*. Retrieved July 12, 2011, from http://www.wcfia.harvard.edu/fellows/papers/2003-04/fernandez.pdf.

Figueroa Ibarra, C., and S. Martí y Puig. 2007. "Guatemala: From Political Struggle to a Divided Left." In Deonandan, K., D. Close, and G. Prevost, eds., *From Revolutionary Movements to Political Parties: Cases from Latin America and Africa*. New York: Palgrave MacMillan.

Fischer, Edward. 2001. *Cultural Logic and Global Economics: Maya Identity in Thought and Practice*. Austin: University of Texas Press.

Fischer, Edward. 2008. "Introduction: Indigenous Peoples, Neo-liberal Regimes, and Varieties of Civil Society in Latin America." In Fischer, Edward, ed., *Indigenous Peoples, Civil Society and the Neoliberal State in Latin America*, 1–18. Oxford & New York: Berghahn Books.

Fischer, Edward, and McKenna R. Brown, eds. 1996. *Maya Cultural Activism in Guatemala*. Austin: University of Texas Press.

Fischer, Edward, and Peter Benson. 2006. *Broccoli and Desire: Global Connections and Maya Struggles in Postwar Guatemala*. Palo Alto, CA: Stanford University Press.

Foucault, Michel. 1979. *Discipline and Punish*. New York: Vintage Books.

Foucault, Michel. 1980. "On Popular Justice: A Discussion with Maoists." In Gordon, Colin, ed., *Power/Knowledge: Selected Interviews and Other Writings, 1972–1977*. New York: Pantheon.

Foucault, Michel. 1986. "Text/Context of Other Space." *Diacritic*, *16* (1).

Foucault, Michel. 1991. "Governmentality." In Burchell, Graham, Colin Gordon, and Peter Miller, eds., *The Foucault Effect*, 87–104. Chicago: University of Chicago Press.

Foxen, Patricia. 2007. *In Search of Providence: Transnational Mayan Identities*. Nashville, TN: Vanderbilt University Press.

Fregoso, Rosa-Linda, and Cynthia Bejarano, eds. 2010. *Terrorizing Women: Feminicide in the Américas*. Durham, NC: Duke University Press.

Friedman, Milton. 1962. *Capitalism and Freedom*. Chicago: University of Chicago Press.

Fuentes Díaz, Antonio. 2004. "Linchamiento en México." *Ecuador Debate*, (61), 259–270.

Fuentes Díaz, Antonio, and Leigh Binford. 2001. "Linchamientos en México: Una Respuesta a Carlos Vilas." *Bajo el Volcán*, *2* (3), 143–156.

GAM (Grupo de Apoyo Mutuo). 2009. *Informe sobre la situación de derechos humanos y hechos de violencia, primer semestre 2009 Julio*.

Garcia Canclini, Nestor. 1988. *Hybrid Cultures: Strategies for entering and leaving modernity*, trans. Chiaparri, C. L., and S. L. López. Minneapolis: University of Minnesota Press.

García, Fernando. 2009. *Linchamientos: justicia por mano propia o justicia indígena?*, May 13. Retrieved July 12, 2011, from http://www.cajpe.org.pe/sistemasjuridicos/index.php?option=com_docman&task=doc_download&gid=28&Itemid=13.

García, María Elena. 2005. *Making Indigenous Citizens*. Palo Alto, CA: Stanford University Press.

Garrard-Burnett, Virginia. 2009. *Terror in the Land of the Holy Spirit: Guatemala Under General Efraín Ríos Montt, 1982–1983*. Oxford & New York: Oxford University Press.

Gledhill, John. 2000. *Power and Its Disguises*. London: Pluto Press.

Gledhill, John. 2004. "Neoliberalism." In Nugent, David, and Joan Vincent, eds., *A Companion to the Anthropology of Politics*, 448–467. Oxford: Wiley-Blackwell.

Glick Schiller, Nina. 2004. "Transnationality." In Nugent, David, and Joan Vincent, eds., *A Companion to the Anthropology of Politics*, 448–467. Oxford: Wiley-Blackwell.

Gluckman, Max. 1954 [1994]. *The Judicial Process Among the Barotse of Northern Rhodesia*. New York & London: Berg Publishing Ltd.

Gluckman, Max. 1963 [2004]. *Order and rebellion in tribal Africa: Collected essays with an autobiographical introduction*. New York & London: Routledge.

Goldin, Liliana. 2009. *Global Maya: Work and Ideology in Rural Guatemala*. Tucson: University of Arizona Press.

Goldin, Liliana. 2011. "Labor turnover: the shape resistance takes in late capitalism." *Latin American Research Review*, 46 (3).

Goldman, Francisco. 2004. *The Art of Political Murder*. New York: Grove Press.

Goldstein, Daniel. 2003. "In Our Own Hands: Lynching, Justice and the Law in Bolivia." *American Ethnologist*, 30 (1), 22–43.

Goldstein, Daniel. 2004. *The Spectacular City: Violence and Performance in Urban Bolivia*. Durham, NC: Duke University Press.

Goldstein, Daniel. 2005. "Flexible Justice: Neoliberal Justice and 'Self-Help' Security in Bolivia." *Critique of Anthropology*, 25 (4), 389–411.

Goldstein, Daniel. 2010. "Toward a Critical Anthropology of Security." *Current Anthropology*, 51 (4), 487–517.

Goldstein, Daniel. 2012. *Outlawed: Between Security and Rights in a Bolivian City*. Durham, NC: Duke University Press.

Gomberg-Muñoz, Ruth. 2010. *Labor and Legality*. Oxford & New York: Oxford University Press.

González, Gaspar Pedro. 1995. *A Mayan Life*. Ranchos Palos Verdes, CA: Yax Te' Books.

Gordillo, Gaston. 2002. "Locations of Hegemony: The Making of Places in Toba's Struggle for La Comuna." *American Anthropologist*, 104 (1), 262–277.

Gordillo, Gaston. 2004. *Landscapes of the Devils*. Durham, NC: Duke University Press.

Gramsci, Antonio. 1989 [1971]. *Selections From the Prison Notebooks*. New York: International Publishers.

Grandia, Liza. 2011. *Enclosed: Conservation, Cattle, and Commerce among the Q'eqchi' Maya Lowlanders*. Seattle: University of Washington Press.

Grandin, Greg. 1999. "Bitter Fruit for Rigoberta." *The Nation*, February 8.

Grandin, Greg. 2000. *The Blood of Guatemala: A History of Race and Nation*. Durham, NC: Duke University Press.

Grandin, Greg. 2003. "History, Motive, Law, Intent: Combining Historical and Legal Methods in Understanding Guatemala's 1981–1983 Genocide." In Gellately, Robert, and Ben Kiernan, eds., *The Specter of Genocide: Mass Murder in Historical Perspective*. Cambridge: Cambridge University Press.

Grandin, Greg. 2004. *The Last Colonial Massacre: Latin America and the Cold War*. Chicago: University of Chicago Press.

Grandin, Greg. 2006. *Empire's Workshop: Latin America, the United States, and the Rise of the New Imperialism*. New York: Metropolitan Books.

Grandin, Greg. 2010. "It Was Heaven That They Burned." *The Nation*, September 27.

Grandin, Greg, Deborah T. Levenson, and Elizabeth Oglesby, eds. 2011. *The Guatemala Reader*. Durham, NC: Duke University Press.

Green, Linda. 1999. *Fear as a Way of Life: Mayan Widows in Guatemala*. New York: Columbia University Press.

Green, Linda. 2003. "Notes on Mayan Youth and Rural Industrialization in Guatemala." *Critique of Anthropology*, *21* (1), 51–73.

Greenhouse, Carol J., Elizabeth Mertz, and Kay B. Warren, eds. 2002. *Ethnography in Unstable Places: Everyday Lives in Context of Dramatic Political Change*. Durham, NC: Duke University Press.

Guerrero, Andres. 2001. "Los linchamientos en las comunidades indígenas: La política perversa de una modernidad marginal?" *Ecuador Debate*, *53*, 197–226.

Gupta, Akhil, and James Ferguson, eds. 1997. *Anthropological Locations: Boundaries and Grounds of a Field Science*. Berkeley: University of California Press.

Guss, David M. 2000. *The Festive State: Race, Ethnicity, and Nationalism as Cultural Performance*. Berkeley: University of California Press.

Gustafson, Brett. 2009. *New Languages of the State: Indigenous Resurgence and the Politics of Knowledge in Bolivia*. Durham, NC: Duke University Press.

Gusterson, Hugh. 2004. *People of the Bomb: Portraits of America's Nuclear Complex*. Minneapolis: University of Minnesota Press.

Gutiérrez, Marta Estela. 2003. "Los mecanismos del poder in la violencia colectiva: los linchamientos en Huehuetenango." In Mendoza, Carlos, and Edelberto Torres-Rivas, eds., *Linchamientos: ¿barbarie o "justicia popular"?*, 175–210. Guatemala City: Colección Cultura de la Paz.

Gutiérrez, Marta Estela, and Paul Hans Kobrak. 2001. *Los linchamientos: Pos conflicto y violencia colectiva en Huehuetenango, Guatemala*. Guatemala City: CEDFOG (Centro de Estudios y Documentación de la Frontera Occidental de Guatemala).

Gwynne, Robert, and Crístobal Kay. 1999. *Latin America Transformed: Globalization and Modernity*. New York: Arnold.

Habermas, Jurgen. 1989. *The Structural Transformation of the Public Sphere: An Inquiry into a Category of Bourgeois Society*, trans. Thomas Burger. Cambridge, MA: The MIT Press.

Hale, Charles. 2002. "Does Multiculturalism Menace? Governance, Cultural

Rights and the Politics of Identity in Guatemala." *Journal of Latin American Studies*, *34*, 485–524.

Hale, Charles. 2005. "Neoliberal Multiculturalism: The Remaking of Cultural Rights and Racial Dominance in Central America." *PoLAR*, *28* (1), 10–28.

Hale, Charles. 2006. *Más Que Un Indio: Racial Ambivalence and Neoliberal Multiculturalism in Guatemala*. Santa Fe, NM: School of American Research Press.

Hall, Stuart. 1977. "Culture, the Media, and the 'Ideological Effect.'" In J. Curran et al., eds., *Mass Communication and Society*. London: Edward Arnold.

Hamrick, Robert. 2003. "Nicknames and their Currency in Santa Caterina Palopó." Paper read at the Annual Meeting of the American Anthropological Association. Chicago.

Handy, Jim. 1984. *Gift of the Devil: A History of Guatemala*. Boston, MA: South End Press.

Handy, Jim. 1994. *Revolution in the Countryside: Rural Conflict and Agrarian Reform*. Chapel Hill: University of North Carolina Press.

Handy, Jim. 2004. "Chicken Thieves, Witches, and Judges: Vigilante Justice and Customary Law in Guatemala." *Journal of Latin American Studies*, *36*, 87–104.

Hanks, William. 1990. *Referential Practice: Language and Lived Space Among the Maya*. Chicago: University of Chicago Press.

Harley, J. B. 1988. "Maps, Knowledge, and Power." In Cosgrove, Denis, and Stephen Daniels, eds., *The Iconography of the Landscape*. Cambridge: Cambridge University Press.

Harvey, David. 1993. "From Space to Place and Back Again: Reflections on the Condition of Postmodernity." In Bird, John, Barry Curtis, Tim Putnam, and Lisa Tickner, eds., *Mapping the Futures: Local Cultures, Global Change*, 3–29. London: Routledge Press.

Harvey, David. 1989. *The Condition of Postmodernity*. London: Basil Blackwell.

Harvey, David. 1996. *Justice, Nature, and the Geography of Difference*. London: Blackwell Publishers.

Harvey, David. 1996. *The Condition of Postmodernity*. London: Blackwell Publishers.

Harvey, David. 2005. *A Brief History of Neoliberalism*. Oxford & New York: Oxford University Press.

Harvey, David. 2010. *The Enigma of Capital and the Crises of Capitalism*. New York: Oxford University Press.

Harvey, Neil. 1998. *The Chiapas Rebellion: The Struggle for Land and Democracy*. Durham, NC: Duke University Press.

Hendrickson, Carol. 1995. *Weaving Identity: Construction of Dress and Self in a Highland Guatemalan Town*. Austin: University of Texas Press.

Hervik, Peter. 1999. *Mayan People Within and Beyond Boundaries*. Amsterdam: Harwood Academic Publishers.

Hill, Robert, and John Monaghan. 1987. *Continuities in Highland Maya Social Organization*. Philadelphia: University of Pennsylvania Press.

Hinton, Alexander, and Kevin O'Neill. 2009. *Genocide: Truth, Memory and Representation*. Durham, NC: Duke University Press.

Holland, Dorothy, and Jean Lave. 2001. Introduction. In Holland, Dorothy, and Jean Lave, eds., *History in Person: Enduring Struggles, Contentious Practice and Intimate Identities*. Santa Fe, NM: School of American Research Press.

Holston, James, and Arjun Appardurai. 1996. "Cities and Citizenship." *Public Culture, 8,* 187–204.

Huggins, Martha. 1991. *Vigilantism and the State in Modern Latin America: Essays on Extralegal Violence.* New York: Praeger.

Human Rights Watch. 2012. World Report: Guatemala. Retrieved March 1, 2012, from http://www.hrw.org/world-report-2012/Guatemala.

IACHR (Inter-American Commission on Human Rights). 2005. *Justice and Social Inclusion: The Challenges of Democracy in Guatemala.* Country report, Organization of American States.

IDIES (Instituto de Investigaciones Económicas y Sociales). 1999. *El Sistema Jurídico Mam.* Guatemala City: Universidad Rafael Landívar.

Ikeda, Mitsuho. 1999. *The Cultural Involution of Violence: A Guatemalan Highland Community and Global Economy.* Osaka University, Center for the Study of Communication-Design.

INE (Instituto Nacional de Estadística). 1996. *Censo 1994: Departamento de Huehuetenango.* Guatemala City: Instituto Nacional de Estadística.

INE (Instituto Nacional de Estadística). 2003. *Censo Nacional XI de Población y VI de Habitación 2002.* Guatemala City: Instituto Nacional de Estadística.

James, Erica. 2010. *Democratic Insecurities: Violence, Trauma and Intervention in Haiti.* Berkeley: University of California Press.

Jonas, Susanne. 2000. *Of Centaurs and Doves: Guatemala's Peace Process.* Boulder, CO: Westview Press.

Joseph, Gilbert M., and Daniel Nugent. 1994. *Everyday Forms of State Formation: Revolution and the Negotiation of Rule in Modern Mexico.* Durham, NC: Duke University Press.

Kay, Cristóbal. 2001. "Conflictos y violencia en la Latinoamérica rural." *Nueva Sociedad, 174,* 107–120.

Kearney, Michael. 1995. "The Local and the Global: The Anthropology of Globalization and Transnationalism." *Annual Review of Anthropology, 24,* 547–565.

Kearney, Michael. 1996. *Reconstructing the Peasantry: Anthropology in Global Perspective.* Boulder, CO: Westview Press.

Kearney, Michael. 2004. *Changing Fields of Anthropology: From Local to Global.* New York: Rowman and Littlefield Publishing.

Kingfisher, Catherine, and Jeff Maskovsky. 2008. "The Limits of Neoliberalism." *Critique of Anthropology, 28* (2), 115–126.

Kipnis, Andrew. 2008. "Audit Cultures: Neoliberal governmentality, socialist legacy or technologies of governing?" *American Ethnologist, 35* (2), 275–289.

Kirsch, Stuart. 2002. "Rumour and Other Narratives of Political Violence in West Papua." *Critique of Anthropology, 22* (1), 53–79.

Kleinman, Arthur. 2000. "The Violence of Everyday Life: The Multiple Forms and Dynamics of Social Violence." In Das, Veena, Arthur Kleinman, Mamphela Ramphele, and Pamela Reynolds, eds., *Violence and Subjectivity.* Berkeley: University of California Press.

Kobrak, Paul Hans. 1997. *Village Troubles: The Civil Patrols in Aguacatán, Guatemala.* Ph.D. dissertation, University of Michigan, Department of Sociology.

Kobrak, Paul Hans. 2003. *Huehuetenango: Historia de una guerra.* Huehuetenango: CEDFOG (Centro de Estudios y Documentación de la Frontera Occidental de Guatemala).

Konefal, Betsy. 2010. *For Every Indio Who Falls: A History of Maya Activism in Guatemala, 1960–1990*. Albuquerque: University of New Mexico Press.

La Farge, Oliver, and Douglas Byers. 1931. *The Year Bearer's People*. Tulane University, Department of Middle American Research, New Orleans.

Lancaster, Roger. 1992. *Life is Hard: Machismo, Danger, and the Intimacy of Power in Nicaragua*. Berkeley: University of California Press.

Lancaster, Roger. 2008. "State of Panic." In Collins, Jane, Micaela di Leonardo, and Brett Williams, eds., *New Landscapes of Inequality: Neoliberalism and the Erosion of Democracy in America*. Santa Fe, NM: Society for American Research Press.

Lancaster, Roger. 2011. *Sex Panics and the Punitive State*. Berkeley: University of California Press.

Landolt, Patricia. 2001. "Salvadoran economic transnationalism embedded strategies for household maintenance, immigrant incorporation, and entrepreneurial expansion." *Global Networks, 1* (3), 217–241.

LeFebvre, Henri. 1991 [1974]. *The Production of Space*, trans. Nochilson-Smith, Donald. Oxford: Wiley-Blackwell.

LeFebvre, Henri. 1992. *The Production of Space*. UK and Malden, MA: Wiley-Blackwell.

Lem, Winnie, and Belinda Leach, eds. 2002. *Culture, Economy, Power: Anthropology as Critique, Anthropology as Praxis*. Albany, NY: SUNY Press.

Levenson-Estrada, Deborah. 1994. *Trade Unionists Against Terror: Guatemala City, 1954–1985*. Chapel Hill, NC: The University of North Carolina Press.

Levenson-Estrada, Deborah. 2003. "The Life That Makes Us Die/The Death That Makes Us Live: Facing Terrorism in Guatemala City." *Radical History Review*, (85), 94–104.

Levenson-Estrada, Deborah. 2011. "Living Guatemala City, 1930s–2000s." In O'Neill, Kevin, and Kedron Thomas, eds., *Securing the City*. Durham, NC: Duke University Press.

Levenson-Estrada, Deborah. 2013a. "Guatemala's Maras: from life to death." In Nelson, Diane, and Carlota MacAllister, eds., *Aftermath: War by Other Means in Post-Genocide Guatemala*. Durham, NC: Duke University Press.

Levenson, Deborah. 2013b. *Adiós, Niño: The Gangs of Guatemala City and the Politics of Death*. Durham, NC: Duke University Press.

Levitt, Peggy. 2000. *The Transnational Villagers*. Berkeley: University of California Press.

"Linchamientos." 2000. *El Periódico*, July 30.

Little, Walter E. 2004. "In Between Social Movements: Dilemmas of Indigenous Handicrafts Vendors in Guatemala." *American Ethnologist, 31* (1), 43–59.

Little, Walter E. 2004. *Mayas in the Marketplace: Tourism, Globalization and Cultural Identity*. Austin: University of Texas Press.

Little, Walter E. 2008. "New Spiritual Clients and the Morality of Making Money." In Browne, Katherine E., and Lynn Milgram, eds., *Economics and Morality: Anthropological Approaches*. Plymouth, UK: Altamira Press.

Little, Walter E., and Timothy J. Smith, eds. 2009. *Mayas in Postwar Guatemala: Harvest of Violence Revisited.* Tuscaloosa: University of Alabama Press.

López García, Julián. 2003. "Abordando los linchamientos en Guatemala: Del autismo capacitador a consensos negociados." In Mendoza, Carlos, and Edelberto Torres-Rivas, eds., *Linchamientos: ¿barbarie o "justicia popular"?* Guatemala City: Colección Cultura de la Paz.

Loucky, James, and Marilyn M. Moors, eds. 2000. *The Maya Diaspora.* Philadelphia: Temple University Press.

Lovell, George. 1992. *Conquest and Survival in Colonial Guatemala: A Historical Geography of the Cuchumatán Highlands, 1500–1821.* Montreal & Buffalo, NY: McGill and Queens University Press.

Lovell, George. 1995. *A Beauty That Hurts.* Toronto: Between the Lines.

Low, Setha. 2001. "The Edge and the Center: Gated Communities and the Discourse of Urban Fear." *American Anthropologist,* 103 (1), 45–58.

Lubkemann, Steven. 2008. *Culture in Chaos: An Anthropology of the Social Conditions in War.* Chicago: University of Chicago Press.

Lyon, Sarah. 2011. *Coffee and Community: Maya Farmers and Fair-Trade Markets in Guatemala.* Boulder: University Press of Colorado.

MacLeod, Murdo. 1973. *Spanish Central America, 1520–1720.* Berkeley: University of California Press.

Mallon, Florencia. 1995. *Peasant and Nation: The Making of Postcolonial Mexico and Peru.* Berkeley: University of California Press.

Mamdani, Mahmood. 1997. *Citizen and Subject.* Princeton: Princeton University Press.

Manz, Beatriz. 1988. *Refugees of a Hidden War: The Aftermath of the Counterinsurgency in Guatemala.* Albany, NY: SUNY Press.

Manz, Beatriz. 2004. *Paradise in Ashes: A Guatemalan Journey of Courage, Terror, and Hope.* Berkeley: University of California Press.

Marx, Karl. 1963 [1852]. *The Eighteenth Brumaire of Louis Bonaparte.* New York: International Publishers.

Massey, Doreen. 1984. *Spatial Divisions of Labor: Social Structures and the Geography of Production.* New York: Methuen.

Massey, Doreen. 1994. *Space, Place, and Gender.* Minneapolis: University of Minnesota Press.

McAllister, Carlota. 2003. *Good People: Revolution, Community and Conciencia in a Maya-K'iche' Village in Guatemala.* Ph.D. dissertation, Johns Hopkins University, Department of Anthropology.

McAllister, Carlota, and Nelson, Diane. 2013. Introduction. In *Aftermath: War by Other Means in Post-Genocide Guatemala.* Durham, NC: Duke University Press.

McConahy, Mary Jo. 2003. "Next Guatemala President Must Decide on Official Story." *Pacific News Service,* November 10.

McCreery, David. 1994. *Rural Guatemala 1760–1940.* Palo Alto, CA: Stanford University Press.

McIlwaine, Cathy, and Caroline Moser. 2004. *Encounters with Violence in Latin America: Urban Poor Perceptions from Colombia and Guatemala.* New York & London: Routledge Press.

Menchú, Rigoberta. 1998. *Crossing Borders.* London & New York: Verso.

Mendoza, Carlos. 2003. "Violencia colectiva en Guatemala: una aproximación teóretica al problema de los linchamientos." In Mendoza, Carlos, and Edelberto Torres-Rivas, eds., *Linchamientos: ¿barbarie o "justicia popular"?*, 275–327. Guatemala City: Collección Cultura de la Paz.

Mendoza, Carlos, ed. 2011. *Linchamientos en Guatemala.* Retrieved July 12, 2011, from http://linchamientos.blogspot.com/.

Mendoza, Carlos, and Edelberto Torres-Rivas, eds. 2003. *Linchamientos: ¿barbarie o "justicia popular"?* Guatemala City: Colección Cultura de la Paz.

Menjívar, Cecilia. 2011. *Enduring Violence: Ladina Women's Lives in Guatemala.* Berkeley: University of California Press.

Merry, Sally Engle. 2001. "Spatial Governmentality and the New Urban Social Order: Controlling Gender Violence Through Law." *American Anthropologist*, 103 (1), 16–30.

MINUGUA (Misión de Verificación de las Naciones Unidas en Guatemala). 2003. *Fourteenth Report on Human Rights of the United Nations Verification Mission in Guatemala.*

MINUGUA (Misión de Verificación de las Naciones Unidas en Guatemala). 2003. "Los Linchamientos: un flagelo que persiste." In Mendoza, Carlos, and Edelberto Torres-Rivas, eds., *Linchamientos: ¿barbarie o "justicia popular"?*, 275–327. Guatemala City: Colección Cultura de la Paz.

Montejo, Victor. 1999. "The Year Bearer's People: Repatriation of Ethnographic and Sacred Knowledge to the Jakaltek Maya of Guatemala." *International Journal of Cultural Property*, 8 (1), 151–166.

Montejo, Victor. 2002. "The Multiplicity of Mayan Voices." In Warren, Kay B., and Jean Jackson, eds., *Indigenous Movements, Self-Representation, and the State in Latin America.* Austin: University of Texas Press.

Moodie, Ellen. 2010. *El Salvador in the Aftermath of Peace.* Philadelphia: University of Pennsylvania Press.

Namuth, Hans. 1989. *Los Todosanteros.* New York: Nishen Press.

Narotzky, Susana. 2007. "'A Cargo del Futuro'—Between History and Memory: An Account of the 'Fratricidal' Conflict during Revolution and War in Spain (1936–39)." *Critique of Anthropology*, 27 (4), 411–429.

Narotzky, Susana. 2010. "Regulation and Production in a Globalized World: What Ethnography Brings to Comparison." *Ethnology*, 48 (3), 175–193.

Nash, June. 1970. *In the Eyes of the Ancestors: Belief and Behavior in a Maya Community.* New Haven, CT: Yale University Press.

Nash, June. 2001. *Mayan Visions: The Quest for Autonomy in an Age of Globalization.* New York & London: Routledge Press.

Navaro-Yashin, Yael. 2012. *The Make-Believe Space: Affective Geography in a Postwar Polity.* Durham, NC: Duke University Press.

Nelson, Diane. 1999. *A Finger in the Wound.* Berkeley: University of California Press.

Nelson, Diane. 2009. *Reckoning: The Ends of War in Guatemala.* Durham, NC: Duke University Press.

New York Times. 2000. "Guatemalans Kill Japanese and Tour Driver," May 1.

Nordstrom, Carolyn. 1997. *A Different Kind of War Story.* Berkeley: University of California Press.

Nordstrom, Carolyn, and Antonius C. G. M. Robben, eds. 1995. *Fieldwork Under Fire*. Berkeley: University of California Press.

Nugent, David. 2010. "States, secrecy, subversives: APRA and political fantasy in mid-20th-century Peru." *American Ethnologist*, 37 (4), 681–702.

Oakes, Maud. 1951. *Beyond the Windy Place: Life in the Guatemalan Highlands*. New York: Farrar, Strauss and Young.

Oakes, Maud. 1951. *The Two Crosses of Todos Santos*. New York: Bollingen Foundation (Pantheon Books).

OAS (Interamerican Commission on Human Rights). 1981. *Report on the Situation of Human Rights in the Republic of Guatemala*. Retrieved May 20, 2011, from http://www.cidh.oas.org/countryrep/Guatemala81eng/chap.2.htm.

Offit, Tom, and Garrett Cook. 2010. "The Death of Don Pedro: Insecurity and Cultural Continuity in Peacetime Guatemala." *Journal of Latin American and Caribbean Anthropology*, 15 (1), 42–66.

Oglesby, Elizabeth. 2007. "Educating citizens in postwar Guatemala: historical memory, genocide, and the culture of peace." *Radical History Review*, 97, 77–98.

Oglesby, Elizabeth, and Amy Ross. 2009. "Guatemala's Genocide Determination and the Spatial Politics of Justice." *Space & Polity*, 13 (1), 21–39.

O'Neill, Kevin Lewis, and Kedron Thomas, eds. 2011. *Securing the City: Neoliberalism, Space and Insecurity in Postwar Guatemala*. Durham, NC: Duke University Press.

Ong, Aihwa. 1999. *Flexible Citizenship*. Durham, NC: Duke University Press.

Ong, Aihwa. 2006. *Neoliberalism as Exception*. Durham, NC: Duke University Press.

Orellana, Sandra. 1984. *The Tz'utujil Mayas: continuity and change, 1250–1630*. Norman: University of Oklahoma Press.

Orlove, Benjamin. 1991. "Mapping reeds and reading maps: the politics of representation in Lake Titicaca." *American Ethnologist*, 18, 3–38.

Orlove, Benjamin. 2002. *Lines in the Water: Nature and Culture at Lake Titicaca*. Berkeley: University of California Press.

Paerregaard, Karsten. 2010. "The Show Must Go On: The Role of Fiestas in Andean Transnational Migration." *Latin American Perspectives*, 37 (5), 50–66.

Paley, Julia. 2001. *Marketing Democracy: Power and Social Movements in Post-Dictatorship Chile*. Berkeley: University of California Press.

Palma, Gustavo, and Juan Pablo Gómez. 2010. "Seguimos atrapados en la finca." *InforPress Centroamericano*, March 19–26. Interview by Andrés Porasier. AVANCSO (Asociación para el Avance de las Ciencias Sociales en Guatemala).

"Pandillas asuelan en Todos Santos. Medida: Alcaldes de Huehuetenango denuncian inseguridad." 2003. *Prensa Libre*, February 22.

Payeras, Mario. 1991. *Los fusiles de octubre: ensayos y artículos militares sobre la revolución guatemalteca, 1985–1988*. Mexico City: J. Pablos.

Peacock, Susan C., and Adriana Beltrán. 2003. *Hidden Powers: Illegal Armed Groups in Post-Conflict Guatemala and the Forces Behind Them*. Washington Office on Latin America, Washington.

Pearce, Jenny. 1998. "From Civil War to 'Civil Society': Has the End of the Cold War Brought Peace to Central America?" *International Affairs*, 74 (3), 587–615.

Perera, Victor. 1989. "The Long Journey Home: Pablo Fernandez and the Discovery of La Rochela." *Grassroots Development*, *13* (2), 16–25.

Perera, Victor. 1993. "The Crosses of Todos Santos." In Victor Perera, *Unfinished Conquest: The Guatemala Tragedy*, 135–153. Berkeley: University of California Press.

Perera, Victor. 1995. *Unfinished Conquest: The Guatemalan Tragedy*. Berkeley: University of California Press.

Perry, Richard. 2000. "Governmentalities in City-Scapes." *PoLAR*, *23* (1), 65–73.

Pew Hispanic Center. 2011. "Hispanics of Guatemalan Origin in the United States, 2009." May 26. Downloaded June 20, 2011, from http://pewhispanic .org/files/factsheets/76.pdf.

Philpot-Munson, J. Jailey. 2009. "Peace Under Fire: Understanding Evangelical Resistance to the Peace Process in Post-war Guatemala." In Little, Walter E., and Timothy J. Smith, eds., *Mayas in Postwar Guatemala Harvest of Violence Revisited*. Tuscaloosa: University of Alabama Press.

Ponciano González, Jorge Ramón. 2013. "Whiteness and the Criminalization of the Dark Plebeian." In Nelson, Diane, and Carlota McAllister, eds., *Aftermath: War by Other Means in Post-Genocide Guatemala*. Durham, NC: Duke University Press.

Poole, Deborah. 2004. "Between Threat and Guarantee: Natural and Legal Jurisdictions on the Margins of the Peruvian State." In Das, Veena, and Deborah Poole, eds., *Anthropology in the Margins of the State*. Santa Fe, NM: School of American Research Press.

Poole, Deborah, and Gerardo Renique. 2003. "Terror and the Privatized State: A Peruvian Parable." *Radical History Review*, (85), 150–163.

Pop Barillas, P., and J. F. Lara. 2000. "Turba mata a turista." *Prensa Libre*, April 30.

Popol Wu'uh. 1996. *Popol Vuh: The Definitive Edition of the Mayan Book of the Dawn of Life and the Glories of Gods and Kings*, trans. Tedlock, Dennis. New York: Touchstone Books.

Postero, Nancy. 2006. *Now We Are Citizens: Indigenous Politics in Post-Multicultural Bolivia*. Palo Alto, CA: Stanford University Press.

Pratten, David, and Atreyee Sen, eds. 2007. *Global Vigilantes*. London: Hurst & Company.

Pred, Allan, and Michael Watts. 1992. *Reworking Modernity: Capitalisms and Symbolic Discontent*. New Brunswick, NJ: Rutgers University Press.

Preti, Alessandro. 2002. "Guatemala: Violence in Peacetime—A Critical Analysis of Armed Conflict and the Peace Process." *Disasters*, *26* (2), 99–119.

Ramírez Espada, A., and M. Acabal. 2000. "Primeras capturas podrían efectuarse hoy." *Prensa Libre*, May 2.

Ramos, Alcida. 2002. "Cutting Through State and Class: Sources and Strategies of Self-Representation in Latin America." In Warren, Kay B., and Jean Jackson, eds., *Indigenous Movements, Self-Representation, and the State in Latin America*. Austin: University of Texas Press.

Reina, Rubén. 1966. *The Law of the Saints: A Pokomam Pueblo and its Community Culture*. Indianapolis & New York: The Bobbs-Merrill Company.

REMHI ([Proyecto Interdiocesano de] Recuperación de la Memoria Histórica).

1998. *Guatemala: Nunca Más*. Guatemala City: Oficina de Derechos Humanos del Arzobispado.

Remijnse, Simone. 2003. *Memories of Violence: Civil Patrols and the Legacy of Conflict in Joyobaj, Guatemala*. West Lafayette, IN: Purdue University Press.

Reynolds, Pamela. 1997. "The Ground of All Making: State Violence, the Family and Political Activists." In Das, Veena, Arthur Kleinman, Mamphela Ramphele, and Pamela Reynolds, eds., *Violence & Subjectivity* (pp. 141–170). Berkeley: University of California Press.

Robinson, William. 1996. *Promoting Polyarchy: Globalization, U.S. Intervention and Hegemony*. Cambridge: Cambridge University Press.

Robinson, William. 2003. *Transnational Conflicts: Central America, Social Change and Globalization*. London: Verso.

Rodgers, Dennis. 2007. "Joining the Gang and Becoming a 'Broder': The Violence of Ethnography in Contemporary Nicaragua." *Bulletin of Latin American Research*, *26* (4), 444–461.

Rodgers, Dennis. 2009. "Slum wars of the 21st century: Gangs, mano dura, and the new urban geography of conflict in Central America." *Development and Change*, *40* (5), 949–976.

Rodriguez, Nestor P., and Jacqueline M. Hagan. 2000. "Maya Urban Villagers in Houston: The Formation of a Migrant Community from San Cristóbal Totonicapán." In Loucky, James, and Marilyn M. Moors, eds., *The Maya Diaspora*. Philadelphia: Temple University Press.

Rofel, Lisa. 1999. *Other Modernities: Gendered Yearnings in China After Socialism*. Berkeley: University of California Press.

Rojas-Perez, Isaias. 2008. "Writing the Aftermath. Anthropology and Post-Conflict in Latin America." In Deborah Poole, ed., *A Companion to Latin American Anthropology*. Malden, MA: Blackwell Publishing Ltd.

Rosaldo, Renato. 1997. "Cultural Citizenship, Inequality and Multiculturalism." In Flores, William V., and Rina Benmayor, eds., *Latino Cultural Citizenship: Claiming Identity, Space and Rights*, 27–38. Boston, MA: Beacon Press.

Rosales, E., and M. Morales. 2000. "Anuncian capturas en caso de turistas japonesas." *Siglo XXI*, May 1.

Rose, Nikolas. 1999. *Powers of Freedom: Reframing Political Thought*. Cambridge: Cambridge University Press.

Rose, Nikolas. 2001. "The Politics of Life Itself." *Theory, Culture and Society*, *18* (6), 1–30.

Roseberry, William. 1989. *Anthropologies and Histories*. New Brunswick, NJ: Rutgers University Press.

Roseberry, William. 1994. "Hegemony and the Language of Contention." In Joseph, Gilbert M., and Daniel Nugent, eds., *Everyday Forms of State Formation*, 355–366. Durham, NC: Duke University Press.

Roseberry, William. 1998. "Social Fields and Cultural Encounters." In Joseph, Gilbert M., Catherine LeGrand, and Ricardo D. Salvatore, eds., *Close Encounters of Empire*, 515–524. Durham, NC: Duke University Press.

Roseberry, William. 2004. "'Para calmar los ánimos entre los vecinos de este lugar': comunidad y conflicto en el Pátzcuaro del Porfiriato." *Relaciones: Estudios de historia y sociedad*, *25* (100), 107–135.

Rothenburg, Daniel. 1998. "Los Linchamientos—The Meaning of Mob Action in the Wake of State Terror in Guatemala." *Native Americas, 15* (1), 1–7.

Rouse, Roger. 1991. "Mexican migration and the social space of postmodernism." *Diaspora, 1,* 8–23.

Rouse, Roger. 1995. "Questions of Identity: Personhood and Collectivity in Transnational Migration to the United States." *Critique of Anthropology, 15* (4), 351–380.

Rundstrom, Robert. 1990. "A Cultural Interpretation of Inuit Map Accuracy." *Geographical Review, 80,* 155–168.

Rus, Jan. 2010. "Comment: Financing Undocumented Migration and the Limits of Solidarity: Unsettling Findings from Guatemala." *Latin American Perspectives, 37,* 145–147.

Rus, Diane L., and Jan Rus. 2008. "La migración de trabajadores indígenas de los Altos de Chiapas a Estados Unidos, 2001–2005: el caso de San Juan Chamula." In Villafuerte, Daniel, and María del Carmen García, eds., *Migraciones en el Sur de México y Centroamérica,* 343–382. Mexico City: Miguel Ángel Porrúa Editores.

Samper, David. 2002. "Cannibalizing Kids: Rumor and Resistance in Latin America." *Journal of Folklore Research, 39* (1), 1–32.

Sanchinelli, Luis Lima, and Mynor Cortez. 2009. "Anatomía de un linchamiento." *El Periódico,* December 26.

Sandoval, M. A. 2000. "El linchamiento de un turista japonés pone de rodillas a la industria turística." *Prensa Libre,* May 2.

Sandoval, Marta. 2009. "El linchamiento del sastre." *El Periódico,* May 10.

Sanford, Victoria. 2003. *Buried Secrets: Truth and Human Rights in Guatemala.* New York: Palgrave MacMillan.

Sanford, Victoria. 2008. "From Genocide to Feminicide: Impunity and Human Rights in Twenty-First-Century Guatemala." *Journal of Human Rights, 7,* 104–122.

Sanford, Victoria. 2009. "What Is an Anthropology of Genocide? Reflections on Field Research with Maya Survivors in Guatemala." In Alexander Hinton and Kevin O'Neill, eds., *Genocide: Truth, Memory and Representation.* Durham, NC: Duke University Press.

Santamaria, Gema. 2012. "Taking Justice Into Their Own Hands: Insecurity and the Lynching of Criminals in Latin America." *ReVista,* Winter. Cambridge, MA: David Rockefeller Center for Latin American Studies, Harvard University.

Scheper-Hughes, Nancy. 1992. *Death Without Weeping: The Violence of Everyday Life in Brazil.* Berkeley: University of California Press.

Scheper-Hughes, Nancy, and Phillippe Bourgois. 2004. Introduction. In Scheper-Hughes, Nancy, and Phillippe Bourgois, eds., *Violence in War and Peace: An Anthology,* 1–31. London: Blackwell Publishing.

Schirmer, Jennifer. 1998. *The Guatemala Military Project: A Violence Called Democracy.* Philadelphia: University of Pennsylvania Press.

Schlesinger, Stephen, and Stephen Kinzer. 2005. *Bitter Fruit: The Story of the American Coup in Guatemala.* Cambridge, MA: David Rockefeller Center for Latin American Studies, Harvard University.

Scott, James C. 1976. *The Moral Economy of the Peasant: Rebellion and Subsistence in Southeast Asia*. New Haven, CT: Yale University Press.

Scott, James C. 1998. *Seeing Like a State: How Certain Schemes to Improve the Human Condition Have Failed*. New Haven, CT: Yale University Press.

Scott, Winston. 2012. "Beyond Coffee Plantations: Coffee Production, Emerging Economic and Social Spaces, and Q'eqchi' Maya in Senahú, Guatemala." Ph.D. dissertation, University at Albany–SUNY, Department of Anthropology.

Sharp, Ellen. 2008. "Vigilante Order, the State of Exception and la Primera Capitana." Paper presented at the meeting of the American Anthropological Association, San Francisco, CA.

Sharp, Ellen. 2012a. "The Battle over Alcohol: Grassroots Justice versus the Guatemalan State." Paper presented at the meeting of the Latin American Studies Association, San Francisco, CA.

Sharp, Ellen. 2012b. "Between Justice and Vigilantism: Organizing to Confront Crime in Post-War Guatemala." *Grassroots Development*.

Sieder, Rachel. 1998. "Customary Law and Local Power in Guatemala." In Seider, Rachel, ed., *Guatemala After the Peace Accords*, 97–115. London: Institute of Latin America Studies.

Sieder, Rachel. 2001. "Rethinking Citizenship: Reforming the Law in Postwar Guatemala." In Hansen, Thomas Blom, and Finn Stepputat, eds., *States of Imagination: Ethnographic Explorations of the Postcolonial State*. Durham, NC: Duke University Press.

Sieder, Rachel. 2007. "The judiciary and indigenous rights in Guatemala." *International Journal of Constitutional Law*, 5 (2), 211–241.

Sieder, Rachel. 2008. "Legal Globalization and Human Rights: Constructing the Rule of Law in Postconflict Guatemala?" In Pitarch, Pedro, Shannon Speed, and Xochitl Leyva-Solano, eds., *Human Rights in the Maya Region*. Durham, NC: Duke University Press.

Sieder, Rachel. 2011a. "Contested sovereignties: Indigenous law, violence and state effects in postwar Guatemala." *Critique of Anthropology*, 31 (3), 1–24.

Sieder, Rachel. 2011b. "Building Mayan authority and autonomy: The 'recovery' of indigenous law in post-peace Guatemala." *Studies in Law, Politics, and Society*, 55, 43–75.

Sitler, Robert. 2001. "Understanding Death in a Mayan Market." *Community College Humanities Review*, 22 (1), 88–98.

Smart, Alan. 2001. "Unruly Places: Urban Governance and the Persistence of Illegality in Hong Kong's Urban Squatter Areas." *American Anthropologist*, 103 (1), 30–44.

Smith, Carol. 1984. "Local History in Global Context: Social and Economic Transitions in Western Guatemala." *Comparative Studies in Society and History*, 26 (2), 196–228.

Smith, Carol, ed. 1992. *Guatemalan Indians and the State: 1540–1988*. Austin: University of Texas Press.

Smith, Gavin. 1999. *Confronting the Present*. Oxford & New York: Berg.

Smith, Gavin, and Susana Narotzky. 2006. *Immediate Struggles: People, Power and Place in Rural Spain*. Berkeley: University of California Press.

Smith, Timothy J. and Adams, Abigail, eds. 2011. *After the Coup: An Ethnographic Reframing of Guatemala 1954*. Champaign: University of Illinois Press.

Smith, Waldemar. 1977. *The Fiesta System and Economic Change*. New York: Columbia University Press.

Snodgrass Godoy, Angelina. 2002. "Lynching and the Democratization of Terror in Postwar Guatemala: Implications for Human Rights." *Human Rights Quarterly*, *24* (3), 640–661.

Snodgrass Godoy, Angelina. 2004. "When 'Justice' is Criminal: Lynchings in Contemporary Latin America." *Theory and Society*, *33*, 621–651.

Snodgrass Godoy, Angelina. 2006. *Popular Injustice: Violence, Community and Law in Latin America*. Palo Alto, CA: Stanford University Press.

Speed, Shannon. 2006. "At the Crossroads of Human Rights and Anthropology: Toward a Critically Engaged Activist Research." *American Anthropologist*, *108* (1), 66–77.

Speed, Shannon. 2007. *Rights in Rebellion: Indigenous Rebellion and Human Rights in Chiapas*. Palo Alto, CA: Stanford University Press.

Stadelman, Raymond. 1940. "Maize Cultivation in Northwestern Guatemala." *Contributions to American Archaeology*, *33*, 83–263.

Stephen, Lynn. 2001. "Culture as Resource: Four Cases of Self-Managed Indigenous Craft Production in Latin America." In Dominguez, Jorge, ed., *Mexico, Central America and South America: New Perspectives. Volume 5: Race and Ethnicity*. New York & London: Routledge Press.

Stephen, Lynn. 2002. *Zapata Lives*. Berkeley: University of California Press.

Stephen, Lynn. 2007. *Transborder Lives: Indigenous Oaxacans in Mexico, California, and Oregon*. Durham, NC: Duke University Press.

Stoler, Ann. 2002. *Carnal Knowledge and Imperial Power: Race and the Intimate in Colonial Rule*. Berkeley: University of California Press.

Stoll, David. 1993. *Between Two Armies in the Ixil Towns of Guatemala*. New York: Columbia University Press.

Stoll, David. 1999. *Rigoberta Menchú and the Story of all Poor Guatemalans*. Boulder, CO: Westview Press.

Stoll, David. 2010. "From Wage Migration to Debt Migration? Easy Credit, Failure in El Norte, and Foreclosure in a Bubble Economy of the Western Guatemalan Highlands." *Latin American Perspectives*, *37* (1), 123–142.

Striffler, Steve. 2007. "Neither Here Nor There: Mexican Immigrant Workers and the Search for Home." *American Ethnologist*, *34*, 674–688.

Taracena Arriola, Arturo. 2002. *Etnicidad, estado y nación en Guatemala. Volumen 1: 1808–1944*. Antigua, Guatemala: CIRMA (Centro de Investigaciones Regionales de Mesoamérica).

Taracena Arriola, Arturo. 2004. *Etnicidad, estado y nación en Guatemala. Volumen 2: 1945–1985*. Antigua, Guatemala: CIRMA (Centro de Investigaciones Regionales de Mesoamérica).

Taussig, Michael. 1992. *The Nervous System*. New York & London: Routledge Press.

Taussig, Michael. 1999. *Defacement: Public Secrecy and the Labor of the Negative*. Palo Alto, CA: Stanford University Press.

Tavico Leguarca, Oscar I. 1995. *Caracteristicas del Actual Proceso de Desarollo en*

Todos Santos Cuchumatán. Tesis de Maestria, Universidad de San Carlos, Guatemala City.

Tax, Sol. 1937. "The Municipios of the Midwestern Highlands of Guatemala." *American Anthropologist*, *39* (3), 423–444.

Taylor, Matthew, and Michael Steinberg. 2011. "Controlling People and Space." In *Mapping Latin America*. Jordana Dyn and Karl Offen, eds. Chicago: University of Chicago Press.

Tedlock, Dennis (translator). 1996. *Popol Vuh*. New York: Simon and Schuster.

Theidon, Kimberly. 2001. "Terror's Talk: Fieldwork and War." *Dialectical Anthropology*, *26* (1), 19–35.

Theidon, Kimberly. 2003. "Disarming the Subject: Remembering War and Imagining Citizenship in Peru." *Cultural Critique*, *54*, 67–87.

Theidon, Kimberly. 2003. "La Micropolítica de la Reconciliación: Practicando la Justicia en Comunidades Rurales Ayacuchanas." *Revista Allpanchis*, *60*, 113–142.

Theidon, Kimberly. 2012. *Intimate Enemies: Violence and Reconciliation in Peru*. Philadelphia: University of Pennsylvania Press.

Thomas, Kedron, Kevin O'Neill, and Thomas Offit. 2011. "Securing the City: An Introduction." In O'Neill, Kevin, and Kedron Thomas, eds., *Securing the City: Neoliberalism, Space and Insecurity in Postwar Guatemala*. Durham, NC: Duke University Press.

Thompson, Edward P. 1971. "The moral economy of the English crowd in the eighteenth century." *Past and Present*, *50*, 76–136.

Thompson, Edward P. 1978. "Eighteenth Century English Society: Class Struggle Without Class?" *Social History*, *3* (2), 133–165.

Thompson, Ginger. 2004. "Tattooed Warriors: The Next Generation; Shuttling Between Nations, Latino Gangs Confound the Law." *New York Times*, September 26.

Time magazine online. 2011. "The Deadliest Zone: Hilary Clinton Visits Central America's Narco-Nightmare." Retrieved July 12, 2011, from http://www.time.com/time/.

Tomuschat, Christian. 2001. "Clarification Commission in Guatemala," *Human Rights Quarterly*, *23* (2), 233–258.

Torres, M. Gabriela. 2008. "Imagining Social Justice Amidst Guatemala's Post Conflict Violence." *Studies in Social Justice*, *2* (1), 1–11.

Torres, M. Gabriela, and David Carey Jr., 2010. "Precursors to Femicide: Guatemalan Women in a Vortex of Violence." In *Latin American Research Review*, *45* (3), 142–164.

Torres-Rivas, Edelberto. 1998. "Sobre el terror y la violencia política en América Latina." In *Violencia en una sociedad en transición*. San Salvador: PNUD (Programa de Naciones Unidas para el Desarollo).

Trouillot, Michel-Rolph. 1995. *Silencing the Past: Power and the Production of History*. Boston, MA: Beacon Press.

Trouillot, Michel-Rolph. 2003. *Global Transformations: Anthropology and the Modern World*. New York: Palgrave MacMillan.

Tully, James. 1995. *Strange Multiplicity: Constitutionalism in an age of diversity*. Cambridge: Cambridge University Press.

UNDP (United Nations Development Program). 2008. Assessment of Development Results in Guatemala. Downloaded June 24, 2011, at www.undp.org /execbrd/pdf/ADR-Guatemala.pdf.

Ungar, Mark. 2002. *Elusive Reform: Democracy and the Rule of Law in Latin America*. Boulder, CO: Lynne Rienner Publishers.

UNICEF. 2008. "Protecting Girls from Sexual Exploitation in Guatemala." www .unicef.org/infobycountry/guatemala.46566.html.

Valencia Caravantes, Daniel. 2011. "La comunidad que lincha." *El Faro*, July 17. Retrieved July 20, 2011, from http://www.salanegra.elfaro.net/es/201107 /cronicas/4764/.

Valenzuela Arve, J., A. Nateras Dominguez, and R. Reguilo Cruz. 2008. *Las Maras: Identidades Juveniles al Limite*. Mexico, DF: Casa Juan Pablo.

Van Cott, Donna. 2000. *The Friendly Liquidation of the Past*. Pittsburgh, PA: University of Pittsburgh Press.

Van Vleet, Krista. 2003. "Partial Theories: On Gossip, Envy and Ethnography in the Andes." *Ethnography*, 4, 491–519.

Vela, Manolo, Alexander Sequén-Móchez, and Hugo Antonio Solares, eds. 2001. *El lado oscuro de la eternal primavera: violencia, criminalidad y delincuencia en la posguerra*. Guatemala City: FLACSO (Facultad Latinoamericana de Ciencias Sociales).

Veltmeyer, Henry, and Anthony O'Malley, eds. 2001. *Transcending Neoliberalism: Community-based development in Latin America*. Bloomfield, CT: Kumarian Press.

Veltmeyer, Henry, James Petras, and Steve Vieux, eds. 1997. *Neoliberalism and Class Conflict in Latin America: A Comparative Perspective on the Political Economy of Structural Adjustment*. New York: St. Martin's Press.

Vilas, Carlos M. 2001. "(In)justicia por mano propia: Linchamientos en el México contemporáneo." *Revista Mexicana de Sociología*, 63 (1), 131–160.

Vilas, Carlos, M. 2008. "Lynching and Political Conflicts in the Andes." *Latin American Perspectives*, 35 (5), 103–118.

Von Clausewitz, Carl. 1984 [1976]. *On War*, trans. Howard, Michael, and Peter Paret. Princeton: Princeton University Press.

Warren, Kay B. 1989. *The Symbolism of Subordination*. Princeton: Princeton University Press.

Warren, Kay B. 1996. "Reading history as resistance: Mayan public intellectuals in Guatemala." In Fischer, Edward, and R. McKenna Brown, eds., *Maya Cultural Activism in Guatemala*, 89–106. Austin: University of Texas Press.

Warren, Kay B. 1998. *Indigenous Movements and Their Critics: Pan Mayan Activism in Guatemala*. Princeton: Princeton University Press.

Warren, Kay B. 2003. "Indigenous Activism across Generations: An Intimate Social History of Antiracism Organizing in Guatemala." In Holland, Dorothy, and Jean Lave, eds., *History in Person*. Santa Fe, NM: School of American Research Press.

Washington Office on Latin America (WOLA). 2006. *Youth Gangs in Central America: A WOLA Special Report*. Washington, DC:

Washington Office on Latin America, November. http://www.wola.org/media /gangs_report_final_nov_06.pdf.

Watanabe, John. 1990. "Enduring Yet Ineffable Community in the Western

Periphery of Guatemala." In Smith, Carol, ed., *Guatemalan Indians and the State*. Austin: University of Texas Press.

Watanabe, John. 1992. *Maya Saints and Souls in a Changing World*. Austin: University of Texas Press.

Watanabe, John. 1995. "Unimagining the Maya: Anthropologists, Others and the Inescapable Hubris of Authorship." *Bulletin of Latin American Research*, 14 (1), 25–45.

White, Luise. 2000. *Speaking with Vampires: Rumor and History in Colonial Africa*. Berkeley, CA: University of California Press.

Williams, Raymond. 1973. *The Country and the City*. Oxford: Oxford University Press.

Williams, Raymond. 1976. *Keywords: A Vocabulary of Culture and Society*. Oxford: Oxford University Press.

Williams, Raymond. 1977. *Marxism and Literature*. Oxford: Oxford University Press.

Williams, Raymond. 1989. *Resources of Hope: Culture, Democracy, Socialism*. London & New York: Verso.

Wilson, Richard. 1995. *Maya Resurgence in Guatemala: Q'eqchi' Experiences*. Norman: University of Oklahoma Press.

Wilson, Richard. 1997. "Representing Human Rights Violations: Social Contexts and Subjectivities." In Wilson, Richard, ed., *Human Rights, Culture and Context: Anthropological Perspectives*, 134–160. London: Pluto Press.

Wolf, Eric R. 1957. "Closed Corporate Peasant Communities in Mesoamerica and Central Java." *Southwestern Journal of Anthropology*, 13 (1), 1–18.

Wolf, Eric R. 1982. *Europe and the People Without a History*. Berkeley: University of California Press.

Wolf, Eric R. 1999. *Envisioning Power: Ideologies of Dominance and Crisis*. Berkeley: University of California Press.

Wood, Elisabeth. 2003. *Insurgent Collective Action and Civil War in El Salvador*. Cambridge: Cambridge University Press.

World Travel and Tourism Council (WTTC). Retrieved February 24, 2012, from http://www.wttc.org/research/economic-impact-research/country-reports/g/guatemala/.

Yashar, Deborah. 2005. "Contesting Citizenship in Latin America: The Rise of Indigenous Movements and the Postliberal Challenge." London & New York: Cambridge University Press.

Zapeta, Estuardo. 2000. "Turismo y cultura: oportunidad en la crisis." *Siglo XXI*, May 5.

Zilberg, Elana. 2011. *Spaces of Detention: The Making of a Transnational Gang Crisis between Los Angeles and San Salvador*. Durham, NC: Duke University Press.

Zur, Judith. 1998. *Violent Memories: Mayan War Widows in Guatemala*. Boulder, CO: Westview Press.

Index

Italic page numbers indicate material in tables or figures.

CPSIA information can be obtained
at www.ICGtesting.com
Printed in the USA
FFOW02n2333170718
47459101-50705FF

Maya after War